MALCOLM
FORBES

MALCOLM FORBES

The Man Who Had Everything

Christopher Winans

ST. MARTIN'S PRESS
New York

To KathyAnn, Benjamin, and Spencer

Grateful acknowledgment is made for permission to reprint the following:

"First Fig" by Edna St. Vincent Millay. From *Collected Poems*, Harper & Row. Copyright 1922, 1950 by Edna St. Vincent Millay. Reprinted by permission of Elizabeth Barrett, Literary Executor.

Design by Richard Oriolo

Library of Congress Cataloging-in-Publication Data
Winans, Christopher.
    Malcolm Forbes: the man who had everything/by Christopher Winans.
        p.   cm.
    "A Thomas Dunne book."
    ISBN 0-312-05134-4
    1. Forbes, Malcolm S.   2. Forbes magazine.   3. Businessmen—United States—Biography.   4. Capitalists and financiers—United States—Biography.   I. Title.
    HC102.5.F67W56   1990
    338.7'61070572'092—dc20
    [B]   90-37255
                                                            CIP

First Edition: September 1990

10 9 8 7 6 5 4 3 2 1

Contents

PREFACE

When I began to research this book in 1988, I wrote Malcolm Forbes a letter in which I informed him I was working on a book about him, his family, and his business. I asked if he would agree to be interviewed or, at least, to be available for the fact-checking process. He wrote back cordially declining my request. He noted that he was working on his own biography—to be published in "a couple of volumes"—and therefore viewed anyone else working on a similar project as a rival not to be assisted. He commented that he was sorry, "but I am sure there are other, and perhaps more colorful and widely appealing Names who are not engaged in their own autobiographical undertakings." A number of sources close to Mr. Forbes also declined to speak to me as a matter of loyalty. If Malcolm was doing his own biography, they reasoned, he would not be pleased to discover they had helped a competitor.

While it would have been much better to do the book with the full cooperation of the Forbes family, the lack of it did not render the task impossible. Still, I hoped somehow to get Malcolm Forbes's input. My strategy was to proceed with the research, write a rough draft of the book, and then request an interview, by which time I would have a better grasp of the subject.

The first draft was about two-thirds completed when Jeannie Williams, a reporter for *USA Today,* called for an interview on how the book was going. By chance, this was a few days before Malcolm died. The main thing she wanted to know was whether the book would say that Malcolm was gay. Indeed, that was what nearly everyone I interviewed for the book wanted to know, and I told Ms. Williams that. Then I responded as I always did in response to the question: I asked her if in fact *she* knew whether Malcolm was gay. Everybody says he is, she replied, but she conceded she had no proof. She tried to get me to confirm that the book would explore the matter, but all I would say was that because the question had been raised by so many sources, I would have to deal with it. But I wouldn't say how. She struggled with whether she would write a story, but apparently decided she didn't want to be the first journalist to report rumors about Malcolm's sexuality.

A few days later, Malcolm died. *Outweek,* a gay weekly that had been pursuing the same question, decided to run a story saying Malcolm was indeed gay. A week or so after the death, Ms. Williams ran a story previewing the *Outweek* story, combining it with notes from her interview with me. The Forbes family concluded this book would focus on Malcolm's sex life and cited that assumption in explaining why they would not agree to be interviewed. Hence, all hope of gaining any cooperation even in the final stages of writing the book was lost.

Before publication, however, the Forbeses somehow obtained a copy of the unedited rough draft. They contacted the publisher through a lawyer to express their concerns about certain elements of the book.

Actually, all of the details they objected to had been fully researched long before Malcolm's death, and it was my hope to get his response to them. I fantasized that when confronted with my toughest questions, Malcolm—with his legendary knack for converting potentially bad press into good press—would rise to the occasion.

Based on what I had learned of his personal integrity, I believed he wouldn't deny anything that was true. I believed that, had he agreed to answer my questions, he would have answered them forthrightly.

His death, however, left me somewhat in the position of the reporter-narrator of the film classic *Citizen Kane.* Like Kane, Malcolm was a highly public publishing mogul whose death left behind a clearly delineated public persona, but whose private side suggested a different portrait. And, alas, like Kane, Malcolm Forbes died before this reporter-narrator could ask him what he felt was the most telling anecdote in his life that would illuminate why he lived the way he did—his "Rosebud."

My candle burns at both ends;
  It will not last the night;
But ah, my foes, and oh, my
  friends—
  It gives a lovely light!
—Edna St. Vincent Millay,
"A Few Figs from Thistles"

1 | THE HAPPIEST MILLIONAIRE

King Tutankhamen achieved immortality not because of what he was but because of the artifacts he left behind. This impressed Malcolm Forbes, who didn't have much patience for museums and antiquities. He liked owning his own museums, but when it came to visiting them, he liked to get in and get out and get on to the next thing. It was more important to have fun than to take time to ponder the awesomeness of anything. The pyramids of Egypt were no exception. Viewing the pyramids, the largest of which rises to 482 feet, he turned to one of his sons and joked, "You don't have to do something like that for me when I die." Everyone laughed.

A few days later, the group was in Luxor. The air was hot, dry, and still in the Nile valley, where monuments to fallen kings have stood for thousands of years. Under a cloudless sky, Malcolm was his usual jovial self. But visiting all those tombs in Giza and now in

Luxor was starting to get to them—especially to Malcolm, with his legendary short attention span for such things.

It was early 1984. Malcolm, sixty-four years old, and the rest of his Capitalist Tool team—about ten young men—were visiting Egypt on one of Malcolm's many Friendship Tours to various countries on motorcycles and in hot-air balloons. They were all wearing their uniforms—bright yellow pants and bright red tops emblazoned with the Forbes Capitalist Tool logo (a motorcycle with wings suspended from a balloon), required dress throughout these tours.

Malcolm—who once said, "History isn't chiseled in stone; it's what some guy did at the time"—trekked down the long narrow passageways to view the tomb of King Tut but didn't linger long. In less than a half hour, he was out of there. What struck him most about Tut's tomb was not what he saw, but what he learned from the tour guide. King Tut's fame had endured for thousands of years not because he was a great monarch—he wasn't—or because the tombs had withstood the ravages of time, but because his burial vault, bulging with artifacts, somehow had escaped the notice of a long procession of grave robbers.

As Malcolm emerged into the blazing sun with team member and then Forbes staffer Jay Gissen at his side, he lapsed into a rare reflective mood. King Tut was practically a kid who accomplished little, yet thousands of years later his name was a household word. Why? Dumb luck had saved his treasures for all the world to marvel at. While other tombs were stripped bare by looters, Tut's survived.

As Malcolm and Gissen headed back to the cafeteria and the vans that had brought them from their hotel a few miles away, Malcolm turned and asked in uncharacteristic earnestness, "Do you think I'll be remembered after I die?"

The gravity of the question took Gissen a little by surprise. Such private, pensive moments were rare on these tours. Typically, Malcolm was "on" nearly 100 percent of the time, keeping a nonstop schedule of speeches and toasts, exchanging T-shirts, pinning Forbes pins on local mayors. He never seemed to lose his enthusiasm for these events, despite repeating the same speeches word for word. Small wonder. The outpouring of affection and admiration that the

Egyptians generated for Malcolm's group along the way was almost shocking, Gissen says.

"People would wait for hours to catch a glimpse of us cycling past, as though we were a motorcade of important dignitaries," he says. They were accorded the cheers normally reserved for royalty when Malcolm's gang roared into a stadium filled with ten thousand people and inflated a huge yellow balloon in the shape of a sphinx.

Would Malcolm be remembered? Gissen, failing to think of anything momentous to say, replied, "Well, you'll at least be an entry in the encyclopedia."

That snapped the spell. Malcolm laughed and responded with a characteristic "Double your salary." The moment was over. On to the next thing, joking all the way.

On the sixth anniversary of the day the Egyptian trip began, February 24—a day Gissen marked each year by calling a few of his former fellow travelers to reminisce—Malcolm Forbes quietly and quite unexpectedly died in his sleep, just as he had wished, of a heart attack at his New Jersey home. He was seventy years old.

Everyone knew Malcolm Stevenson Forbes. He was the rich macho magazine publisher with a big, loving family, a perpetual ear-to-ear smile and glinty eyes behind black-rimmed glasses. Elizabeth Taylor was his girlfriend, and virtually every chairman of every major company on the planet was his buddy. He was the Hugh Hefner of the business world, the darling of the gossip columns. His multimillion-dollar parties were envied because he and his guests had such unbridled fun reinforcing the image of a man spending money as fast as he could. He loved the press, and the press loved him back, cataloguing for all the world his outrageous excesses.

But away from the paparazzi, the big-top extravaganzas, the celebrities, behind the broad smile resided a different Malcolm. The urbane charm and wit faded a little. Instead there was a hint of discontent in this luckiest of men who was envied for having everything. Behind a hidden door off his office at *Forbes* magazine was a secret sauna-equipped apartment festooned with artwork depicting mostly naked men. While Malcolm had the Elizabeth Taylors and the Henry Kissingers and the Donald Trumps and, yes, even the Rolling Stones seemingly at his beck and call, while he had hundreds of millions of dollars and trophy real estate and fleets of motorcycles, planes, and boats, and more Fabergé eggs than the Kremlin and more fame than a pope, he pursued yet another passion he was less willing to share with his admiring public—a passion for the company of young men.

On May 27, 1987, Malcolm threw a gargantuan party at Timberfield, his seventy-five-acre estate in Far Hills, New Jersey. It was big even by Forbes standards, though it would be dwarfed two years later by an even bigger blowout at the family's Moroccan palace that would embody many of the qualities of an elaborate three-ring circus. This 1987 party was less unusual because it was similar in many respects to one Malcolm threw twenty years earlier. In both cases, the purpose was to generate ad sales for a special issue of *Forbes* magazine the following September. Billed as the seventieth anniversary celebration of the financial biweekly his father founded, this party was also a self-tribute to the genius of Malcolm Forbes. Without him, this once obscure, frequently struggling journal might well have had no reason to call attention to itself after seventy years.

The Forbes empire in 1987 bore little resemblance to what it was when Malcolm took complete control in 1964. Then it was a workhorse of modest income, a journalistic dwarf alongside the Big Two, *Fortune* and *Business Week*. It had growth promise, but Malcolm would whip it into a publishing sensation, much to the surprise of family members who had quickly sold out, some of them fearing he would spend it into oblivion. Instead, he transformed *Forbes* into the house organ of capitalism, the cornerstone of a family fortune founded on his marketing brilliance and instincts for manipulating the media. Malcolm Forbes deserved the credit. Using an odd mixture of self-promotion and one of the most admired formulas in business journalism, he made his magazine a must-read for every corporate executive who accepted the premise that individuals make the difference in business. Malcolm was one of those individuals.

Surely he couldn't have done it without the help of four cooperative sons, or without the vast talents of top-notch editors, writers, ad sales people, and financial wizards. But just as surely none of it would have happened without Malcolm running the show, plunking down his money, betting on his instincts and winning nearly every time.

And what a show he ran!

Everything was a production, and as with theater, success was measured in the sheer volume of positive press notices. Cynical journalists would marvel at the extent to which their colleagues gave the Forbeses exactly the kind of coverage they craved; yet these same cynics often turned out to be easy converts. How did the family manage to get universally loving coverage from so many journalists? Reporters pride themselves on their streetwise skepticism, turning over rocks in search of that which reduces the high and mighty to the dimensions of mere mortals. No hero is sacred. So how did the head of *Forbes* get this surly crew to cooperate?

When *Newsday* reporter David Firestone set out to do a feature on Malcolm in 1987, he fully expected to find enough evidence to write about a shallow, selfish man obsessed with superficialities like appearances and possessions. It didn't work out that way. He ended up producing the kind of soft, friendly story commonly known among journalists as a puff piece. Malcolm had converted another skeptic.

"I don't remember being turned around," Firestone says. "I remember being fairly cynical based on superficial knowledge. Having met him, I didn't feel especially kindly toward him, but I felt he was fairly sincere in his pursuit of pleasure—that it wasn't just promotion. His rapport with bikers was remarkable. He talked sincerely with them. I was surprised to see that. Eventually, I didn't find a great deal in his personality to be critical of."

In fact, it became clear that despite his many quirky passions, Malcolm had his finger on the magazine's editorial mission. "It's impossible to be objective," Malcolm told Firestone, "but you've got to be fair. . . . Fairness means understanding what motivated somebody and regretting that it didn't work. But it doesn't mean on the one hand and on the other hand. You go in with a clear mind, but you have to come out with a conclusion."

Beyond that, Malcolm knew what other journalists wanted. He truly was one of them, and he'd spare no expense to give it to them.

The Timberfield party was the ultimate example of this special skill—the ability to unapologetically pull out all the stops in a massive publicity grab that doesn't pretend to be anything else. And yet few of the thousand or so ruling-class guests and journalists would publicly exhibit the slightest inclination to suggest there was anything weird or distasteful about such deliberately conspicuous consumption. It was the definition of ostentation, yet the fact that it was Malcolm doing it seemed to make it merely delightfully amusing.

"Mr. Forbes is a man of unlimited dimensions," gushed party organizer Ruth Schwartz at the time, "and that's how we look at this party—a party of unlimited dimensions."

One reason the Forbeses could escape criticism for such overkill is that this occasion was not a social event so much as a business meeting—a corporate convention of news and advertising sources. As such, the whole thing was a business expense. The "guests" actually were there on business. A link with *Forbes* magazine—the standard-bearer of unadulterated capitalism—was good for the image. The corporate giants also were here, perhaps in some cases for the rare opportunity to meet one another. It is also possible some of them figured that agreeing to be an ad-buying player in a few of Mr. Forbes's PR productions today might be useful tomorrow as a bargaining chip to derail, or at least tone down, a negative story in the magazine.

But it was a myth that Malcolm ultimately pulled all the strings, that he could send a pack of reporters like bloodhounds after a company resisting an ad sales rep's advances—or kill an unfriendly story about a faithful advertiser.

What was certainly true was that Malcolm did little to dispel the notion. If that's what people with big advertising money wanted to think, fine. That image, regardless of the fact that it had little basis in reality, was what created the most conflict in the minds of self-respecting journalists who honed their skills at *Forbes* under the tutelage of editor James W. Michaels, a short balding UPI veteran universally recognized as a genius. (Before *Forbes,* Michael's great claim to fame was breaking the news in 1948 that Gandhi had been assassinated. He did it by monitoring state radio broadcasts in his New Delhi hotel room rather than hanging around the scene with the rest of the press corps. In his office hangs a framed copy of the story with his byline on it as it appeared on the front page of a major New York newspaper.)

Here was Malcolm at his home in Far Hills, the perfect New Jersey executive-bedroom community. The eight-bedroom colonial house itself was modest in the context of such estates. But after eight weeks of preparation, he had lured all manner of corporate and government titans, past and present, to wallow in glorious overabundance.

Malcolm was basking in this carefully orchestrated atmosphere. Even the weather cooperated, though the production typified opulence bordering on the vulgar. When the overriding theme for a six-hour party for a thousand mostly rich people is that money is no object, it's probably impossible to avoid at least a little tackiness. To blunt the inevitable question of taste, the air was spiced liberally with the self-effacing humor that was a Forbes trademark. The message, as always, was that the Forbeses weren't pompous. They were just out here having lighthearted fun. They were spending it now because you can't take it with you. They were showing the world how to enjoy wealth in a carefree manner, all the while making sure that the assets kept growing. The basic message: We work hard, we play hard, we don't take ourselves too seriously, yet we're kind of classy in an irreverent way.

Of course, how the world judged the Forbeses mattered a lot. In many ways, as was the case since B. C. Forbes founded the magazine, the name had always been perhaps the family's most valuable asset. Their image was a large part of what they sold—that of happy millionaires miraculously spending it all and having it all. The fact that they were a close-knit, warm, loving family made the picture nearly perfect. And this was the image journalists consistently focused on when covering the Forbes family.

Now here were the rich and famous gathering at Timberfield in the moonlit twilight of the Reagan eighties, a time of unprecedented economic expansion. They were there for what one guest called "the ultimate celebration of gratuitous wealth," which Malcolm personalized more than anyone in this century, having found a way to make money out of the phenomenon of money.

For hours the private helicopters flew in and out of the estate, delivering load after load of superrich corporate giants. At one point thirty-eight of them were parked there. A convoy of limousines delivered the merely rich who couldn't or wouldn't spring for a chopper.

The scene: a huge tent hung with silk tapestries sporting the Forbes crest, a stag. A tract house could have been stuck in one corner of the tent and not been noticed. Half an army of bagpipers and drummers—121 of them—came marching out of the woods through an artificial mist manufactured along with a miniature Scottish village for the occasion. In tribute to the kilted Malcolm, they played a medley of Scottish airs, followed by "Amazing Grace," Malcolm's personal favorite. The whole show reportedly cost $2 million. Milling about Malcolm were 1,100 recognizable socialites, corporate honchos, media moguls, and stars. Lost in the throng were the likes of Carl Icahn, Barbara Walters, David Rockefeller, and Sir James Goldsmith—people seldom found anywhere but center stage. Malcolm had the audacity to invite then President Ronald Reagan to be the keynote speaker. Granted, Reagan and Malcolm were friends who praised each other publicly and privately, but the President declined. He was replaced with a trio that, taken as a whole, probably carried almost as much prestige: then Secretary of the Treasury Howard Baker, then New Jersey governor Thomas Keane, and U.S. Senator Bill Bradley (who drew polite applause when he mentioned the problems of poverty and the homeless).

The crowd included a broad cross section of the rich, famous, and powerful from Wall Street, big business, national politics, national media, and high society: James Robinson of American Express, Donald Marron of PaineWebber, Felix Rohatyn of Lazard Frères, Rand Araskog of ITT, Roger Smith of General Motors, former White House adviser Robert Strauss, former White House cabinet member Cyrus Vance, former U.S. senators Abraham Ribicoff and Paul Laxalt, U.S. Information Agency director Charles Wick, CIA director William Webster, U.S. attorney general Edwin Meese, former ambassador Walter Annenberg, Washington Post Company chairman Katharine Graham, *New York Times* publisher Arthur Sulzberger, William Paley of CBS, Helen Gurley Brown of *Cosmopolitan*, Christie Hefner of *Playboy*, Bob Guccione of *Penthouse*, Eppie Lederer (Ann Landers), model Jerry Hall (boyfriend Mick Jagger had to cancel because of a recording date), television personality Regis Philbin, writer Fran Lebowitz, Oscar de la Renta, Dina Merrill, Jerome Zipkin, Beverly Sills, and Lee Radziwill.

This was Malcolm's finest hour, a celebration of his unqualified success as a journalist and businessman. On his arm was the modern world's Cleopatra, Elizabeth Taylor. The rest of the world was at his feet, the crowd long since won by this brash and charming aristocrat. Perhaps never before had the world seen such a concentration of the rich and powerful outside of a superpower summit or a royal wedding.

Forbes stepped forward to acknowledge this tribute of his own making. It was the climactic moment of this masterpiece of social self-stimulation. (As his friend William F. Buckley would later comment, "When you viewed his Fabergé eggs, you were doing *him* a favor.") It was time for the valedictory, and Malcolm, who commanded a small army of talented writers and editors, might be expected to deliver a momentous speech.

Instead, with Taylor at his side, he pulled out of his pocket a $1 million check and handed it to her for the American Foundation for AIDS Research, which she chaired. "I can't believe this," Liz said, appearing genuinely surprised. "The check is for one million dollars. That really leaves me quite speechless!"

But helping to cure AIDS seemed almost incidental to Malcolm's stated purpose: "to give the *Forbes* magazine celebration more significance than just a social event." Drawing so much attention to a philanthropic gesture wasn't really Malcolm's style. Indeed, he made donations to many other charities—including Memorial Sloan-Kettering Cancer Center, Meals on Wheels, the Police Athletic League, the New-York Historical Society—without calling attention to himself.

Giving money for AIDS research, however, had perhaps more significance than even Malcolm realized.

"At that moment, a check for AIDS!" recalls Christopher Byron, then an assistant managing editor at Forbes. "There they were arrayed before him, the people from whom all the money had come, and that was the one gesture he thought to make. It was as if at that moment he still was undecided what to do."

Byron was referring to that element of Malcolm's private life that everyone seemed to know about but that no talked about, despite the numerous times it had imposed itself, often on the unsuspecting. On the one hand, Malcolm and his family strove mightily to present a certain image. They were to be seen as lovable aristocrats without a shred of pretension—salt of the earth and living proof of the good things in store for the family that stays together. And to a large extent, this image was an accurate reflection of reality. On the other hand, Malcolm had a nonpublic life that kept bubbling to the surface—a life he recklessly pursued nearly in the open while at the same time struggling to conceal it. He seemed simultaneously tired of hiding yet frightened of being found out, lest the news somehow damage his integrity and his financial empire.

There was another side to Malcolm that seldom won public notice, an occasional insensitivity that appeared unintentional. Malcolm had the whole Far Hills extravaganza videotaped and requested that the magazine's staff come to view it at a New School auditorium near the office. Viewing the family's home movies was an annual compulsory event for Forbes employees around Christmas time.

"How delightful that in this day and age someone thought this appropriate," says one former editor.

This time Malcolm opened with a little speech about rough times ahead. Ad volume was down, profitability was hurting. All would have to tighten their belts a little, he said, then stepped aside to show everyone the tape of what some had come to recognize as one of the most conspicuous examples of wasteful extravagance to date.

This was a typical Malcolm vulgarity, in this case "inviting" the staff essentially to pay tribute to the tribute to himself. This would have been just another vaguely insulting but amusing diversion for the staff had he not preceded it with the chat about how frugal everyone was going to have to be.

In reality, the party in May 1987 more than paid for itself. Major advertisers essentially paid their way in by agreeing to place ads in Forbes's seventieth anniversary issue, which Malcolm later boasted generated a record $10 million in revenue. Perhaps the party wasn't such a waste of money after all, but Forbes's timing left a few staff members feeling they'd been treated to more pre-Christmas irony than they could stomach.

In such gestures are more than a hint of the self-absorbed pomposity Malcolm's own father exhibited with his employee years before.

Bertie Charles Forbes was proud of his own success. He combined dogged hard work, uncompromising frugality, and his own brand of financial cunning to build a business out of raw skill. In a paternalistic way, he rewarded loyalty among his employees with an annual event called Veterans Day that some found belittling. It was mandatory for the entire staff to attend a picnic at his home in Englewood, New Jersey, an occasion that would include what for many was a humiliating tradition of lining up to have B.C. personally hand them each an envelope containing a bonus. The amount usually wasn't large enough to be considered more than a token reminder that your paycheck comes not from your labors but from the goodness of the boss's heart.

Surely B.C. viewed this event as a special opportunity to show his gratitude for staff who'd hung around five years or longer. But the way he handled it left just the opposite impression—that he was cheap and had an overblown sense of how much his employees admired him.

But the small, frugal gesture was in keeping with his personality. The idea of investing millions in a life-style was foreign to him. What you invested was time and effort, and the money you risked was other people's. Strutting around with Hollywood stars, duplicating the life-style of a decadent Roman emperor, would never have struck B.C. as sound business strategy.

For Malcolm, it was. But the terms of B.C.'s will established a trust with the requirement that Veterans Day be reenacted year after year. Malcolm made the best of it in terms of making it entertaining and eschewing the paternalistic aspect that B.C. probably intended to pass on. That was enough immortality for B.C.

But Malcolm was different. He may have been curious about how history would remember him, but his business goal was to establish himself as a legend in his own time. He wanted to be to capitalism what Casey Stengel was to baseball: the game's most colorful proponent and purest practitioner.

Making Elizabeth Taylor part of the formula was a stroke of genius, though initially it was Taylor's idea. Fresh from divorcing the mother of his four sons and a daughter, Malcolm must have sensed that such a match-up would be the stuff of supermarket tabloid dreams. Getting the Forbes name into the scandal rags might seem counterproductive, something that could hurt the magazine's sterling reputation in advertising and journalism circles. It wouldn't be long before the *National Enquirer* would be trumpeting the news that Malcolm wanted to marry Taylor and that Taylor was thinking about it.

This solved a problem for the voracious publicity hound in Malcolm. You can achieve fame within certain circles, but achieving notoriety in many circles is tricky. One way is to get elected president of the United States, and Malcolm had already tried and failed at that. But a famous media mogul is not often known outside the business. You can be a sports hero, but to people who don't follow sports, you're unknown. Malcolm had certainly established himself as a major luminary in magazine publishing. He'd even made a name for himself as an eccentric rich guy. But his celebrity status was still outside the realm of superstardom. How could he broaden his appeal? The answer was to use what writer Julie Baumgold called "the borrowed fame of Elizabeth Taylor."

It may have seemed tacky at the time, but as executives at the magazine would later concede, the alliance vastly expanded Forbes's name recognition. But the rumors of a marriage proposal reported in the tabloids revived a far different kind of rumor in close-in circles—the rumor that Malcolm preferred young men. The Taylor thing struck insiders as dishonest. It's okay to be gay and hide it. But to be gay, hide it, and then actively promote the idea that you're the right man for one of the world's most famous sex symbols? That irked people who knew better.

John Anderson, an intern who started working at Forbes shortly after the Far Hills anniversary party in 1987, wasn't irked. He was awed by Malcolm. Anderson had recently graduated from the University of Texas. He went to work under Harry Seneker on the Forbes 400 Rich List in June 1987, about a month after the seventieth anniversary party. In view of all the hoo-ha about Malcolm and Taylor, he was a little puzzled when fellow staffers warned him about Malcolm's thing for young men.

Still, Anderson was determined to meet this legend and was willing to take the risk that Malcolm might misinterpret his motive, which was to see what a multimillionaire celebrity was like up close.

"The first time I met him, I knew all the rumors," he says. Another staffer who'd had direct experience had filled him in on the details of his own encounter and told him how to fend off unwanted advances.

Anderson instigated his own close encounter with Malcolm. He and another intern that summer "decided we wanted to meet Malcolm before we left," Anderson says. "We sent him a letter that we wanted to take him to lunch and he called us down to his office. If it were two twenty-year-old women interns, I don't know if they'd get in. We got into his office and started chatting."

This wasn't just any old office. This was the former board room for Macmillan Publishing Company's U.S. headquarters in which receptions were held for such authors as Margaret Mitchell and Winston Churchill. Malcolm had it crammed with English antiques, Oriental rugs, and an eclectic array of art by the likes of Rubens, Gauguin, Renoir, Bellows, Homer, and James Bama, whose favorite topic was ruggedly virile cowboys. Malcolm's work was organized in a diamond-studded Fabergé folder, and he summoned secretaries with jade Fabergé push buttons on an intercom.

Malcolm asked the two young men where they were from, where they were living, how they liked New York.

"He asked me, 'What do you do at night? Do you like to go to singles clubs?' I said, no, I don't have the money or time or something like that. I didn't think anything about it," Anderson says.

The meeting ended without a lunch date, and the two interns returned to work. About six months later, Anderson, now a full-time employee, found an excuse to request another meeting with Malcolm. Malcolm had gotten hold of some preliminary research the young reporter had done on a candidate for the Rich List, an annual list that ranks the four hundred richest people in the United States. Anderson's editor had passed the information on to Malcolm, and Malcolm had alluded to it in his Fact and Comment column as a sort of plug for list.

Anderson was worried because he hadn't yet double-checked some of the information. His concern turned into a good excuse for asking to see the boss once again.

"I figured the more times I could see Malcolm, the better," Anderson said. "I called his secretary because I was worried about why I wasn't contacted first before he used the material."

Malcolm explained that mentioning the possibility of someone making it to the Rich List was harmless and seemed a good way to promote the list, one of Malcolm's more brilliant concoctions.

Then Malcolm asked casually, "Do you ride motorcycles?"

"No," Anderson said.

"Would you like to?" Malcolm said.

"Sure." A secretary who sits by Malcolm then handed Anderson a piece of paper and said, "Here. Write your address. Just put down your home phone number and address."

Anderson complied, but he didn't hear from Malcolm any time soon after that. "At this point, Malcolm must have thought I was interested in him," Anderson concedes.

About two months later, Malcolm called Anderson into his office on a Friday about nine A.M. "I forgot," he said to Anderson, "but did you say you'd like to bike?"

"Yeah," Anderson said.

"Well, how about if we go bike riding next week?" Malcolm said.

"Okay, sounds good to me."

Malcolm told Anderson to meet him next door at his town house at 5:30 P.M. Monday. "We'll have dinner and go out for a ride," he said.

As he stood there in Malcolm's palatial office surrounded by "all these paintings and Russian trinkets on his desk worth millions," Anderson began to wonder, How am I going to get out of this thing? He wanted to be able to say he'd shared an evening of fascinating banter over an elegant meal with this legendary capitalist—but without having to take a bath with him.

When 5:30 Monday came around, Anderson met Malcolm at his office and followed him into the house part of the town house—two floors connected by a spiral staircase. A camera crew was setting up equipment in the living room. Malcolm made two screwdrivers, gave one to Anderson and suggested they go into the bedroom since the living room was occupied.

Oh, great! Right into the bedroom, Anderson thought. The only place to sit was on the bed. Anderson sat on the end. Malcolm half lay on it with one leg on the bed and one leg off. Anderson couldn't help but notice the life-size statue of a teenage boy in a loincloth—"like a junior Tarzan."

Malcolm made small talk along the exact same lines as that first time when Anderson and the other intern were in his office. Where was Anderson from? Where did he live? Did he like New York? This went on for about a half hour. They talked about how the rich list was going and about the quality of the people working on the project. Then the subject of dinner came up.

"John, I like to take a sauna before I go to dinner," Malcolm said matter-of-factly and invited Anderson to join him.

Anderson used the excuse he learned from the other reporter: "No thanks," he said. "I was just on the fourth floor [the location of the in-house gym] before I came down." The lie was meant to indicate that he'd just had a workout and a shower and wasn't in the mood for getting sweaty and taking another shower.

"Are you sure?" Malcolm said. "The sauna's just right in back."

Anderson declined, and Mr. Forbes dropped the idea altogether. The decision probably cost Anderson a chance to view what one former staffer called the world's best collection of pornographic art.

Malcolm then pulled out a manila folder from a drawer next to the bed. It was full of Malcolm's own restaurant reviews and some menus. "Where'd you like to eat?" he asked, but then ignored Anderson's choice and selected a restaurant himself—a place on Third Avenue on the Upper East Side.

Malcolm called the security guard and said, "Hey, get out one of my Harleys."

The two men, dressed in suits, headed for the street, stopping by a rack loaded with gloves and helmets on the way to the elevator. The Harley—license plate MSF2—was ready for them on Twelfth Street. Malcolm got on and Anderson climbed on the back, grabbing onto Malcolm. They took off for Third Avenue and headed uptown.

"When you ride a motorcycle and you're on the back," Anderson explains, "you're kind of at the whim of the driver. I don't think he was doing it on purpose, but I noticed that every time he'd take off from a light, my reflex would be to shoot forward to stay on the bike and run right into him."

They didn't talk much, but at one stoplight, Anderson asked Malcolm about his highly publicized friendship with Liz. "It was all over the office that she was supposed to be his beard."

"Yeah," he said, "she's coming to town. We're going to see *The Phantom of the Opera.* I've got to get tickets. We'll see who has more pull around here."

Malcolm wore a helmet without a mask, so people on the street and in taxis could recognize him—which they did.

His manner was unpretentious. There was no entourage, no servants. When they reached the restaurant, he backed the Harley into a parking space on the street between cars. They walked in and took a table in the front by the door. The reservation was made under the name Malcolm Stevenson.

During dinner, Malcolm seemed subdued, almost brooding. "I almost started feeling bad," Anderson says. "Maybe he thought he was going to get something from me that he wasn't going to get. Here he was spending a hundred and twenty bucks for dinner and probably wondering, What am I doing going out with this cub reporter?"

After the meal, they got back on the Harley and headed down Fifth Avenue. Damn, Anderson thought. We're going back to the town house. I'm in trouble again.

But Malcolm stopped at one point and asked, "Where do you live?" This would be the third time Malcolm had asked him this question.

"Seventieth on the West Side," Anderson said.

"You should have told me sooner so I could drop you off," Malcolm said. Instead, he stopped at Columbus Circle. As Anderson said goodbye, Malcolm reached into his pocket, pulled out a wad of cash, and said, "Here."

It was $100. Anderson tried to refuse it, but Malcolm insisted he take it.

"You were working tonight," he said. "You were my security."

Anderson returned his helmet and gloves to Malcolm's secretary the next morning and included a note thanking him. Some co-workers told Anderson the next day the $100 should be viewed as hush money; others believed it was a simple act of generosity.

The experience puzzled Anderson. What was Malcolm up to? Did he simply want to give this young kid from Texas a lifelong memory? What's wrong with an older man inviting a younger man to share a sauna bath before dinner? "He was a nice guy," Anderson says. "I liked him. He was accessible. I knew I could meet with him in his office if I needed to."

Anderson was amazed at how widespread the talk was of Malcolm's sexual preferences at the office, yet the outside world seemed oblivious. "His divorce raised a lot of eyebrows," Anderson says, referring to conversations he had with subjects for the rich list. "I'd call these guys and they'd say, 'What's the deal with Malcolm getting a divorce? Why?' They didn't seem to have the slightest inkling."

Anderson wasn't the only young man Malcolm ever asked to dinner for no apparent reason. In fact, after one new staffer's mind-boggling experience in the 1970s, it became standard procedure to brief attractive young men on how to deal with Malcolm's invitations.

One twenty-two-year-old who started at Forbes in 1983 says he was warned. Someday Malcolm will show up in your office unannounced for no apparent reason, he was told. He'll talk awhile about nothing in particular, then ask you to dinner. You'll go, meeting him first at the town house to look at all his erotic gay art. He'll invite you into the sauna. Then you'll have to fight him off, assuming you're not inclined.

After three months at Forbes, this new employee's picture and bio appeared in "The Piper," the in-house bulletin. As predicted, Malcolm showed up in his office, noting that the announcement had attracted his attention. He chatted about that for a while. It was clear he had no particular reason to be there. Then he asked the staffer out to dinner, possibly to rate a restaurant.

The young man had been coached on the proper response.

"Gee, I can't," he said. "My fiancée is making dinner for me Friday night." At the time, he had no fiancée.

"Okay, maybe some other time," Malcolm said.

That was the first and last time this employee ever talked to Malcolm Forbes, though he would work there six years before leaving in 1989. Though the encounter was harmless, he resented it.

"It bugged me," he says. "I was nervous. If I hadn't been warned, I would have thought, Wow, Malcolm Forbes wants to get to know me. But you don't turn down the chairman of the company, so I felt that having to do that was a pain in the ass. Probably more women than men have to deal with this. And it was more intrusive for me, because I was warned."

Indeed, from the employee's point of view, the experience bordered on harassment. Several young men who had similar experiences say they felt the same. When your boss shows interest in you, it's usually a sign that he likes the job you're doing. That's exciting. When it becomes clear that it's you he likes—and his interest in your work is probably marginal—it can be threatening. It's a dilemma: reject him on a personal level and it may hurt your career. Some men at Forbes have stumbled through this awkwardness and come away with razor-sharp images of the stark contrast between appearances and reality, though it never seemed to hurt their careers.

But the rumors about his sexuality swirled for decades. Virtually everyone interviewed for this book raised the question without being prompted. They wanted to know whether someone, at last, was going to provide a glimpse of the Forbeses that everyone seemed to know about but wouldn't discuss publicly. Or would this be simply a rehash of the family's carefully orchestrated stream of media notices about awesome charm, wealth, and connections?

"It was obvious what Malcolm's preferences were," Anderson says. "In all his escapades, his cooks and staff all look very handsome. It seemed to be well known, yet you never read one word that Liz was a beard. You wonder how many fifty-year-old white males would still want to subscribe knowing this. Yet he wasn't very discreet."

Even in the early 1960s, before the sexual revolution, the rumors were out there. Steve Quickel, who worked at Forbes then, says, "I remember a box maker from Brooklyn, a big, gruff guy, at lunch leaning over and saying, 'So what's this I hear about Malcolm being queer?' You'd hear about it like that, but that was about it."

Malcolm wanted it both ways: he wanted to be a star among the world's high and mighty, yet ride a motorcycle down New York's predominantly gay Christopher Street in full riding leathers with a handsome young man clinging tightly to his back and not be publicly noticed by the wrong people. And in the end, Malcolm had it both ways.

In the mid-1970s at the palace in Morocco, when former *Forbes* staffer Arthur Jones was working on a biography of Malcolm, he asked him about the rumors that he was bisexual.

"Christ!" Malcolm replied. "What sort of book is this?" And that pretty much brought to an end the extensive cooperation Jones had enjoyed to that point in researching the book.

2 | "BE SOMETHING"

A perceptive teacher's simple word of encouragement can make the difference between success and failure— or, at least in the case of Bertie Charles Forbes, success and fortune.

"My headmaster led me to believe I could write," B. C. Forbes wrote of Gavin Grieg, headmaster at Whitehill, the little school in New Deer, Scotland, that B.C. attended to age fourteen. The ability to write, then, became the focus for this ambitious little Scotsman of seemingly boundless energy. It would become the fertile ground from which would spring unbounded wealth.

B.C. was born in 1880, the sixth of ten children raised by Robert Forbes and Agnes Moir in a little house called Cunnieknowe in Aberdeenshire. B.C.'s father was the village tailor; he also ran the general store and sold beer.

"My father," B.C. wrote, "managed to get along somehow until the family multiplied much faster than his meager earnings did.

Long before the tenth came along, the sledding was painfully hard." It was a rare reference to his father.

At fourteen, having completed eighth grade, B.C. left the fold for Peterhead, twenty-five miles away, where he worked several months as a bookkeeper before taking a stab at what he thought would be a writing job with the *Peterhead Sentinel* newspaper. It was Grieg, an occasional contributor to the *Sentinel,* who gave B.C. the confidence that writing was a job he could do. His first attempt, however, backfired. He applied for a seven-year apprenticeship as a compositor, thinking the word meant one who writes compositions—not one who sets type.

Undaunted, he took a shorthand course—then a requirement for would-be reporters—and did well enough that, at sixteen, he landed a job with the *Dundee Courier.* He worked as an assistant to a reporter in Perth for the equivalent of $2.50 a week, lived in a garret in a tenement boarding house, and literally fed on the boarders' leftover scraps. He worked from nine to midnight, filing reports to his supervisor from interviews and meetings he attended and from the checks he made with hospitals and the police.

Within six months he got his reward, having impressed the home office with skillful writing—for example, the amazing tale of a long-distance swim across the Tay River, a murder trial, and the visit of Queen Victoria. At age seventeen, B.C. was given his own district, Brechin, and went there at double the pay as a senior reporter, bringing with him a cousin, Charlie Moir, to be his assistant.

During the next four years, B.C. honed his journalistic skills and instincts, nurtured a passion for card playing, and took up golf. He also fell in love with a woman—a Forbes of no direct blood relation. Even after he was transferred far away to Dundee, he courted her, but to no avail. She married someone closer to home. B.C. was heartsick.

"I shook the dust of Scotland off my feet, and sailed for the remotest corner of the world I could think of, South Africa, then in the close of the Boer War," he wrote in the *American* magazine, "where I figured I could find enough excitement to assuage my black, black woe."

He took with him a shorthand notebook with a photo of Andrew Carnegie pasted on the inside front cover. And on the inside rear cover was a poem called "Be Something." It read in part: "Be something in this living age / And prove your right to be / A light upon some darkened page . . ."

It took B.C. seven months to land a newspaper job in South Africa, and he was practically broke when he started at the *Natal Mercury* in 1902. Within a few weeks he was backing up the paper's top writer and soon after was hired away to be the number-two senior reporter for the *Rand Daily Mail*, the new name of a failing Johannesburg paper just taken over by a South African mine promoter. The editor was hero journalist Edgar Wallace, whose great claim to fame was breaking the news that the Boer War was over.

B.C. thrived, earning a good salary, saving several thousand dollars, and further focusing his ambition. By 1904, at the age of twenty-three, he had developed a particular interest in business news. "He was learning how to make money, he was meeting men who knew how to make more," wrote Arthur Jones, a former *Forbes* editor and author of a 1977 biography of Malcolm Forbes. B.C., who had grown up in a Scotland that participated financially in the American railroad boom, decided America was the place to seek his own fortune.

He arrived in New York in September 1904. It took a week—and a Scottish connection—to get a serious interview, with John W. Doddsworth, managing editor of the *Journal of Commerce and Commercial Bulletin*. Doddsworth asked B.C. why he should hire someone who didn't know the difference between Wall Street and Broadway.

Bertie's answer: "Because, sir, I'll work for nothing."

He was hired at $15 a week and immediately made a mark. He did it in dry goods. One of his topics was raw silk. The paper would publish the importers' prices, but B.C. decided to report actual selling prices—the deals importers cut with buyers. This caused a storm of complaints to B.C.'s bosses, much to the benefit of his career. B.C. already was redefining business journalism by reporting not just on superficialities but by digging up what until then had been considered proprietary information—news that moves the market. In this case, the reports' impact was to create a more competitive silk market; published prices fell.

This aggressive approach was a reflection of B.C.'s energy and ambition. He was intensely competitive. Perhaps the best example of how confident he was in his own ability to convert his skills into success was his decision to move from a $10-a-week boarding house in Brooklyn into a room at the Waldorf-Astoria that cost him more than he was earning. Why? Because the Waldorf was one of the most popular places for businessmen to stay over in New York. And while B.C. would later concede that the payoff in terms of stories was less than expected, schmoozing at the Waldorf led him to conclude that businessmen were often more interesting than their businesses.

As a journalist, B.C. was clearly distinguishing himself in four noticeable ways. First, he brought enterprise reporting to business journalism, uncovering and reporting market-moving information, using a variety of investment-banker types as confidential sources, thus establishing himself as an influential force in business. Second, he introduced the human element, focusing on the people and personalities shaping companies. Third, his writing was lively and readable. Fourth, he did the work of a multitude of journalists.

In fact, it was his insatiable appetite for work that gave birth to a column concept that survives today under the signature of a grandson. It was called Fact and Comment, "a daily column of notes." Forbes started it after becoming assistant financial editor at the *Journal of Commerce* as a way to do "more than the job called for."

His prodigious output drew the attention of the editor at the *Commercial and Financial Chronicle,* who asked if B.C. would be willing to write that publication's weekly money-market review, in addition to everything else he was doing. He obliged, and that brought his talents to the attention of William Randolph Hearst in 1911.

Hearst wanted to improve the financial pages of his *New York American,* a morning daily. The search for talent centered on columnists at two different publications, both of which turned out to be using the same writer: B. C. Forbes.

B.C.'s decision to join the *American* quickly paid off. Not only was he earning and saving more money than ever before, he was gaining a notoriety unlike that of any financial journalist before him. He did it by putting flesh and blood on the dry bones of business news. In so doing he established a readership that newspaper business pages previously hadn't known. And that in turn established Forbes as a power to be reckoned with on Wall Street. He knew this, and he used it to curry favor with some of the rich men he admired and from whom he would soon borrow money to let him start his own magazine.

But before going into business for himself, B.C. would once again find romance. This time, it would last a long time—long enough, at least, to raise a family.

When John Stevenson struck out on his own in native England, it was to become a priest. He entered a Jesuit seminary, but it wasn't right for him. He quit, became a pharmacist, and emigrated to the United States, setting up shop in the Bay Ridge section of Brooklyn, a popular neighborhood for the well-to-do Irish of the day. It was there that he met the widowed Adelaide Keegan, a third-generation American of Irish descent with three children, Katherine, Adrian, and Harry. Her first husband, John Tracy, who was in the barge business, had died of pneumonia less than a year after Katherine was born. Family legend has it that Tracy, who loved to drink, became ill after spending a night out in the cold.

In 1896, Adelaide Keegan Stevenson—who owned a lot of land and made a small fortune on mortgage certificates—had her fourth child and named her Adelaide. (Years later, after Stevenson died, his widow married John Foley, who survived her, inherited Adelaide's fortune, and left it to his mother, who was living in a nursing home. Adelaide's family fortune vanished soon after with the death of Foley's mother.)

By the age of eighteen, daughter Adelaide Stevenson was a tall, stately beauty with auburn hair and her red-headed mother's charm and wit. She was also ready for marriage—or so her mother believed. The Stevensons held regular card parties at their home, and it was to one of these parties in 1914 that some friends brought the eligible bachelor and well-known financial columnist B. C. Forbes, then thirty-four. B.C. fell for the gorgeous young Adelaide. In fact, his ardor was so strong, it overcame any misgivings he might have had about one very basic difference between them: she was staunchly Catholic and he was staunchly Presbyterian. They married a year later—in the sacristy of Our Lady of Angels Church in Bay Ridge, Brooklyn. Because of the religious difference, they could not be married at the church's main altar, and the rest of their lives together would be troubled by religious conflict.

In 1917, when B.C. decided to launch a publication of his own, he intended to name it Doers and Doings. Walter Drey, whom Forbes had asked to join him in the venture, knew better. He agreed to enter the partnership with one condition—that the magazine be named after its founder. Drey, general manager of the *Magazine of Wall Street,* knew the Forbes name would open advertisers' doors—a prophetic observation. Forbes had already made his name synonymous with informative, people-oriented business journalism.

To start the venture, B.C. gave up an annual income—including salary from Hearst and payment for numerous other articles— roughly equivalent in 1990 to $185,000. And though he certainly had amassed sizable personal wealth, not one penny of it would be dedicated to the magazine. Instead, he borrowed all necessary funding, including whatever he needed to sustain the level of his family's personal wealth. And much of the borrowings came from the men he featured in his book *Fifty Men Who Are Making America.* Such a financial arrangement today would be condemned as a potential conflict of interest. Even under Malcolm the perception persisted that an ad in *Forbes* might lessen the advertiser's vulnerability to harsh editorial treatment, though the evidence suggests otherwise.

From the first issue of *Forbes* (September 15, 1917, "devoted to doers and doings"), it was clear that being on B.C.'s good side meant generous praise. Being on his bad side made one a potential target of the kind of hard-hitting, biting indictments that characterize many a modern-day *Forbes* story.

The first issue's Fact and Comment column led with this quote:

"With all thy getting, get understanding." It was attributed to Robert Burns, honored son of B.C.'s beloved Scotland. Of course, it wasn't Burns; it was the Bible, Proverbs 4:7.

B.C. went on to state that the purpose of business is to "produce happiness, not to pile up millions." Never mind that piling up millions happens to be what makes countless business people and their stockholders happy. This was typical of B.C.'s simplistic brand of wisdom, a formula that would survive his passing through his son Malcolm.

B.C. admitted in that first issue that he would never shrink from heaping praise on a subject, declaring, "Give a man full credit for being liberally and unselfishly inclined, and the tendency is for him to try to live up to his reputation." Sure enough, the issue contained such puffery—a piece about what a great employer B. F. Goodrich Company was. This also was a reflection of another of B.C.'s pet concepts: that productivity ultimately depended on harmony between employers and employees.

None of these cracker-barrel adages, however, mattered a whit compared to the thrust of the tough stories B.C. fashioned. He established a formula that survives today as the single distinguishing characteristic for which *Forbes* is most admired in journalism. The inaugural issue contained this piece by B.C.: "High-Placed Misfits. George Jay Gould, the Nicholas Romanoff of American Finance. The Tragic Story of How the Gould 'Empire,' the Greatest Patrimony Ever Left a Young American, Has Been Dissipated."

Forbes unblinkingly ripped into his prey, indicting him for "his narrowness of vision, his unreasoning jealousy, his chronic suspicion, his distrust of both subordinates and rivals. He would neither run his properties himself nor give others freedom and authority to do so."

As Arthur Jones wrote in 1977, the story on Gould embodied the Forbes formula: "the sharp attack, supported by some carefully marshaled facts, the quick aside to sketch in an element of the subject's character, the anecdote or piece of physical description to give the reader an insight into the manner or bearing of the subject. The feisty, aggressive, acidic *Forbes* story had come into its own."

Not the sort of piece captains of industry look forward to reading about themselves or their companies. What Forbes offered the prospective subject was a clear choice between being portrayed as hero or villain. B.C.'s simplified view of the world left no room for gray areas, and to a large extent that tradition would survive intact. And later generations would measure the magazine's future prospects by its ability to maintain its feistiness.

From 1916 through 1928, Adelaide filled the big house on Fountain Road with five sons. She had a maid to help with the cleaning and a nanny to assist with the two youngest, Gordon and Wallace. They all were born in the age of overnight stock-market fortunes that nurtured *Forbes* magazine in its infancy. B.C.'s personal wealth grew accordingly, permitting him to repay backers and reinvest profit.

The firstborn was Bruce, in 1916, then Duncan in 1918, Malcolm a year later, Gordon in 1923, and Wallace in 1928. To deal with the religious conflict between the parents, the Forbes boys were baptized alternately in the Catholic and Presbyterian faiths, with Bruce leading off as a Catholic. Ultimately, this strategy probably all but ruined the boys' ability to develop a sense of faith in any religion, with Bruce and Malcolm attending Mass at Saint Cecilia's Church with their mother, and Duncan and Gordon going with their father to the First Presbyterian Church in Englewood. To begin with, the practice was hypocritical; it violated principles of both churches. Adding to the religious fuzziness was the occasional insistence by B.C. that Bruce and Malcolm, on returning from early-morning Mass, join him and the other brothers for a second Sunday service.

The religious rivalry between B.C. and Adelaide was so intense that even in the face of Duncan's death as a teenager in a car crash in 1933, the baptismal scorecard was a matter of real concern. To keep the Catholics from gaining such a wide lead over the Protestants, Wallace—originally slated for Catholicism according to the formula—would be reassigned a Protestant.

"We all believed, however, that our mother must have snuck us out to be baptized in the Catholic church without my father knowing it," says Wallace. "She would have thought we'd all end up in hell if she didn't."

"We five brothers were pretty rivalrous," Malcolm once said.

"We had to learn a new hymn every Sunday. My father would sit there playing poker with his friends and we had to recite a hymn before we could go out to play. We got ten cents for it."

Duncan's death in a car, with Bruce at the wheel, was a major turning point in the family. The happy days of the prosperous 1920s had already given way to the austere 1930s. The magazine was costing B.C. more to produce than it was taking in and could easily have been folded for sound financial reasons.

B.C. had successfully predicted the crash of 1929 and kept it from hurting his own immediate investments, but *Forbes* was an investor's magazine and as the supply of investors dwindled, so did the magazine's own fortunes. Just as significant was the creation of the first business magazine to compete with *Forbes: Fortune,* the invention of *Time* magazine founder Henry Luce. "The field which lies open is as immense and as rich as was ever offered to journalistic enterprise," Luce said at the time. In fact, it has been suggested that whatever success *Forbes* magazine had enjoyed to that point was a reflection not of its quality, but of the lack of anything else with which to compare it.

B.C.'s partner, Walter Drey, was wiped out by the crash, suffered a nervous breakdown and eventually left as *Forbes* business manager and vice president. When the market plunged again in 1931, B.C. got stung, having gobbled up some bargains in the wake of the 1929 crash.

With the depression in full force in 1932, *Forbes*'s circulation hovered around 60,000, with B.C. blithely running cover stories on "men who are making America" despite widespread evidence of economic decay. The Forbes boys spent their free time working in the mail room.

Whether the pressures of business had any influence isn't clear, but about this time, the marriage of B.C. and Adelaide, while rich and pleasurable in some ways, was increasingly marred by running domestic quarrels—about Adelaide's spending and B.C.'s card games, drinking, and supposed womanizing. Duncan's death put the family's unity to the ultimate test, and it wouldn't survive.

Duncan was well liked because he was so warm. The freckle-faced fifteen-year-old had established his role among the brothers as "engineer and inventor"—the orchestrator of mischief and pranks. Duncan was like Peck's bad boy. He looked like Alfred E. Newman. "He was a very special guy," recalls a cousin. "He was a Huck Finn and very, very funny."

B.C. and Adelaide were vacationing at Yama Farms in the Adirondacks in New York with W. Walton Jones, the Cities Service Oil Company executive, and his wife. Bruce had just gotten a new convertible for his seventeenth birthday and decided with Duncan to drive the one hundred miles or so to Yama Farms.

The boys rounded a bend on Storm King Highway and found it blocked by two cars, one with a flat and another that had stopped to help. Bruce veered to avoid them. The tires on one side slipped onto the soft shoulder. The car flipped over, and Duncan suffered a broken neck and died. Bruce was arrested briefly and was jailed until his uncle, Frederic Bruce, bailed him out. Though Bruce Forbes was never charged, the incident surely added to his trauma. Throughout his life, he would occasionally wake up in a sweat dreaming about it. Even if Bruce didn't blame himself for Duncan's death, he would live with the belief that his mother held him responsible and never forgave him.

Deepening Adelaide's anguish was B.C.'s rush to bury Duncan. While others in the family were emerging from shock and overwhelmed by grief, B.C. was intent on seeing to it that no one dwelt too long on the tragedy. Toward that end, he had Duncan buried the next day. "Adelaide was aghast," recalls one family member. She wanted him buried in the Catholic cemetery. "It seemed to her his disposition was being handled no better than if he were a pet." Indeed, Duncan was her pet, and the dispute over his burial did permanent damage to Adelaide's love for B.C. It was the beginning of the end of their marriage.

The incident left Bruce feeling permanently separated from his mother's love. As for Malcolm, it was the loss of his closest sibling—a boyhood companion and co-conspirator in numerous projects and adventures.

The incident brought out the worst in the parents. B.C.'s Victorian inclination not to wallow in emotion left his children and wife alone to deal with their own despair. In fact, his response to the tragedy was to sign the family on for a trip to Scotland, back to New Deer, to attend for the first time in person the annual picnic he funded there. Little space or time was allowed for the survivors to share their grief over the loss of Duncan.

B.C.'s effort to put the tragedy behind the family wasn't enough to save his marriage. If anything, the rush to bury Duncan sealed off any hope of recovery. It was another example of B.C.'s Victorian insensitivity to the feelings of others. He was a great one for promoting the virtues of ambition, discipline, and hard work and for rewarding success, but in matters of the heart, he was awkward. And in his relationship with Adelaide he was just as Victorian, much to her dissatisfaction.

B.C. was the quintessential chauvinist, recalls one family member who knew him. He came and went as he pleased, but expected his wife to be there at all times. He depended on her to entertain his mogul friends, and she was good at it. Though not an extrovert, she was poised and witty—a great raconteur and charmer. Yet B.C. also expected her to oversee the household duties of cooking and cleaning and to raise the boys.

Gradually, after Duncan's death, the affection between them ran out on both sides and they began to snap at each other.

They decided to transfer Malcolm from Englewood Junior High to a prestigious boarding school, Hackley, in the fall of 1934, perhaps partly to shield him from the battles on the home front. It is at this age, some have speculated, that a part of Malcolm's emotional development stopped. It would become evident in later life in the things and activities that seemed to give him the greatest pleasure.

It was at Englewood that Malcolm published his first schoolboy newspaper, a continuation of similar activities he'd initiated at home. One example: "The City of Dunc Weekly News," named in memory of Duncan, was founded to report news "dealing with the happenings of two cities built by Malcolm and Gordon Forbes in the cellar of their home out of cardboard boxes, with cellophane windows and electric lights." It was co-edited by schoolmate "G. P. Shultz," the future secretary of state under Ronald Reagan, and printed on the $35 duplicator Malcolm got for his thirteenth birthday.

At Englewood he used the paper to conduct a poll to find out whom the students deemed the most popular, best dressed, best looking, and so on. Malcolm bagged best dressed, most humorous and, prophetically, best host. That summer he used the duplicator to put out the *Eagle Scout,* a newspaper he launched at the suggestion of his scout leader.

Malcolm was not happy about leaving home to join his brother Bruce at Hackley in Tarrytown, New York. He liked living at home. He liked his mother's company. But what Malcolm wanted wasn't considered. Once there, he struggled to shine in the shadow of his popular brother, whose natural gregariousness and ability at sports were qualities Malcolm comparatively lacked. What brought Malcolm out of himself was the opportunity to lead.

The solution for Malcolm was to involve himself again in a newspaper project, first a short-lived one he called the *Underclassmen's Voice,* then the *Hackley Eagle* with which he caused a flap by inadvertently printing an off-color joke in a regular column of schoolboy humor.

The joke: "Did you hear about the absent-minded professor who kissed the trolley and jumped on his wife and went to town?" Malcolm said he wasn't aware of the sexual innuendo, but school officials were shocked and even considered kicking him out. Instead it was decided the paper must be vetted by the faculty. After a few issues, young Malcolm grew frustrated with what was being expunged and threw in the towel with this announcement: "We admittedly made mistakes, but we will not make the mistake of printing what is not our opinion as we wanted it expressed. No, we can discontinue rather than that."

With that, the *Hackley Eagle* died, but it won for Malcolm a note of warm praise. "I admire your fearless independence of spirit," B.C. wrote him. "Naturally, I'm an ardent believer in the freedom of the press." Though the letter didn't say so, B.C. may also have been pleased that Malcolm was dropping this academic distraction.

*   *   *

On September 20, 1943, Adelaide would leave B.C. and sue for a legal separation, custody of then fifteen-year-old Wallace, and financial support. In a thirteen-page affidavit, she accused B.C. of occasional drunkenness and brutality. She called him a "bully, egotist, tyrant and boor." B.C. wasn't pleased to see all this reported in detail in the *New York Times,* and moved fast to reach a settlement. He agreed to pay Adelaide $100 a week plus expenses for Wallace and $1,500 in legal fees.

Among Adelaide's suspicions was that B.C. had been carrying on an affair with his longtime secretary, Gertrude Weiner. It was a logical assumption. They probably spent more time together than B.C. and Adelaide. B.C., after the breakup, even had her accompany him on his trips back to Scotland. But while Weiner increasingly became B.C.'s irreplaceable assistant during her career at Forbes starting in 1919 at the age of sixteen, the two apparently never became lovers, as insiders had suspected. She simply was a typist who turned out to be the one who could tolerate his fussiness and understand his brogue. "Oh, I had to fight him off once or twice," she once said, "but that's not unusual in a business office."

They were friends. They played gin rummy till late in the evening when B.C. didn't want to go home. She brought her boyfriends to him for his approval (he liked none of them, and she remained single until the day she died in January 1990 at age eighty-seven). He was generous with words of praise and promises of raises when times got better, but he never came through. Still she would stay on till the day he died, suffering his irritability and his annoying habit of persisting in telling her dirty jokes she didn't want to hear. In the end, she would be the only nonfamily employee ever given a share of ownership in the company—granted, a tiny one, but big enough so that years later it would put her at odds with a certain single-minded heir.

B.C. convinced himself that Adelaide's legal action did him no personal damage. He was confident his friends believed his assertion that she had lied in the affidavit. He linked Adelaide's decision to a friendship with a woman who convinced her it was a sin to live with a Protestant. And he believed he had overindulged her and that eventually she would admit her mistake and return to him.

But in the eleven years that followed, ending with B.C.'s death in 1954, they would remain legally married. And as a practicing Catholic, Adelaide considered herself married, as to some extent did B.C. He used his legally married status, perhaps, as a shield against any other romantic involvements. Not that he possessed great sex appeal. While he had a great mind, he was not physically attractive. He was corpulent and smelled of cigars. Still, women would make a play for him and he seemed to enjoy that, but he stopped short of settling down with anyone.

During their years of separation, B.C. stayed in touch with Adelaide. He occasionally would infuriate her by showing up unannounced at her residence in Manhattan with a bottle of gin. "He'd be interested in having a little romance, but she wasn't," says one family member. It didn't happen very often, but he seemed to believe that because he was supporting her, he had the right to arrive at any time. Clearly he'd gotten impatient—maybe even a little lonely—waiting for Adelaide to come crawling back home. She never did return.

3 | "A QUIET CHAP NAMED MALCOLM"

Of the four sons who lived to adulthood, Malcolm was the most obvious choice to succeed his father. Early on, Malcolm strove to emulate B.C. Soon after he got his first typewriter, at age eight, he was writing and printing a household newspaper. The year before Duncan was killed, when Malcolm was thirteen, he got his own printing press, and by age fifteen had published newspapers for home, school, and scouts. At Princeton, when he failed to get elected to the staff of the *Daily Princetonian,* he launched the *Nassau Sovereign* magazine—against his father's advice. The *Sovereign,* billed as the campus *Fortune,* eventually put a competitor, the *Princeton Tiger,* out of business.

But Malcolm did not want to succeed his father, who once said, "I never met a rich man's son who was worth a damn." His goal was more ambitious: he wanted to be president of the United States. "It's the Holy Grail," he once said, "the gold at the end of the rainbow." It was an idea he had even as a grade-school student. "In fifth grade someone else in my class was interested in public life, and I regarded him as a potential rival for the presidency," he said.

His older brother, Bruce, had less awesome goals. He may not have had the editorial ambitions and instincts to succeed B.C., but he certainly had the right disposition to cheerfully step into the family business. His greatest asset was superb salesmanship, but his obsession with ad sales caused him to turn the auto companies—especially General Motors—into sacred cows at Forbes. He was determined to win them over as steady advertisers at all costs. As a salesman, it didn't hurt that he was handsome, athletic, and charming. He had the natural wit of his mother. People enjoyed dealing with him.

"Everyone says how funny Malcolm was," one relative says, "but his was not a spontaneous wit. He constantly used and reused other people's lines. And at dinner on the *Highlander,* he'd say these things for the umpteenth time and everyone would laugh uproariously, but it's the emperor's-clothes situation. No one would tell him he's naked."

Bruce, a mediocre student, graduated from Hackley in 1935 and went on to the University of Michigan where he played football until an injury sidelined him. That same injury also kept him out of the military during World War II. Instead he did war work for Bendix.

One of Bruce's younger brothers, Gordon, also was barred from regular military service in the war by an injury. When Gordon was about ten years old, he was hit by a car on a gravel driveway in Englewood, leaving a foot permanently maimed. He spent the war with the American Field Service in North Africa helping mop up the carnage in the wake of Field Marshal Erwin Rommel. From there Gordon—who, unlike Duncan, Malcolm, and Wallace, avoided transfer to Lawrenceville, opting to finish high school in Englewood and buy a car instead—would go to Yale to major in drama. Like the rest of his brothers, Gordon had spent summers working in the mail room of Forbes. As sometimes happens when children are pressed into working for family, Gordon developed a strong aversion to the family business and made a firm commitment not to get involved.

Bruce had no such commitment. He went on from Bendix after

the war to join his father's business by opening up an ad sales office in the General Motors building in Detroit to help capture some of the big ad dollars car makers were spending. The auto tycoons adored him. They played golf, wined and dined together at favorite haunts like the Greenbriar resort in West Virginia. They valued Bruce's friendship and showed it by advertising in *Forbes*.

He married a model from California, Marsha McLean, around the time the United States entered World War II and set up housekeeping in Detroit. The marriage lasted through the war years and produced a child, Bonnie, who would get caught up in the counterculture upheaval of the late 1960s and lose her life in the midst of it (many family members say they don't know how she died). By then, Bruce himself would already have died, and Bonnie's mother, remarried and living back in California, would be a dim memory in the Forbes clan.

Some family members felt that while Marsha was lovely, attractive and sweet, she placed more importance on being Mrs. Forbes than it deserved at the time. "She wanted to be Madam Queen," one family member says. "B.C. didn't like that. He was going to stay in control and run things until the end."

Compared with Malcolm, Bruce had modest ambitions: he simply wanted *Forbes* to flourish. His main contribution to that end was an immense congeniality with potential advertisers. But away from business, he sought simple pleasures.

"We went to Twenty-one every night during the week," his second wife, Ruth, recalls, "and got to know everyone in business. But Friday night, we'd go home, take the phone off the hook, drink iced tea, and make love all weekend. It was very romantic."

B.C. may have felt Malcolm had good ideas, but he was doubtful of his ability to see them through. Bruce on the other hand had proved himself effective in Detroit. He had developed lasting friendships with the likes of General Motors executive Semon "Bunky" Knudsen, Governor Thomas E. Dewey of New York, and David Mahoney, then of Colgate-Palmolive and later of Norton Simon.

While Bruce was cultivating business contacts, Malcolm was plotting a political career. His first business endeavor out of college was intended to put him on the road to the White House. In 1941, two days after graduating from Princeton, Malcolm, with his father's friends' help, bought two weekly newspapers in Lancaster, Ohio—the *Fairfield Times* and the *Lancaster Tribune*. Why Ohio? Aside from Virginia, it had produced the most presidents.

"I was burning with political ambition and thought if I built a chain of weeklies in a state like Ohio, with its blend of agriculture and industry, it would give me a strong political base," he said. "I soon discovered I just didn't have time for my weekly column. I was breaking up pages, sweeping up newsprint, running around to sell ads and then collecting for them on Thursday so I could pay the help on Friday."

The plan failed. Running a nonessential business in the midst of an all-consuming war was too hard. There were newsprint shortages, machine-part shortages and labor shortages. Despite drawing no salary for himself and eating free at a restaurant in return for publishing its menu, Malcolm couldn't make a go of it. After Pearl Harbor, he enlisted in the army, cheating on the eye exam by wearing then-newfangled contact lenses. The newspaper operation continued through 1942, with Corporal Forbes filing reports on army life, but the following year, he shut it down, with B.C. eventually helping him handle outstanding financial obligations.

After a failed romance with a Lancaster girl, and a near fatal stint as a soldier in Germany, Malcolm returned to the United States in a body cast to face the possibility of losing his left leg. The thigh had been splintered by enemy machine-gun fire while Malcolm was searching for a missing unit that was supposed to be backing up his unit. During his nine-month convalescence in 1945, Malcolm, recipient of a Bronze Star and Purple Heart, started to focus his attention on the family business. He had definite ideas on how to improve the magazine's sagging image.

Though he had always winced at the idea of going to work for his father ("I vowed never to work for him because I thought we'd never get along," he once said), the April 15 issue announced a new column called "A Soldier Speaks: What GI's are expecting after victory." Malcolm, who had been earning $90 a month in the military, had been lured in with a $100-a-week job offer.

It was also in 1945 that Malcolm met Roberta Remsen Laidlaw at a cocktail party in Englewood to celebrate the impending surrender of the Japanese. He proposed to her that night and they would marry a year later on September 21. She was twenty, he was twenty-seven. B.C. "raised me to a hundred ten a week in a burst of largess," Malcolm said. "I must say money went farther then, but not that much farther." Less than two years later, on July 18, 1947, the couple had their first child, a son. They named him Malcolm Stevenson Forbes, Jr., and called him Steve. He would be the first of four sons and finally a daughter.

Malcolm soon turned his attention to another non-*Forbes* project that would quickly prove to be a big money loser: *Nation's Heritage,* a $150-a-year coffee-table art book–quality magazine featuring the finest printing and binding money could buy—and no advertising. It was never clear to anyone how the thing could possibly make money. The mission was to generate, six times a year, an oversized picture book full of images intended to appeal to national pride at a time when America was feeling particularly righteous, having just saved the world from fascism.

Malcolm hired Robert K. Heimann, an ambitious Princetonian who endeared himself to Malcolm by seeking permission in 1946 to revive the *Nassau Sovereign.* In fact, Wallace Forbes acted as business manager on the *Sovereign.* Malcolm liked the job Heimann, a native of Queens, New York, did with the *Sovereign* and hired him to edit *Nation's Heritage.*

Small wonder B.C. had doubts about Malcolm's ability to run the magazine. His efforts were scattered, his success rate spotty. While running *Nation's Heritage* into the ground, Malcolm was putting his political career back on track, managing to get himself elected to the Bernardsville Borough Council in 1949. At the same time, he remained involved in the family magazine, making three major contributions.

The first, in 1947, the year Malcolm was named a Forbes vice president, was the creation of Investors Advisory Institute (IAI), a sort of newsletter of suggestions for stock-market pickers. At the time, *Forbes* circulation stood at a mere 67,000, up only 7,000 from the Depression years when B.C. kept the magazine alive with income from his syndicated Hearst column, which was finally canceled in 1943 after twenty-three years. *Fortune* and *Business Week* had long since left *Forbes* behind. Meanwhile, IAI would quickly grow to $51,000 in aftertax profit by 1950, when B.C. would describe it as "our star money maker."

Malcolm's second and third contributions would be of a much longer-lasting nature—and better indications of his magazine-business instincts. He convinced B.C. that in order to improve quality and, therefore, circulation, *Forbes* must hire its own editorial staff, rather than rely on freelancers, to establish consistency of quality and focus. Hiring Heimann in 1949 as managing editor was a step in that direction. Heimann's greatest contribution was to place a high premium on the kinds of hard negative stories that get readers' attention.

Finally, Malcolm suggested to B.C. that the usually ad-poor January 1 issue be used to introduce a feature grading the nation's top corporations. The idea—inaugurated five years before *Fortune* magazine started its now-famous list of top industrial concerns—would evolve into an annual in-depth ranking of five hundred corporations by profitability, revenue, and return on equity. The issues would soon attract millions of dollars worth of ads.

These all were highly profitable ideas, but where was Malcolm headed in terms of *Forbes* magazine? B.C. had to wonder in 1949 as he paid off the last of the debts Malcolm had rung up creating *Nation's Heritage* and watched as his son continued to be drawn into politics.

In fact, Malcolm was about to embark on a seven-year quest for high political office. He started it with a successful campaign in 1951 for the state senate seat for Somerset County and added to his activities a personal commitment to do whatever he could to convince General Dwight Eisenhower to run for president and then to do his bit to ensure victory in the 1952 New Jersey primary.

Perhaps Malcolm felt he owed Ike a tribute. It was Ike, after all, who in 1949 presented the Freedoms Foundation gold medal and $1,500 to Malcolm for "bringing about a better understanding about the American Way of Life." How did Malcolm do this? By publishing, however unprofitably, *Nation's Heritage*. The commendation yielded Malcolm, the politician, and *Forbes,* the magazine, invaluable publicity. The lesson was not lost on Malcolm. In fact, he was gradually becoming a master of self-promotion, and he was starting to show an inclination to try unconventional ploys.

It was in 1949, for example, that he first used his brilliant white-space gimmick. To air a dispute with his ad agency over his desire to see more white space around Forbes ads, Malcolm took out a two-page ad in *Advertising Age* and left them blank except for these small-type words in one corner: "Agency clashes with client. See story page 28." He would recycle the idea years later, running two blank pages in *Forbes* and calling it an editorial containing all that could be said about a particular secretary of state's success in promoting U.S. interests abroad.

These were highly unconventional uses of space that could easily contain decent feature-length stories, not to mention a couple of valuable full-page ads. But for Malcolm, they were calculated risks. The shock value of squandering two costly pages in a magazine would more than make up for the apparent waste of space by getting *Forbes* talked about. It would generate more public notice than any conventional ad or editorial, no matter how cleverly written.

But in politics, he would learn, it's not enough just to play a good game. His strategy for winning an election was to go after the independent voter, to present himself as independent of clubhouse politicians. This was a good approach for garnering public notice, but he lacked a coherent platform. Malcolm wanted political power, but he (and the voters) didn't know why.

Ruth Blake, a blue-eyed brunette from Flushing, New York, was a secretary in GM's public relations office. One day in 1951 she was having coffee in the Fisher Building when a mutual friend introduced her to Bruce Forbes. Ruth thought he was a knockout. "It was love at first sight for me," says Ruth, who, like Bruce, was divorced.

Bruce was a frequent visitor to the PR office, and Ruth was determined to get to know him better. One day he stopped in to chat with GM's PR chief, Ruth's boss. She made up her mind to force an encounter.

"I literally bumped into him on his way out," she says, "almost knocked him over."

Bruce took the bait. He asked her out to dinner that night. Though she had no plans, she was careful to decline the offer, but accepted his invitation to go out the following evening. It was the start of a three-month courtship and a storybook romance that Ruth says lasted until the day he died.

On their first date, when Bruce took her home and they walked to her door, he started to kiss her, but stopped. He didn't like the idea of kissing her at first, he told her, because his former mother-in-law was also named Ruth. As they stood there, Ruth five feet three, Bruce six feet one, Bruce said, "You're Shorty." They kissed, and from then on, she was Shorty to everyone.

At Christmas time, Ruth returned for the holidays to her parents' home in Cliffside Park, New Jersey, about ten miles from Englewood, the Forbeses' hometown. Bruce called her from Detroit Christmas Eve and proposed to her, and she accepted.

Bruce jumped on a plane in Detroit just as a snowstorm was getting started, and at five A.M. Christmas Day, Ruth met him at La Guardia Airport. They visited their families to break the news, then returned to Detroit and got married at City Hall a few days later in the middle of a blizzard.

They had been living in Detroit for about a year when B.C. told Bruce in late 1952 that he needed him to get directly involved in running the magazine, and the couple moved into a $150-a-month apartment at Fifth Avenue and Eighth Street, a few blocks down from the office.

B.C.'s reason for calling Bruce back to the home office was his own that he was slowing down. He would soon be making it into the office only a couple of days a week. He was suffering a numbness in his right arm—a numbness like that which preceded his own father's death. He needed someone besides Malcolm in place to be ready to take the reins.

Malcolm had sharpened the magazine's editorial focus, and the new managing editor, Robert Heimann, was capable of putting the magazine's new formula to work: more hard-hitting stories about companies and the people who run them. "Heimann figured if you kick ass hard enough, you'll get people's attention," a former colleague says. The staff generally respected him, though there was a sense he was competing with Malcolm, trying to demonstrate that he was brighter than his boss.

But in 1952, Malcolm was working for Eisenhower, who had declared himself a candidate on January 7 and had gone on to win the New Hampshire primary. At the same time, Malcolm was convincing himself that he had enough support to make a run for governor. He saw himself following the path of Woodrow Wilson to the White House via the New Jersey governorship.

Meanwhile, Heimann, who liked to wear a trench coat and a homburg, was vacillating about which way he wanted to go with his own career. But with Malcolm increasingly out of the office and Bruce necessarily getting more involved in editorial matters in his absence, Heimann, Malcolm's man, would soon leave, in 1954, to begin a steady climb to the top of the executive heap at American Tobacco. Byron (Dave) Mack, Bruce's man, would succeed him. Mack, like Bruce, did not get along well with Malcolm. The reason was that while Mack could fool Bruce into thinking everything was hunky-dory on the editorial side, he could not win Malcolm's trust. Malcolm knew that Mack had serious problems getting along with staffers. But for the time being, Mack's tenure was secure, because Malcolm increasingly was a politician and less a Forbes executive.

In 1953, Bruce was taking charge at *Forbes.* His primary mission: get control of operations and establish a strategy for promoting the magazine. His reputation for intelligence, however, wasn't good— certainly not as good as Malcolm's. At one point, some editorial staffers took to derisively referring to Bruce as "My Own Brucie" after a champion cocker spaniel of the day.

Meanwhile, the stock market had turned down, the magazine's fortunes were flagging as a result, income from IAI dropped sharply, and B.C. seemed to be fading.

"He was sort of an embarrassment," says a former writer. "He'd shuffle through in his slippers at five P.M. to turn off all the fans.

Quite a contrast to Malcolm all neatly dressed in tweedy Princeton style."

Amid all this, Malcolm declared himself a Republican candidate for governor. But without the party's support, he lost that spring. He did not then throw himself into his work at *Forbes*. Malcolm's attention span was short on any project over which he could not exercise complete control. Having to share power with Bruce as well as B.C. was totally uninspiring.

Among his diversions that summer were trips on his 42-foot yacht, *Wings*, with Heimann and six-year-old Steve Forbes. Their goal was to reach Labrador and return, a 2,500-mile journey. They did it by taking a series of long weekends between June and September, flying to meet the boat for each leg. The trip ended in near disaster. On the way down from Nova Scotia, the engines—which had to be rebuilt during the trip because of Malcolm's decision to ignore warnings not to use a certain type of diesel fuel—died about a hundred miles east of Boston. The boat drifted for half a day before the Coast Guard rescued them, and it was quickly sold thereafter.

The episode had three results. First, on the down side, Malcolm had diverted his and Heimann's time away from the magazine when it least could afford it. Two, media reports of the incident provided Malcolm yet another example of how to get publicity: stage an adventure. Three, it gave Malcolm the idea of having a corporate yacht on which to entertain advertiser and corporate executives.

Still, Malcolm was not devoting his energies to *Forbes*. His political career wasn't dead. He was a state senator and remained convinced he could still be a successful gubernatorial candidate. He continued to indulge his wanderlust. And at *Forbes*, the management structure would have to change drastically for Malcolm to get more enthusiastically involved. As it stood, writing Fact and Comment was his main contribution. For all anyone else could tell who worked there at the time, Malcolm had no other role in the business.

Near the end of 1953, B.C., then a short, heavyset seventy-three-year-old who favored gold-tipped cigarettes, decided not to wait another year for his biennial return to his beloved New Deer in

Aberdeenshire, Scotland. He must have known his time was running out fast, and so must have the people of New Deer. In the church at Maud where B.C. worshiped and gave generously, there were tears in everyone's eyes during a service he attended; it was clear this would be his last visit.

The end came late in the day on May 5, 1954, nine days before B.C.'s seventy-fourth birthday. It was long past quitting time in the magazine's rented offices at 80 Fifth Avenue. The place was empty and quiet, but Andy, the elevator operator, noticed the lights were still on in B.C.'s office. He poked his head in, discovered Forbes dead on the floor, and notified the family. "And they didn't give me a goddamn nickel for it," he bitterly told a co-worker the next day.

For the next ten years, *Forbes* magazine—debt free at the time of B.C.'s death—essentially belonged to Bruce. And from 1954 to 1958, the magazine's circulation doubled to 265,000, with Mack as editor and Jim Michaels—whom Mack had hired originally as a reporter in 1954 after Michaels had first knocked on the door at *Fortune*—as managing editor. Malcolm was still casting about for a purpose in life. He owned a third of the magazine, Bruce a third, and their two younger brothers the remaining third. But Malcolm's share meant nothing to him, because it wasn't control. Further limiting his influence was the fact that staffers generally liked Bruce more than they liked him.

"Bruce and Malcolm were two different kinds of people," one former veteran staffer said. "Bruce was warm. He made a lot of friends easily. Malcolm was cold and calculating."

After B.C.'s passing, Bruce became president and Malcolm publisher and editor in chief. They battled briefly over who would move into B.C.'s office. Malcolm lost. Whatever the titles meant, Malcolm's role remained limited. He was the quiet, intellectual type who would remain hidden away in his office, a somewhat shadowy figure. Many people were unsure exactly what his influence was around the magazine.

The contrast with Bruce made Malcolm's character seem even murkier. "There was Bruce, this big, hardy, slap-on-the-back kind of guy, and in the other office on the other side there was this quiet chap named Malcolm," recalls former staffer Steve Quickel.

Despite B.C.'s death, Malcolm was still tentative in the amount of time he was willing to commit to the magazine. He traveled to Europe on the *Ile de France* and met Premier Mendès-France and West German chancellor Konrad Adenauer. He also spent time campaigning for U.S. Senator Clifford P. Case and managed to retain his own state senate seat—but by a slim four hundred votes, a sharp contrast with his wide margin of victory the first time around.

In 1956, Malcolm told Bruce he intended to run for the Republican nomination to oppose incumbent Robert B. Meyner as governor of New Jersey.

"I'll back you all the way," Bruce told him, "but if you lose, don't expect to come back in here and take over." Bruce knew Malcolm's inclination was to be in charge of whatever he was involved in. It was an aspect of Malcolm he didn't like and one of the reasons the two were never close.

Malcolm managed to win the Republican party nomination in 1956, but he was unable to unseat Meyner, and in 1957 lost by a landslide. Malcolm responded by abruptly ending his political career.

In fact, the night of the election, Forbes held a dinner to celebrate the magazine's fortieth anniversary. Numerous captains of industry had been persuaded to attend. In front of this highly prized audience Malcolm stood up and announced that in light of his defeat, he'd be stepping back into the fray at *Forbes* magazine. With that, as a gag, he presented a gold watch to Bruce, praised him for the wonderful job he'd been doing and wished him well in his retirement. Bruce was visibly shaken by the scene Malcolm had created in front of all those important people.

"The Forbeses were always pretty rough with one another," says one former staffer.

While many politicians see the name recognition that flows from a high-profile race as an asset to be invested in future contests, Malcolm simply wanted to cut his losses. He was disenchanted in part because of the amount of time it took him away from his family.

But Malcolm apparently still harbored a desire for some kind of role in government. Following his gubernatorial defeat, he launched a series of long-winded puff pieces on the various branches of the military, hoping for an appointment as secretary of one of them.

Malcolm was aggressive on these reporting trips. Upon meeting the top brass at various bases, he'd always make a point of telling them immediately that he was a machine-gun sergeant in World War II. That would always get their attention. Then if they started to treat Malcolm to a presentation of charts and statistics, he'd stand up in the middle of it and say, "We're not here for this; we want to see the troops in the field." End of presentation.

The military appointment never happened, but Malcolm would never quit politics entirely. For example, he acted as a delegate-at-large to the Republican convention in 1960 and helped with fund-raising efforts—a role that would pave the way to presidential audiences, invitations to White House events, and finally a presidential commendation in 1989.

The 1957 gubernatorial defeat, however, had sent him into a deep funk, and part of the reason may have been his inability to get past Bruce, who remained firmly ensconced despite the gold-watch prank. Generally, Malcolm seemed to wander aimlessly and took so many long afternoon naps that he confided in one staffer he wouldn't be surprised if he started to get bedsores.

Since college, Malcolm had succeeded at little. He was rapidly becoming the kind of rich man's son B.C. talked about—the heir who simply spends the inheritance without enhancing it. And his deal with Bruce blocked him from achieving even a consolation prize: top man making a creditable mark in the family business. As long as Bruce stayed in charge—and it appeared he planned to remain indefinitely—Malcolm's options for growth within *Forbes* were limited.

Meanwhile, the magazine's personality was still gradually coalescing into a crisp, clear image, but it faced two major perceptual obstacles. First, part of B.C.'s legacy was that many business people viewed him as a blackmailer: They believed failure to buy advertising in *Forbes* could result in punishment by editorial lambasting.

Though one would be hard pressed to prove this ever happened, the perception affected *Forbes* staffers' ability to report. It's hard to get interviews from people who assume you're there to crucify them. The second obstacle was that while Heimann did much to turn the magazine's focus to companies and away from the stock market, the product remained woefully imperfect. It was under Heimann, says one former staffer, that *Forbes* developed a reputation for being "terribly inaccurate but irreverent."

Combine these two perceptions—a penchant for vindictiveness and a tendency to be inaccurate—and the result is a decidedly chilling effect on a potential source's willingness to cooperate. Add to that a sense that the magazine's influence is negligible, and you have to wonder why anyone in the early 1950s would ever talk to a writer for *Forbes*. "I'd tell people who I was and where I worked and they'd say, '*Ford* magazine? What kind of magazine is that?'" recalls one staffer. It made life extremely hard for the *Forbes* writer under orders to knock down Goliaths that deserved to be knocked down—even if the magazine was given credit for adopting many of the best qualities of *Time*.

Dave Mack, who had worked at *Time*, may have been dismal in handling personnel and less than energetic in his own work, but he instituted one change that went far to close the magazine's credibility gap: he hired a staff of research assistants—fact checkers to go over writers' copy to purge inaccuracies of any magnitude. Without that, the magazine could be as brash as it wanted, but no one would take it seriously. Gradually, with assiduous policing, the magazine could acquire an air of genuine authority. With that, irreverence takes on gravity. Stories that make forceful, provocative arguments then can have real impact, the ultimate reward in journalism of any kind.

But the impact has to be justified, and fact checkers can keep a writer from promulgating a thesis that lacks factual underpinnings. The system worked.

Jonathan Greenberg, a writer who worked at *Forbes* years later as a research assistant, remembers one occasion in particular. He had to tell a reporter that a pivotal assumption in his story was wrong, rendering the story itself wrong.

"This was right on deadline," Greenberg recalls, "and this was a story the writer had been struggling with for some time. He broke down and cried, because he knew I was right. There was no way that story could be salvaged. The facts just didn't support the story." For a writer, the experience is like that of an architect whose ill-conceived plans result in a building that collapses under its own weight.

Being the researcher who discovers a fatal flaw is no fun, says Greenberg, but the incentive to do so was compelling. "You were taught that accuracy, fact checking fell to the researcher, and that your job security depended on doing it perfectly." In three years, he would see three researchers fired for failing to catch mistakes.

Dave Mack's major contribution may have been to make *Forbes* editorially honest, but he did little to dispel the notion that it was no place for the fainthearted. In fact, he was one of *Forbes*'s most legendary mean-spirited types.

"The guy was maniacal," one ex-staffer says. "Our desks were in cubicles in a row. When he started firing people, he'd start with whoever was in the cubicle farthest from his office." Once, he decided he wanted one story per day out of everyone. Someone finally responded by handing in a two-sentence story. That sent Mack through the roof.

At one point, Bruce Forbes instituted a training program, a trendy idea he latched on to because of its growing popularity among his General Motors buddies. Mack used the idea as further ammunition in his manage-by-fear arsenal. "You guys are going," he told regular staffers, "because we got these trainees."

His first day on the job in 1959, Sheldon Zalaznick, a reporter at the time who eventually would become managing editor, sat in on an editorial meeting with Mack, Michaels, and the magazine's eight or so other writers. Mack sat behind his desk expressing extreme displeasure about the issue that had just closed. As was his habit, he slowly waved an eighteen-inch metal pica gauge in front of him like a metronome. "I'll spin this staff the way a Buddhist spins his prayer wheel if I have to," he growled.

Mack may have been a brilliant writer and editor, but he was diabolical in his ability to instill fear. On more than one occasion management would tell everyone as work began on a new issue, "By the end of this cycle we're going to have to fire one of you." Of course, no one would want to be perceived as the least productive of the staff at the end of such a cycle. In one instance, one of the staff members got so anxious about who was going to get the ax, he went to Mack and asked, "Give it to me straight, Dave. Is it me you're planning to fire?"

"Well, it wasn't going to be you," Mack told the reporter, "but now that you mention it, it may as well be."

The man was fired on the spot.

On another occasion, Mack called everyone into his office, drew the blinds and turned the lights down low. Waving his pica gauge, he addressed the gathering: "I've heard one of you is writing a book about me, but it will never happen, because none of you can write."

It wasn't clear why anyone would want to write a book about Mack, not that Mack wasn't talented. "I learned a lot about writing under Mack," says Ray Brady, now of "CBS Evening News," "but I lost a lot of blood in the process."

In another display of Mack's ability not to let a little sentimentality crimp his style, he fired someone on Christmas Eve. Sheldon Zalaznick tacked a message to the bulletin board: SANTA STRIKES AGAIN!

Nevertheless—or perhaps partly because of such tough-mindedness—the magazine gained in both stature and circulation. By 1964, *Forbes*, boasting circulation of more than 400,000, was poised to compete seriously with *Fortune* and even *Business Week,* the number-one business magazine. If Mack exemplified the worst elements in the Forbes character, Bruce Forbes embodied the best.

"He had a kind of beaming presence, a bonhomie, onward-and-upward style," Zalaznick recalls. His favorite image of Bruce was a picture on a wall at the office of Bruce in the stern seat of the Forbes yacht, *Highlander,* sitting with former President Herbert Hoover. The idea that he had "the Chief," as Hoover was known, on the *Highlander* was as close to heaven as Bruce probably could imagine being.

It was Bruce's congeniality and gregarious salesmanship that put *Forbes* on a path of dynamic growth. He obviously enjoyed the work and being at the center of a swirl of exciting gains, yet he managed to stay out of the magazine's editorial way. "It was a mark of class on somebody's part," Zalaznick says, "that the average working stiff at the magazine knew goddamn little of Bruce Forbes."

What little contact staffers did have with Bruce tended to be of a positive nature.

"He was one of the most delightful, gorgeous men you'd ever want to meet," says his widow, Ruth. "With the magazine, for example, at Christmas time, they'd give out bonuses. He'd never say, 'Come up to my office to get it.' He went to each person's desk right down to the guy in the mail room. He shook his hand and said, 'If it weren't for you, we couldn't keep this business going.' "

At Christmas time, Bruce would get one hundred crisp, new one-dollar bills and stick them in a breast pocket. "He would walk along, take out these dollar bills and hand them out to people as he passed, saying 'Merry Christmas.' He was the happiest man."

But it seemed Bruce was a little afraid of success. *Forbes* was already on the fast track; promotional mailings were generating huge returns. Yet Bruce seemed reluctant to seize the opportunity and push ahead, at a time when the magazine was strong enough to challenge the competition in several categories—including quality of readership and copy.

Meanwhile, Malcolm was itching for a fight but unable to do anything about it. He was certain *Forbes* could win and keep on winning with an aggressive marketing strategy, but Bruce had seen his brother drift in and out of the business many times in a way that made him wonder, just as his father had, whether Malcolm would ever have the necessary attention span to see a long-term business plan to a successful conclusion.

Malcolm, however, was not a quitter. He was determined to prove them all wrong.

4 | SUPER-MALCOLM

In the early 1960s, *Forbes* may have been ripe for more aggressive promotion, but Bruce remained focused on the foundation. He wasn't ready to invest heavily in a costly ad campaign. The company could easily afford it at that point, but Bruce believed the basic corporate assets still needed firming up. It meant buying the Macmillan building, circa 1925, at 60 Fifth Avenue and an adjoining town house around the corner on Twelfth Street, a first step into what would become one of Forbes's most lucrative profit centers, real estate. It also meant building up a stellar staff.

One of those people was Leslie C. Quick, Jr., later of the discount brokerage firm Quick & Reilly. Bruce hired Quick in 1957 to be his business manager and vice president. At the time, *Forbes* revenue was running about $3.5 million annually, with about $1 million of that coming from ads. The rest was from circulation and services. The services, offered to *Forbes* subscribers, included Investographs,

Investors Advisory Institute, the Forbes Investment Portfolio, the Forbes Stock Market Course (a steady money maker that required practically no overhead), and numerous books by B.C., such as *America's Twelve Master Salesmen.*

Part of Quick's job was to analyze the services to identify the strong and the weak and decide how to make them more profitable. The investment portfolio was one of the worst performers, and Bruce asked Quick to determine whether it could be turned around. Quick concluded that as a nondiscretionary operation—that is, it didn't have its customers' authority to buy and sell securities without their approval—it couldn't be effective. It relied on customers to send in postcards acknowledging that the client had effected the trade recommended by the service. Too often clients simply forgot to send in the postcards, so the Forbes advisers could never be certain about the current status of a customer's account. Today such accounts are practically extinct.

Another area Quick needed to rejuvenate was IAI, Malcolm's brainchild. The IAI Weekly Report was hard to read and the information wasn't fresh. Much of it had been picked up from other published sources. It tended to look at only the bluest of blue-chip stocks. The research lacked coherence, the stock picks were lousy, and there was little follow-up. The eight-page report carried some lame charts on the back, which tracked stocks for growth and income. The renewal rate was, not surprisingly, low. Most of the 8,000 subscribers were first-time, short-term trials at $5 a head at a time when the going annual rate was $54. Quick started looking for a stock-market wizard to turn IAI around.

How do you find wizards to call your own before someone else discovers them and makes them overpriced stars on Wall Street? Luck.

Forbes had recently acquired Investographs, a publisher of charts and graphs for investors and with it its owner, Walt McKibben. McKibben knew what Quick was looking for and thought of Raphael Yavneh, a lawyer who possessed two superb qualities: a proven knack for analyzing businesses and predicting their performance, and a fierce sense of independence from the Wall Street herd.

It was McKibben who lured Yavneh into the stock-picking business in 1958, inviting him to join him at Weisenberger Investment Reports to write about foreign companies, of enhanced interest to investors because of the advent of the European Common Market. Eventually, Yavneh moved on to do similar work at Standard & Poor's Corporation, where he was promised complete editorial autonomy. He was a fast writer and editor and good at translating foreign corporate reports, but he began to encounter requests that all his analysis be corroborated by independent market researchers.

The issue came to a head over a story he'd done about Unilever, the giant Anglo-Dutch consumer products concern.

"Where'd you get these projections?" Yavneh was asked.

"There're mine," he said. "I collected the information and this is my analysis of it."

"Well, can't we get someone on Wall Street to confirm your projection?"

But no one on Wall Street watched the company. Yavneh suggested the fact checker contact Carl Marks & Company, a New York trading house for mostly foreign over-the-counter stocks. Yavneh was surprised that Standard & Poor's got its confirmation and ran the story. He was curious who else out there was making precisely the same per-share earnings projection as he was about Unilever. He tracked the confirmation to the market maker Carl Marks dealt with for Unilever shares.

"How did you arrive at this conclusion?" Yavneh asked.

"Don't you remember?" the market maker replied. "You gave it to me a few months ago when we met at a conference."

The last straw for Yavneh at Standard and Poor's was an editing decision. He had written a glowing report on American South African Gold, but included the warning that the political situation in South Africa and Rhodesia posed a potential threat to the health of the stock. After all, the mines were operating with the benefit of virtual slavery. How long could that last? The warning was deleted. Yavneh quit in June 1960 and eventually went to work for Istel Lepercq, the American money-management arm of Schlumberger.

McKibben showed some of Yavneh's writings to Quick, who was impressed. At Lepercq, Yavneh had proved himself a brilliant stock picker. The major element in his success was his personal prohibition against competing with other stock pickers. Unlike the big stock brokerages, which compete against one another, Yavneh viewed the companies themselves as the competition. They were the game, not other research analysts.

McKibben arranged for Yavneh to meet with Quick for lunch in mid-October 1963. Afterwards, Quick took him to meet Bruce and Malcolm. By the time Yavneh returned to his office, Quick was on the phone with a job offer. They wanted him to start either immediately or on November 1. The offer included a huge salary jump that Istel wasn't ready to match. Yavneh—who grew up in Greenwich Village not far from *Forbes*—took the plunge, sensing an opportunity to run his own operation as a fairly independent unit of Forbes Inc. Bruce Forbes's only instructions were: "Do whatever you want to do, but show it to me after you've done it and explain what you've done."

Yavneh liked Bruce's management style. He'd settle in for the morning with iced coffee at a restaurant across the street and hold court there. He'd meet with one department head after another to find out what was happening in every department, sending each executive back to the office with instructions on who was to meet next with Bruce.

"Though it wasn't called that at the time," Yavneh said, "it was my first power breakfast."

Yavneh's first move was to increase the type size of the report to 10 point from 8 point and insert more space between lines for easier reading. He also ordered the staff of eight or nine people to forget whatever chain of command they were used to, and begin answering to Yavneh. Within six months, IAI had regained its strength, and Yavneh was a much-in-demand stock-market whiz making speeches and consulting on the side.

Mack had quit abruptly in 1961 after learning he had an incurable muscular disease, and Jim Michaels, who succeeded him as editor, had been building his own team, with Malcolm backing his moves to put more emphasis on investigative reporting techniques more common on traditional newspaper beats where rooting out mismanagement and corruption has always been part of the job. To Michaels, stockholders were often unwary consumers to be protected from the inept and corrupt in the corporate community.

It was part of an overall strategy to achieve greater public awareness of the magazine as controversial and outspoken—or arrogant and opinionated, some critics would say. If *Forbes* could promote hard-hitting stories that successfully called conventional wisdom into question, the magazine would have the fodder it needed for an unconventional advertising campaign that would raise eyebrows.

Michaels's recruitment efforts themselves were unconventional. Steve Quickel, for example, was attracted to apply for a job by an item in *Forbes* that practically read like a want ad. At the time, he had recently graduated from the business school at Dartmouth College and was mired in a boring eighteen-month training program at Mellon Bank in Pittsburgh. The item in *Forbes* was Michaels writing about having just hired Wayne Welch and Fritz Schumacher, despite the fact that they had no prior business-journalism experience.

Quickel wrote to Michaels, who responded that the drill at *Forbes* was "up in two years or out." If Quickel was still interested, Michaels would submit his name to the "selection committee."

"The selection committee at that time probably amounted to nothing more than Michaels sitting on the john," Quickel says.

His interview amounted to about two hours of listening to Michaels, a short, owlish man with a slightly whiny voice and a penchant for chewing on the end of his glasses—a man who when he walked sort of leaned forward, charging ahead. Michaels, relatively new to the job of editor, spent most of the interview talking about his magazine.

"This approach wasn't what I expected, having gotten used to a routine that includes a battery of psychological tests," Quickel says. "But at that time, *Forbes* wasn't a very big book (the industry's term for a magazine)—maybe only forty-eight to fifty-two pages."

At the end of the interview, Michaels offered him a job. Quickel said he wanted to think about it. Michaels suggested he have lunch with two other staffers—Welch, one of the people hired in Bruce's trainee program, and Bob Flaherty—to help him decide.

"Wayne said, 'Don't do it,'" Quickel recalled. "He said the pressure was just awful. Bob said, 'Buy it,' touting the opportunity for the board-room education. That was the sales pitch." Quickel decided to give it a try and ended up staying fifteen years.

At the time Quickel was hired, Michaels had in place probably one of the strongest editing teams ever assembled at *Forbes.* The top players were senior editors Dero Saunders, who had come from *Fortune,* and Sheldon Zalaznick, who had been a sports editor at *Newsweek* and had been in public relations about three years when he started at *Forbes* in 1959. Of the two, Zalaznick was the more obviously brilliant. A third major force on Michael's team at the time was Flaherty, a Harvard Business School graduate.

But it was Michaels's talent that impressed staffers the most. He was the ultimate rewrite man. He could sit down with a story with the Standard & Poor's yellow sheet—raw data about a company's earnings and market position—next to it and completely flop the point of view. Using the exact same facts, he could reverse the story's original argument, simultaneously making it shorter and brighter.

"He taught me a lot about objectivity," says Frank Lalli, now managing editor of *Money* magazine. "There's a lot to that expression, 'The facts wouldn't let me tell the truth.'"

Malcolm was pretty quiet in those days, Quickel recalls, especially compared with Bruce, whose office buzzed with activity. Malcolm seemed to stick mainly to writing Fact and Comment. He wasn't the socializer that Bruce was, recalls a former Forbes executive. Malcolm seemed to get along better with his chauffeur than with the kinds of people Bruce hung out with on the links at the Greenbriar.

But Malcolm's decisions were having a major positive impact. Giving Michaels a free hand was crucial to the magazine's future. No one ever disputed Michaels's genius as an editor in being able to spot story ideas that were winners, prod writers to deliver more than they themselves thought possible, and finally to punch up copy—to transform it from dull and boring into riveting entertainment.

In addition to being the kind of editor writers could trust to make copy sing, Michaels generally operated without interference from the family. He was free to make his own hiring and firing decisions, and he was free to reward excellence with excellent raises. The freedom Michaels enjoyed was entirely a function of Malcolm and Bruce's ability to hire good people and let them do their jobs with a minimum of second-guessing. The brothers were able to do that largely because of the smallness of the operation. If something was terribly wrong, it would be spotted by top management in a matter of days, because in the early 1960s, the entire editorial staff consisted of about twenty editors, writers, and researchers—not a huge number of people to keep track of.

By 1964, the *Forbes* formula for success was in place. It was no longer the *National Enquirer* of business publications, as some had seen it, running rumors to titillate rich investors. Instead there were intelligent, tight investigative pieces that exposed the fundamental realities of a company's business, organization, and management. The only thing holding it back from overtaking its old nemesis, *Fortune,* was the uneasy relationship between Malcolm, then forty-four, and Bruce, forty-seven. They did not like each other, and despite Malcolm's preelection agreement with Bruce, it was becoming less clear who was in charge of what. While Bruce ran the business and advertising side, Malcolm seemed to have a free hand on the all-important editorial side.

Malcolm's third son, Christopher, would later tell *AdWeek* that Bruce was not the best of B.C.'s sons for the job. "The oldest was the third-most capable," he said. "I was old enough to be vaguely aware that it was not easy for my father and uncles. . . ." It's better to have one leader, Christopher said, than two leaders with equal authority but with different opinions about how to run a business.

In the spring of 1964, Bruce and Ruth flew to Nassau with Mr. and Mrs. Robert Fluor of Fluor Corporation in the Fluors' private plane. In Nassau, Bruce said, "My back is killing me." He'd just had a top-to-bottom physical a few weeks earlier, and though he was a little overweight, he was in good shape.

They returned to a Fort Lauderdale, Florida, hospital, but the doctor there found nothing. By the time they got back to New York, Bruce was in agony and was admitted to Presbyterian Hospital for a thorough examination. "He was filled with cancer," Ruth says. The diagnosis was inoperable bladder cancer. He had only seven weeks to live.

During that time, Ruth stayed at his side and, toward the end, decided to see if she could arrange for Bruce to enjoy some of his favorite things one last time. One company sent a private plane to fly them to the Greenbriar resort in West Virginia, a favorite hang-out for Bruce, partly because of his friendship with the Greenbriar golf pro, Sam Snead. Sam met them at the door when they pulled up. A band played for him. Every day, Sam would come in to play gin rummy. Bunky Knudsen of General Motors arranged the For-beses' air transportation back to New York. Bruce wanted to see the 98-foot *Highlander II*—the Forbeses' second in a line of corporate yachts—one last time where it was docked in New York.

Soon after, Bruce lapsed into a coma in the hospital and died June 2. The short road to the end was a horror of excruciating pain, and Ruth, forty-one at the time, would never fully get over the loss. "I loved him so much," she says. What made his passing even more painful for her was to watch what happened to the family's public image once Malcolm's big brother was no longer there to restrain him. "That Malcolm stuff," she says, "is so unlike anything Bruce would have done." Yet none of it would be possible were it not for the solid business foundation the conservative older brother had established. It galled her that as Malcolm became a celebrity and *Forbes* prospered beyond anyone's expectation, the work that Bruce had done to make it feasible would rapidly fade from public memory, with Malcolm getting full credit for the success.

In fact, Malcolm frequently acknowledged publicly the benefit of inheriting a healthy, debt-free company and acknowledged Bruce's contribution. Malcolm's frequent response to how he achieved suc-cess was "sheer ability, spelled i-n-h-e-r-i-t-a-n-c-e."

But for Ruth, life with Bruce was a fairy tale, and being able to retire at forty-one without financial worry to live in a Park Avenue apartment would not provide the fun she had accompanying Bruce through the glittering world of postwar corporate America.

At the funeral, Malcolm thanked everyone for showing up. "We all were waiting to see what would happen," Steve Quickel recalls. "At the time, Malcolm didn't seem like someone who would become the leader of the band. Since then I've often referred to him as Clark Kent: he went into the phone booth and came out Super-Malcolm."

After Bruce's death, Malcolm called the staff in for a meeting and said, "I'm glad to be in this new job, but like LBJ, I don't like the way I got it."

Nevertheless, very soon after Bruce's death, Malcolm, who until then had had little involvement in the business side of *Forbes,* swiftly flew into action. In those days, Malcolm wasn't very active entertaining corporate titans on the *Highlander.* That was a job Bruce and Ruth had dominated. In fact, it wasn't unusual that after Bruce and Ruth had spent a night of business entertaining into the wee hours, Malcolm and Roberta would show up bright and early the next morning to take the boat out for their own personal pleasure. Like many things after Bruce's death, that too would change—quickly.

In fact, one of the first excursions Malcolm took was through the Great Lakes to entertain all of Bruce's old friends in Cleveland and Detroit. Malcolm didn't inherit just the magazine, Ruth Forbes says: "Malcolm even inherited Bruce's friends—people like John Kluge, David Mahoney, all those guys were Bruce's friends."

David Mahoney was a Colgate-Palmolive executive who eventually became chief executive of Norton Simon, Inc. John Kluge, the Metromedia chairman, would eventually find himself in the number-one spot on *Forbes's* list of richest Americans.

In fact, Malcolm didn't inherit anything but a title and operational control. Full ownership control would come later—but not much later. Owning 100 percent of Forbes Inc. was important to Malcolm, who reveled in being the top executive and calling all the shots. Not having to answer to one single shareholder was essential to accommodate Malcolm's passion for complete freedom within his universe.

"The joy of being boss is what [chief executives] really like—the battle, the challenge," Malcolm said. "They are free spirits who don't seem to be burdened down by responsibility."

With 100 percent ownership of Forbes Inc., Malcolm could take any risk he wanted without having to answer to anyone. Despite his personal setbacks, he retained enough self-confidence to trust his instincts. And he wanted the freedom to act on them without anyone having the right to second-guess him before, during, or after.

The road to complete ownership would be fairly smooth. There were only four other shareholders to deal with: Ruth Forbes, with 30 percent; Gordon and Wallace, each with 16.5 percent; and Gertrude Weiner, with a 7 percent sliver that would seem insignificant to anyone—except Malcolm, who had the remaining 30 percent. He was determined to prevent even the slightest bit of the family business from escaping his clutches. After years of awkwardly sharing responsibility with his father and Bruce, Malcolm wanted the first and last word on ownership and how it would be used to remove all doubt about who was in charge.

Obviously the top priority was to get Ruth's stake to ensure unchallenged voting control. In the meantime, he invited his youngest brother, Wallace, into the family organization a few months after Bruce died. Wallace accepted and made a deal that would guarantee Malcolm the voting power he would need in the event of a challenge from Ruth. Wallace brought his brother Gordon in on the agreement as well. Together they put their shares in a voting trust under Malcolm's control and gave Malcolm the right of first refusal to buy the shares, with no time limit. Wallace trusted Malcolm, and Gordon, in the movie industry out West, wanted no involvement in the magazine's operation anyway.

"The voting trust was my idea," Wallace says. "I felt we ought to have one person without others applying pressure. We didn't want to have a divisive situation and I was confident in Malcolm's ability." He also was sensitive to the frustration Malcolm had felt sharing power with Bruce after his political career ended.

Wallace had no expertise in the magazine business, but he was possibly the best educated of the brothers in matters of Wall Street, and Malcolm had a logical spot for him—to direct the company's services division.

Wallace, a 1949 Princeton graduate with a degree in civil engineering, had spent five postwar years in the navy, mostly with Seabee units, in the Pacific, the Aleutians, Morocco, the Philippines, and, worst of all, Paris Island. By the time Malcolm offered him a job, he had taken an MBA at Harvard Business School and was a trust officer of Boston-based Bay State Corporation's advisory unit to trust departments of member banks. It was logical to assume he knew something about the investment advisory business and could help run Forbes's own investor advisory services.

It had problems. Investographs, for example, was a sinkhole. On advice from Leslie Quick, he shut it down. The Special Situations Survey, a twelve-times-a-year newsletter of stock picks and rationales, was shifted back to IAI where it began and was placed under Ray Yavneh's control. Then Wallace came in as president of the division, with Yavneh as vice president.

At the time, Malcolm assured Yavneh he would remain in complete control, continuing to manage all investment functions. Wallace's role would be simply that of business manager. From the start, Wallace made it clear he was comfortable with that arrangement, and the two worked well together. "He was good at organizing and planning," Yavneh says. He could boil down reams of paper into concise memos that helped the division achieve its goals. By the end of 1965, the unit had eighteen employees, including twelve analysts.

Meanwhile, Ruth Forbes, who still held three tenths of the company, was getting nervous as Malcolm cleared out Bruce's cronies and replaced them with his own people. And there was the mounting publicity surrounding Malcolm and his aggressive spending on such things as a costly advertising campaign, a $1 million renovation of the town house, and an order for a 117-foot *Highlander III* to replace the 98-footer then being used to impress clients, corporate chiefs, and heads of state.

As Ruth puts it, "I wasn't used to all this crap," referring to Malcolm's high-profile spending and partying with everybody who was anybody. "I went to Malcolm," she says, with the idea that he might like to buy her out.

In 1966, Ruth got $850,000 for a 30 percent stake that, if she'd been able to hold on to it, would have been worth at least 175 times that amount twenty-four years later. For advice on the transaction, she relied on her late husband's lawyer at Shearman & Sterling—the same law firm that generally represented Forbes Inc.—and on some of Bruce's old friends, including David Mahoney. Did she get a good price? Perhaps, in the long run, it doesn't matter. While Ruth still suffers occasional pangs to see how Malcolm was praised as the sole creator of the Forbes fortune, she would never have to work.

For Malcolm, the important thing was that with 60 percent ownership, he effectively had control. As Wallace once observed, "Minority stockholders have very few rights." But Malcolm didn't even want to have to worry about minority owners. Part of his motivation was to eliminate the inhibition of worrying about making a unilateral decision that might hurt someone other than himself—a worry that would resurface years later as his heirs' interests became more immediate.

But in 1965, none of these concerns seemed to be inhibiting Malcolm. He hired the Detroit ad agency Campbell-Ewald to develop what would evolve into one of the most successful corporate-image campaigns ever undertaken. It began with a series of snappy one-line ads in October of that year. Some examples:

MIND YOUR OWN BUSINESS. Advertise in Forbes, where more than 400,000 businessmen pry into other businesses.

MIND OTHER PEOPLE'S BUSINESS. That's what 400,000 readers do with Forbes. Which makes it a smart place to advertise if you want to tell them about your business.

FORBES READERS ARE LOADED. Forbes leads all major magazines in percentage of male readers with household income of $10,000 and over.

FORBES READERS CAN MANAGE WITHOUT YOU. Simmons says Forbes' percentage of professional managerial readers tops Fortune, Business Week, Time or Newsweek. Can you manage without them?

These concepts had many of the elements that would coalesce quickly into a campaign that would win twenty-seven awards the following year. It had feistiness, combative references to the competition, and most important of all, it saw the creation of a catchphrase that would last for decades: FORBES: CAPITALIST TOOL, began the ad in the October 15 *New York Times*. "Superb place to put your company's advertising. More than 400,000 readers use Forbes to find out how businesses are run."

Before long, "Forbes: Capitalist Tool" would appear at the end of virtually every ad for the magazine. It was advertising copywriter Pete Booth's stroke of genius.

"It came about as a result of a series of conversations with the editors and the boss man," said Tom Adams, then of Campbell-Ewald, "and Malcolm was always a strong advocate of capitalism and what it meant to the world as a whole. So this was a natural. He said he'd be proud to call his publication a capitalist tool. The guys working on the presentation picked up on his strong and defiant attitude and we suggested that line."

It certainly was punchier than what preceded it: "Forbes: The magazine that tells businessmen how other businesses are run."

"It has humor," Malcolm would later observe, "but it has its point and really rehabilitated the word 'capitalist' when the word had almost become a cussword. It makes people realize that capitalism means free enterprise."

What quickly evolved was a series of attention-getting, sometimes jarring ads based on a slogan lifted directly from the lexicon of leftist diatribes. But before the "Tool" campaign got going, *Forbes* took an unorthodox shot at *Fortune* that showed a stack of a dozen issues of *Fortune* in the top half of an ad. Beneath was a picture of an executive sitting in a commuter train reading *Forbes.* The headline: "Catch up with it on your next vacation?" The tagline: "Keep up with it on your way home." The body copy touted *Forbes*'s hard-working researchers and writers, but especially its editors. It noted the magazine's guaranteed circulation had risen to 425,000, within striking distance of Fortune's 430,000.

This clearly was a bid for the *Fortune* reader tired of the long-winded corporate profiles they hadn't the time to get through. It was an excellent example of breaking the rules of advertising—that you don't mention your competitor in your own ad—and getting away with it. And this ad didn't merely mention *Fortune* in passing. The competitor's name dominated the entire ad.

On the way to winning numerous awards, the "Capitalist Tool" campaign crossed the border into tastelessness in search of shock value. One of the first of the ads was viewed by some critics as appallingly exploitative. The full page ad in the *New York Times* showed an Asian man—a real one—curled up lying on his side and clearly very close to death from starvation, a photo as shocking as any that ever came out of Biafra or Ethiopia. "Hey mister," the headline said. "Want to buy a shiny new car with white walls, air-conditioning, full power, and stereo?" Appalling, but attention-getting. You had to read it to resolve the discomfort caused by this disturbing juxtaposition. It was an ad touting a story titled "Feeding the world's hungry millions: How it will mean billions for U.S. business."

This was followed immediately by another eye-catching full page a few days later. It featured a nearly life-sized close-up of the front end of a huge, slightly soiled hog. The headline was simply CAPITAL-IST PIG, one of the most insulting epithets being hurled at business-men of the day. Again, an ad that said, Read on. This one was promoting a piece in *Forbes* on meat-packing companies like Armour and how they were coping in the increasingly unprofitable meat market.

An ad focusing on a story about how the United States was losing the race for space because of military spending on the Vietnam War showed a skinny, barefoot soldier standing proudly next to a puny-looking automatic rifle. The headline read, "This Vietcong guerrilla helped shoot down an American space ship." Remember, this was in 1966, when the United States was fast approaching its goal of putting a man on the moon and the Vietnam War was just begin-ning to bother a few people. The story itself was the sales pitch, and the ad hit the reader over the head with it.

The same year, *Forbes* ran an article about how American Greet-ings Corporation's earnings had grown 200 percent over ten years largely because of its willingness to bring "kookie, fresh, original thinking" to the greeting card business with zany, humorous greet-ing cards. Full-page ads in the *Wall Street Journal* and *New York Times* promoting the story showed the office of American Greet-ings' "Hi Brow" cards staff. It looked like an album cover for an acid rock group, with one guy using a bedpan for an ashtray, pop art on the walls, a guitar sitting on a chair in the foreground, and no one looking dressed for work or particularly sober. The label under the photo: "The brain center of a 94 million dollar corporation." The copy concluded with this comment: "What Forbes is trying to tell you is that even if your board room doesn't look like a psycho ward, maybe your company could use a little way-out thinking."

This was 1966. The counterculture movement was still in its infancy. Yet here was *Forbes* writing about the hip and turning it into fascinating ad copy. *Forbes* and Campbell-Ewald clearly had the scent of things to come.

The ad format was designed to promote the magazine's best editorial quality: incisive stories almost belligerent in tone and characterized by bold assertions. Underlying it all was the message that *Forbes* was the cheerleader of free enterprise. With this ad campaign, Malcolm turned an anti-American slogan into a killer tagline and an enduring corporate identity. And how it was handled was very much a product of Malcolm's involvement, along with that of James J. Dunn, the ad executive he had just hired away from *Life* magazine to fill the void left by Bruce and the people Bruce had hired and Malcolm was firing.

"Dunn was really symbolic of the change" under Malcolm, says Wayne Welch. "He was right out of central casting. He was tall with silver hair and blue eyes."

Malcolm and Jim Dunn both were more involved than the average client in developing ad campaigns, says Adams of Campbell-Ewald. "Malcolm enjoyed this kind of thing, as did Jim Dunn," Adams said. "They stated they knew as much about advertising as anyone, not that they were overbearing. They made real contributions."

But financially, *Forbes* was still running on the strength of advertising from Bruce's pals—including his auto executive golfing buddies who placed their car ads in *Forbes*. Malcolm, however, was bringing science to this process. Where he lacked Bruce's hail-fellow-well-met personality, he made up for it with careful calculations and deadly accurate instincts. Over time he would cultivate his own brand of infectious charm, but for truly impressing people, he would always rely more heavily on the things he did and had rather than the way he was.

"Malcolm was most sensitive in the area of what's hot, popular, and trendy and how to manipulate that to the company's best advantage," Ray Yavneh says. "He understood publications better than anyone else in the business. Intellectually, Steve [Malcolm's oldest son] is superior, but Malcolm was a genius in terms of understanding what's current in publications."

Unlike Bruce, who kibitzed with his managers over iced coffee at the corner diner, Malcolm held monthly circulation meetings at which he demonstrated repeatedly his instinct to do the right thing at the right time. "He sensed the wind as no one else could, and followed it without hesitation," Yavneh says.

By the end of 1965, Malcolm acknowledged that IAI was providing the wherewithal to nurture the magazine's growth. The sources of IAI's revenue were the weekly report, Special Situations, sales of Forbes's how-to books, and stock-market courses written by Yavneh. All of these were low-overhead operations. The staff was small and took up little space. The mailing lists from which IAI derived its subscribers came from the magazine's subscriber list. The self-teach courses—which amounted to a large loose-leaf book with a three-inch thick spine and about three hundred pages—added no significant costs. The name of the subsidiary was changed to Forbes Investors Advisory Institute, which published Forbes Special Situations Survey and the Forbes Investor, formerly IAI Weekly Report.

There was one more crucial element in the re-formation of Forbes Inc. into the personal product of Malcolm Forbes. Much as forming a team including Jim Dunn and Jim Michaels was Malcolm's major coup in advertising and editorial respectively, positioning Leonard Yablon as Malcolm's top financial man was the last step in creating an essentially perfect management force. Yablon, a five-foot-three Brooklyn native with the appearance of a low-level ward heeler, was soon to be recognized as the architect of Malcolm's successful dealings with the Internal Revenue Service and an aggressive commitment to real estate investment. Yablon had been an outside auditor for Forbes Inc. until 1963, when Bruce Forbes hired him as controller. He quickly became Malcolm's Merlin with the numbers.

In 1967, Malcolm the introvert burst on the social scene with a splash that amounted to a coming-out party. It was billed as a fiftieth anniversary party for the magazine, but for the owner it was more than just an event to garner public notice. It was a brilliantly used sales tool. Top corporate officers were invited, but on the condition that they purchase at least one full-page ad in the fiftieth anniversary issue. At $8,000 a page and 750 guests, this party was the ultimate combination of business and pleasure. Far from groveling for orders, Malcolm was the pied piper. He wasn't asking people to buy ads; he was creating an atmosphere that endeared corporate media buyers to Malcolm and *Forbes*. They liked being entertained, and that predisposed them to take *Forbes* a little more seriously when considering where to advertise.

Malcolm, as he said often, was in the catbird seat. It was his show now, and no one else was going to tell him how to run it. A Forbes employee who helped organize the fiftieth anniversary event at Malcolm's Far Hills estate recalled the boss's reaction when only a handful of people had arrived by the 7:30 starting time.

"Why haven't we got things started?" Malcolm asked.

It was explained that many guests were still en route, delayed perhaps by the traffic jam the party was causing on the narrow road that led to the Forbeses' house.

"I don't care," Malcolm said. "Start the pipers." And with that a regiment of bagpipers marched over the hill at Timberfield.

The party, with a star-studded guest list of the rich and powerful—many of whom had paid their way—was sufficiently sumptuous, elegant, and extravagant to garner yards of publicity. This was the beginning of Malcolm's successful effort to reinvent himself. Many of the trappings would become fixtures at future Forbes extravaganzas: party tents decorated like castles, orchestras, the pipers, the souvenirs (a silver Tiffany bowl for the ladies, a maroon-bound copy of Malcolm's first book, *The Forbes Scrapbook of Thoughts on the Business Life,* engraved in gold for the men), and exquisite food and drink. One of the main attractions was the guest of honor and featured speaker, then Vice President Hubert Humphrey.

Malcolm also distributed a book full of history and anecdotes about the family and the magazine, including descriptions of all the family members. It even mentioned Adelaide's delightfully eccentric sister, Kitty, the Auntie Mame of the family. (It was Aunt Kitty who years later got tired of her doctor telling her how all her ailments were improving and told him, "Well, Doctor, you can tell the coroner I died of improvement"; within days, she died.) One glaring omission, however, from these family thumbnail sketches was his own mother; inadvertently, Adelaide wasn't mentioned.

"He was so embarrassed he almost died," recalls one family member.

At the time, the party was dubbed the party to end all parties. For Malcolm, it was a dry run on his way to achieving a new goal. Gone were the desires for public officialdom. His new role model was the real-life inspiration for the spy-thriller villain Auric Goldfinger—nearby neighbor Charles W. Engelhard, head of Engelhard Mining and Chemicals. Engelhard, who also attended Princeton, had a private gold-colored airliner. The two had campaigned against each other when Malcolm was in the state senate. Having given up on the presidency, Malcolm was going for a new title—one he believed would lend an air of prestige to his magazine—Living Legend of Capitalism.

5 | EMPIRE BUILDING

By 1969 Les Quick was starting to feel it was time to do something about his career. Lenny Yablon was clearly Malcolm's favored money man, and Quick was ready for a new challenge. He worked out a proposal with Wallace for Forbes Inc. to get back into the investment advisory business, but this time clients' accounts would be discretionary.

Quick presented the idea to Malcolm in early 1969.

"It was you who got us out of this business because it wasn't making any money," Malcolm reminded Quick. "Why do you want us to get back in?"

Quick explained that with discretionary accounts, Forbes Inc. could be faster and therefore more effective in generating positive results for clients.

Malcolm wasn't convinced. In what would prove to be yet another example of his superb instincts, he turned down the proposal.

Wallace Forbes then proposed that he and Quick strike out on their own. Wallace said he would sell his 16.5% stake in the magazine to Malcolm to launch their own investment firm and grant Quick a 20 percent stake in the enterprise to help run it. Quick knew his career path at Forbes was limited not only by Malcolm's affinity for Yablon, but by the existence of four heirs, who stood a good chance of wanting someday to take leadership roles at Forbes. And Forbes offered no profit-sharing incentives for nonfamily members, so there was no chance of ever building up equity.

Malcolm, of course, gave the deal his blessing. He may not have liked losing Wallace's expertise, but he certainly would be thrilled at the prospect of retiring Wallace's stake and eliminating another stockholder who, despite having relinquished voting rights, could still offer the thing Malcolm found hard to take from anyone else— advice. He also would have been pleased to see the way cleared for Yablon to take control of the financial side. Malcolm agreed to pay Wallace about $1.2 million for his one-sixth share and sweetened their departure by offering to indefinitely run for free a half-page ad each month promoting their new venture, Wallace Forbes & Associates.

For Malcolm, the timing was superb. For Wallace and Quick, it couldn't have been worse. They opened up shop in July 1969. At the end of the year, the market plummeted.

"The individual investor disappeared for a long time," Wallace recalls. It would cost him hundreds of thousands of dollars. And in retrospect, selling out to Malcolm at that time was also poor timing. "It wasn't a wise business decision," Wallace says, "but you can't cry over spilled milk."

With a wife, Betts, and three children—Alden, the oldest, Alexandra, and Bruce—Wallace would eventually sell out his interest to Quick and move on to work for Standard & Poor's Standard Research Associates Consultants unit, a firm that evaluated privately held companies.

Quick renamed the firm Leslie Quick & Associates, later joining forces with a New York Stock Exchange member to create the now publicly traded Quick & Reilly discount brokerage.

Meanwhile, Yablon moved up at Forbes. He would become the wizard with the magic to ensure that nearly every one of Malcolm's seemingly frivolous purchases would turn into a brilliant investment. What particularly endeared Malcolm to Yablon was his Brooklyn street-fighter approach to dealing with the Internal Revenue Service and seeing to it that Malcolm's life-style would be a tax-deductible business expense in the tradition of *Playboy* magazine's Hugh Hefner.

A description of Yablon's digs at Forbes offers a little insight into the character of this short, balding accountant who favored white-on-white shirts. The desk in his sprawling office rested on a platform a few inches off the floor. On one side was a stuffed tiger in a glass case, on the other a large electric paper shredder. (Malcolm kept one handy in his office as well.) Dominating the decor was a large blue ceramic cobra poised for attack.

"Yablon could be a very nice guy," says Steve Quickel, "but he could also stick it to you."

In business, men like Yablon traditionally are slow to pay the company's bills but quick to complain about those who don't pay promptly. During the summer, he would run downstairs at five P.M. to turn down the air conditioning. And while Malcolm spent millions on elaborate parties and entertaining, Malcolm hated to spend a penny that didn't stand a chance of coming back with interest. One of Yablon's roles—one he filled with apparent zeal—was standard-bearer of a never-ending austerity drive.

By 1968, Malcolm had purchased his first major Fabergé egg, had discovered motorcycling, and most important of all, had started to build a real estate empire that would quickly blossom into a significant source of revenue.

The egg infatuation had its genesis when Malcolm bought a gold cigarette case—plain except for the double-eagle insignia of imperial Russia—made by the Russian goldsmith Fabergé. He paid $1,000 for it at a jewelry store in London. Soon after, he bought his first egg—white enamel with a red cross—for Roberta at Easter time from a shop in New York that specialized in Fabergé objects. He purchased his first major Fabergé egg in 1965 at a Parke-Bernet sale for $45,000—even though at the time it was valued at $12,000. This was the start of a near obsession.

"At the beginning I only bought things I liked," Malcolm once said, "but as you get into it you figure you need examples of this genre and that, you round out the collection, buy things you wouldn't get just for yourself. It evolves."

In the case of the eggs, it would progress to the point at which his own pay-any-price-to-get-it mentality would drive up the value of the entire collection. It meant that, within certain limits—because eventually he would have twelve of the fifty-eight eggs Fabergé ever made—Malcolm could afford to overpay a little because of the positive influence it might have on an appraisal of the rest of the collection. For his eleventh egg, for example, he would pay $1.76 million at an auction at Sotheby's; the seller had acquired it thirteen years earlier for $196,000, also at an auction. (Of course, when it would come time to value the estate, the family would have to scramble for low appraisals.)

What's strange about the things Malcolm would collect was that none of them were traditional art and antiques—the conservative, mainstream kinds of works you'd expect a multimillionaire to acquire. Fabergé objects, for example, while stunning in all their glittery, jewel-encrusted splendor, weren't widely sought by antique dealers. Says one auctioneer/author: "Fabergé is kitsch. It's not even antiques." And Fabergé is about the most elegant thing Malcolm would get into collecting. Presidential papers, American and Victorian artifacts, toy boats, toy soldiers, balloons, and motorcycles would account for the bulk of other collecting interests. And while he would buy traditional artwork from time to time, he seemed to stay away from categories in which he could never hope to rank among the top collectors.

One reason was the influence of his son Kip, who would write his senior thesis at Princeton on Victorian art and convince his father at the time (1972) that it made more sense to invest in an art category not yet wildly popular. Malcolm wrote later in his book *More Than I Dreamed*—a profusely illustrated record of everything Malcolm ever bought, a book that doubles nicely as the ultimate definition of ostentation—that Kip told him: "Why pay huge prices for less than first-rank works of a school at the peak of its popularity, when major Victorian paintings are going for less than the sales tax on a third-rate Picasso?"

But perhaps more importantly it wouldn't serve Malcolm's ever present dual purpose of business and pleasure to be a lower-echelon buyer in a field dominated by academic experts Malcolm could never hope to contend with.

"I don't know how deep Malcolm's interest was in art," says one former auction-house art historian familiar with the Forbes family's buying habits. "He used it in such an awful flamboyant way. When he would buy anything at all, his public relations people would get on to the [auction house's] PR people and say, 'Now we're planning to put this out and what are you doing to get publicity.' That's not really a collector's thing. Malcolm's main thing was always to get publicity. It's very vulgar. They just drive you crazy with 'Are you going to have a press conference?' And he was always there and available for interviews. It's just the opposite of the average serious collector who typically doesn't want any attention at all and doesn't want anyone to know what he paid for something or what he plans to do with it. Of course, Malcolm would get miles of publicity. He'd pay $200,000 for something and get eight inches in the *New York Times.*"

On Malcolm, the bidder: "He wants to pay a lot. He's not really a shrewd bidder. But he buys wonderful stuff. No doubt he gets good advice. But it doesn't take much shrewdness to buy the most expensive thing in the catalogue."

While garnering publicity may be a major justification for every flamboyant thing Malcolm did or bought, his collecting interests still reflected something about the man.

Says the art historian, "Look at what he collected—lead soldiers, balloons, motorcycles. It's all puberty, all a twelve-year-old's dreams. I found it so striking that in collecting things, this man never went in for really fine furniture, antiques or silver. It's all this very kitschy stuff and very, very boyish things—autographs, soldiers. I often wondered if he had a stamp collection. That would complete the profile of a fourteen-year-old boy."

This same auction-house veteran says of Malcolm's interests in fine art, "It always struck me as strange: Here was this man, with this enormous family, who would come to sales at Sotheby's and buy all the male nudes. People would think that was strange. At American painting sales, he bought James Bama paintings. They're pretty good, but Bama . . . specializes in handsome cowboys. Malcolm was a big fan and paid record prices for them."

All this collecting would mean the stuff had to be housed, so Forbes over the years would end up with four museums to display it all. The one at the office held three hundred Fabergé objects, thousands of toy soldiers (this interest started with the impulse purchase of a box of World War I soldiers at an auction), hundreds of toy and model boats, and Victorian and American artifacts, including Malcolm's collection of presidential papers and signatures begun in earnest when Malcolm was in college. He also would set up a museum in Morocco to display toy soldiers, a ballooning museum at his forty-seven-room Chateau Balleroy in France, and the Victorian art collection at the family's Old Battersea House in London.

In 1968, Malcolm found something else macho that appealed to him: motorcycles.

"I had all the popular misconceptions about motorcycling," he once explained, "until one day my chauffeur borrowed the money from me to buy a motorbike and I got on the back. The next thing I knew I was buying bikes for myself and my sons."

And the next thing he knew—as if all this happened by accident—he'd found a way once again to combine business and pleasure. This time, he started buying every model that struck his fancy and justified the expense by purchasing a motorcycle dealership in Whippany, New Jersey. To Malcolm, riding motorcycles was the modern-day equivalent of cowboys on horseback. He formed a motorcycle club predictably called The Capitalist Tools, and dressed up the members—mostly young men—in appropriately labeled red vests, a sort of sanitized version of the traditional outlaw biker gangs' sleeveless denim jackets, or "colors," emblazoned with malevolent insignia.

No longer was the motorcycle interest just fun. Now it was a business, and a club whose presumably tax-deductible purpose was the creation of human billboards on the highway.

Malcolm was so proud of his new toy he would occasionally zip uptown to East 81st Street where his mother lived with a woman companion. He'd pull up outside her apartment and beep his horn, and she'd come out on the balcony to wave to him. Adelaide told family members she thought it was a crazy hobby for someone of Malcolm's age.

With all the profits from *Forbes* flowing into Malcolm's pocket, such investments were beginning to look increasingly attractive. In 1967, for example, Forbes Inc. revenue had soared to about $7 million. And even before then he was casting around for ways to expand the revenue base. He surely was no Goldfinger, but he had managed to bag virtually all Forbes Inc. stock at bargain-basement prices.

Having gotten Wallace's piece of the business, Gordon's fell to him soon after at about the same price, $1.2 million. Gordon wasn't interested in the magazine, and was pursuing a highly successful career in film production on the West Coast.

After graduating from Yale, Gordon went to work for Republic Pictures in Los Angeles. It was at Republic that Gordon met Claudia Adams, a film editor who had moved to Los Angeles from San Diego with her mother after her father was killed in World War II. She had started her career in Sam Goldwyn's studios. She and Gordon were dating when B.C. died in 1954, and they married later that year. Soon after, Claudia quit working and never went back. She would devote herself to raising their two children, Duncan Charles and Dana Lori. Gordon went on to work for John Wayne's Blackjack Productions for seventeen years before settling in for the duration at Paramount.

"Gordon was never interested in the magazine," Claudia said. "He was interested in the theater and movies—and only the business part of it." At Blackjack and Paramount, he was the executive in charge of the studios' physical operations, with all department heads answering to him. The grips, painters, sign-makers, transportation workers—all the functions necessary to maintain the studios where films were created—were Gordon's responsibility. He enjoyed the work, and his children must have sensed it. Duncan would become a freelance motion picture cameraman, and Dana would become a stage manager at Paramount for "Entertainment Tonight."

Says Claudia, "Gordon looked exactly like Malcolm, but shorter. He constantly was mistaken for Malcolm in restaurants. He was the nicest, sweetest, kindest guy. He was everybody's friend. He was the patriarch of the entertainment business. You knew that whatever Gordon told you was true."

Gordon would die in 1988 of a massive coronary at the age of sixty-five at his modest home in Studio City, California. He had retired just six months earlier as vice president of operations at Paramount, the Gulf & Western unit where he'd worked about ten years. Like his life, the end must have been peaceful; Claudia found him dead in bed the morning after a pleasant evening dining out with friends.

Once Malcolm had eliminated all other family members as stockholders, he turned up the heat on Gertrude Weiner, who was still working at Forbes. He let her know, sometimes publicly, that her persistence in holding her small stake displeased him. She finally would acquiesce in 1972, selling her share to Malcolm for about $100,000, and a year later retiring, ultimately to Florida, after more than fifty years of service.

The prices Malcolm paid for the 70 percent of Forbes Inc. he didn't own by inheritance totaled about $3.4 million—a bargain for a property that would swell in estimated value to well over a hundred times that in twenty years. It was a bargain even at the time, and Malcolm must have known it. For example, at about the same time—a couple of years after Bruce died—Malcolm was prepared to bid a much higher amount—$7 million—to buy a much smaller publication, *Gourmet* magazine, which certainly had nowhere near the 400,000-circulation ad base Forbes boasted at the time.

But Malcolm was still no Goldfinger in terms of personal wealth. Granted he now owned a debt-free business whose value was in the millions of dollars, but his life-style was still a long way from achieving the status of living legend. Nor was he interested in waiting long for that to happen. The ideal solution was to make a lot of money fast. Real estate provided that opportunity, though not in the way he expected.

Malcolm's interest in western American real estate was an outgrowth of Roberta's love of the West. As a child she spent summers in Jackson Hole, Wyoming, on a ranch where Owen Wister had written *The Virginian.* Soon after they were married, the Forbeses bought five acres inside Grand Teton National Park and built a log cabin on it. Years later, they bought about twelve thousand acres in Gardiner, Montana, next to the North Gate of Yellowstone and ran it as a successful cattle ranch, with Roberta supervising its operations. She was as much at home there as she was anywhere else, including Far Hills. Both the Wyoming and Montana properties were owned by the family, but Malcolm was interested in an even bigger chunk of the West—for investment. What he had in mind wasn't exactly your conventional buy-low, sell-high real estate speculation.

In 1969 Forbes Inc. bought 168,000 acres—the Trinchera ranch—on the Sangre de Cristo Spanish land grant, about two hundred miles south of Denver, for about $3.5 million with the idea of turning it into a hunting preserve. Brochures were soon printed with rates explaining how much a hunter would have to pay to bag various game running wild on the tract (buck deer, $500; black bear, $1,000; bull elk, $1,250). Deliveries of fencing, $100,000 worth, had already begun when the state of Colorado ruled that it, not Malcolm, owned the wild life, and that Malcolm couldn't use it to turn the now-renamed Forbes Trinchera into a high-priced shooting gallery. Now what?

With the help of Leonard Yablon, Malcolm quickly found a way out. Within a few years, Forbes would sell a fraction of the tract for many times what he paid for it. The solution: a mail-order operation to retail five-acre chunks of the Trinchera spread for as little as $3,500. That's $700 an acre for land that cost Forbes about $22. Not a bad profit margin. Within seven years, Forbes would sell at least $34 million worth of these mail-order lots. It was a better rate of return than anything he could ever achieve at the time in the magazine business.

"Your own land in the Old Southwest. Sangre de Cristo Ranches, division of Forbes Magazine," the brochures and ads read, carefully linking the real estate to the prestige of a national business publication. It was a connection that made some editorial staffers a little queasy. Even today the ads employ some of the hyperbole of less ethical raw-land retailers. They tout Forbes Colorado land as "the perfect place to acquire a substantial part of the American dream," calling it an "unspoiled paradise" that offers the buyer a way "to guarantee your own substantial heritage in America the beautiful." These are not the kinds of sales techniques one uses on seasoned real estate investors. This is pure hype aimed at the heart, not the head, and it worked.

As Yablon would say, "People like to be able to say in a casual way at the cocktail party, 'Yeah, I've got a bit of land out West myself.' " Clearly the target audience was the hardworking urbanite or suburbanite, the hard-core addicts of the rat race, whose egos might be soothed by owning a bit of "unspoiled paradise." It was just the sort of land exploitation Coloradans feared when the National Park Service lost in its bid to buy Trinchera when it came on the market.

In 1981, Forbes would buy up an additional 88,000 acres in the same area. Later, it would market forty-acre lots on the adjacent Forbes Wagon Creek Ranch, starting at $30,000 each. Also in 1981 Forbes would acquire 12,800 acres in Warsaw, Missouri, in the Lake of the Ozarks region for an estimated $7.3 million, naming it (what else?) Forbes Lake O' the Ozarks and imposing on it the same formula it found so successful in Colorado. A major selling point in that formula was required membership in an owners association and adherence to environmental control rules on what could be built where. At Lake of the Ozarks, for example, no one could cut down a tree of six inches or more in diameter without clearance by an environmental committee.

Robert Forbes, Malcolm and Roberta's second-born son, told Ken Cook of the *St. Louis Business Journal* in 1986 that about half the 11,000 Ozarks lots sold by then were ordered sight unseen through the mail, and to his surprise, not one house had yet been built on *any* of the sites. This, despite the fact that Forbes had put in roads (naming them, by the way, after Forbes veterans of five years or more), lakes and recreational facilities, and limiting camping to a few designated areas.

But why should Robert, vice president of Forbes's real estate operations, care whether anyone was developing their sites? The point of the economic formula masterminded by Yablon was to sell parcels on time payments stretched out over fifteen years at competitive interest rates to ensure a steady source of profitable cash flow. There was no tax benefit to selling off chunks of land for cash. Forbes certainly wasn't paying all cash for these properties, and as one Forbes staffer says, "If you buy something and set up a long payout, it ultimately doesn't matter how much you paid for it, because inflation will always bail you out."

An example of Yablon's ability to identify opportunities to save money: Publications like to swap ad space—supposedly to help one another pad the number of ad pages—but Malcolm got his money's worth out of this arrangement more than his rivals did by running his real estate ads in the international editions of *Time* and *Newsweek*. Why not generate land sales instead of running some lame READ FORBES ad?

In the beginning of the land-retailing operation, the typical deal was $3,500 for five acres, payable in $35 monthly installments at 6 percent interest. It would include a money-back guarantee for any customers who viewed the land within a year after purchase and didn't like it.

In 1983, when the Ozarks lots went up for sale, the willing buyer could get 2.5 acres for $60 down and 181 monthly payments of $60 each. The same year, Sangre de Cristo Ranches earned $2.5 million on revenue of $7 million.

Staffers' angst about the magazine being linked so closely to a business in an industry riddled with sleaziness might have been somewhat justified later when the magazine decided to attack Patten Corporation, one of the largest of the rural-land retail operations.

Gretchen Morgenson would write a hard-hitting piece about Patten in the January 12, 1987, issue of *Forbes* that the casual observer could easily have construed as hypocritical for a magazine that happened to be in the same business—granted, in a much smaller way. Headlined OLD GAME, NEW TWIST, it started this way:

"Forget Florida. Today's undeveloped land hype centers on good old New England. The affluent young and upwardly mobile lust not for perpetual sunshine but for 'unspoiled' woodland and farmland plots close to Boston, Providence, or New York. An urban yearning for the bucolic.

"Who's there to sell wide-open spaces to cramped but credit-worthy city dwellers? Patten Corp., a $35 million installment land sales company based in Stamford, Vt."

The story went on to suggest that Patten's accounting practices were hiding a negative cash flow at a time when the company's stock was flying high on the New York Stock Exchange. It was a fine example of the kind of story *Forbes* does so well. Still, Patten quietly bristled at the hypocrisy of *Forbes* magazine making snide remarks about the business of selling "unspoiled" vacation land to city slickers on the installment plan—the main function of Forbes's Sangre de Cristo Ranches.

Two years later, Morgenson took an even harsher look at Patten Corporation. A December 26, 1988, story, headlined SUCKERING THE CITY BUMPKINS, highlighted some of the legal troubles Patten was encountering just as it was beginning to branch out from its traditional fields of operation in the Northeast. While battling it out with state consumer protection agencies over allegedly deceptive sales pitches, Patten was expanding westward—including Montana, where the Forbes family owned a ranch.

The story quoted two Montanans in a single paragraph saying pretty much the same thing—that Patten posed a threat to the environment. Not that Malcolm had sicced Morgenson on Patten. Her motive for doing the story was simple: Patten was a company with five state attorneys general investigating its sales practices, which was hampering its ability to raise money—an interesting target made even more interesting by its colorful chairman, Harry S. Patten.

This time, Patten wasn't about to quietly grit his teeth. He took out full-page ads in the *Wall Street Journal* and *Barron's* to rebut the *Forbes* story, including an offer to send a point-by-point rebuttal to anyone who asked to see it. Included in that eight-page, single-spaced response was this query: "Is it possible that the criticisms in the article concerning Patten's westward expansion arise out of Mr.

Forbes' concern that we may be competing with his real estate activities in that area?"

Even though this wasn't Morgenson's motive for doing the story, it was the kind of appearance of conflict that can undercut a journalist's credibility in the course of trying to report without consideration for the publisher's other business interests.

Said Michaels of Patten's rebuttal, "He didn't answer our points." As for Morgenson, she cited Patten's dismal stock-market performance as proof that she was right about the company. And less than two months after the Forbes story appeared, the company settled the state inquiries, without admitting guilt, by agreeing to repay buyers who felt they'd been misled.

For Forbes, the real estate formula would make it possible for Malcolm to invest in the kind of trophy real estate that he would use as a backdrop for his rapidly emerging role as a famous rich guy. After all, what's the best way to get such publicity? Put yourself in something highly photogenic in front of, say, a castle and transport the media and their cameras to said castle.

The highly photogenic thing would turn out to be a hot-air balloon, and the castle would turn out to be a seventeenth-century chateau in the beautiful French countryside of Normandy. The creation of the public Malcolm Forbes was, by the 1970s, well under way.

6 | THE BLIMP FACTOR

Forbes circulation had swelled to 625,000 by 1972—the year Malcolm wrested the last few shares from Gertrude Weiner—topping its archrival, *Fortune,* by 75,000 readers. Revenue—from advertising, subscriptions, services, and rent from tenants in the office at 60 Fifth Avenue—was more than $17.5 million.

Now began the acquisition of trophy real estate—a strategy to establish Forbes as a worldwide landholder on whose empire the sun never sets. The first of these trophies was the Palais de Mendoub in Tangier, Morocco. The excuse for this 1970 purchase: a base of operations in the Arab world from which to launch an Arabic edition of *Forbes.* Malcolm's assumption was that oil-rich Arabs had more money than they knew what to do with and would snap up copies of *Forbes* to help them find out. (Even if they were to buy the magazine, selling ads in it would prove nearly impossible, because advertising is a medium the Middle Eastern audience tends to ignore.)

That same year, he acquired the forty-seven-room Chateau de Balleroy in Normandy, France, for less than $350,000 from a couple who had rejected an offer from Bernard Cornfeld, the high-living American investor and founder of International Overseas Securities, a mutual fund that swelled to $2 billion before it collapsed.

The Moroccan property, the former governor's palace, was not the finest example of that region's architecture. It was built somewhat in line with its surroundings, but was designed for the comforts of its European occupants when the British and French were ensconced in Morocco.

"It was incredibly garish," says Jefferson Grigsby, a former *Forbes* executive editor who helped launch the *Forbes* Arabic edition. "It looked like a Westerner designed it, based on some wild idea of what a Mideastern palace should look like." But this was the sort of place that appealed to Malcolm, and Tangier was an international flesh market whose reputation had attracted people like Truman Capote, Tennessee Williams, and William Burroughs.

The entry into Morocco provided Malcolm with yet another close brush with death—the fifth by his count, starting with being shot in the war, two close calls while yachting, and getting out of a helicopter that crashed moments later on takeoff from the deck of the USS *Forrestal.* What happened in Morocco may have been the most harrowing close call.

Malcolm, in July 1971, had wangled an invitation to the stag birthday party of Moroccan king Hassan II, perhaps because Malcolm had given him a motorcycle in an earlier meeting. The party was at the king's summer palace in Skhirat on the Atlantic coast. After hundreds had arrived in chauffeured limousines, soldiers armed with automatic weapons and grenades stormed the palace cutting down everyone in their path. At first the guests inside thought the approaching onslaught was a fireworks display just getting under way. But before it was over, more than a hundred people were killed in the palace courtyard.

Malcolm escaped uninjured by jumping through a smashed window to the beach below and crawling away to a corner of the king's golf course where other guests had fled. But the soldiers rounded them up and marched them back to the palace courtyard passing numerous corpses on the way. Meanwhile, the king had slipped away and was hiding in a lavatory off his throne room. When soldiers discovered him there, he ordered them to obey him. Because they had been duped into participating in the attack by being told they were there to rescue the king, they quickly acceded.

At the time, Kip—"suitably aided by both a current and a future wife," according to *Town and Country* magazine—was entertaining guests at the Forbes palace in Tangier. The current wife was Sondra Irene Simone. The future wife was the German baroness Astrid Mathilde Cornelia von Heyl ze Herrnsheim, whom he'd met when she was working for Warner Dailey, Malcolm's antique trader in London who set up Forbes International, an antiques business. When Kip first learned of the attack, he was informed that Malcolm was among the dead. Incredibly, the incident didn't dim Malcolm's commitment to the palace and the Middle Eastern publishing venture.

Malcolm would go on to set up the Arabic edition, using Mendoub as a base of operations. The costly venture would be killed in 1979 in the wake of the Iranian revolution and hostage crisis and the ensuing complications in Arab-American business relations. But the palace would stay in the Forbes collection and become the scene of a Forbes party so extreme in its lavishness that even gossip columnists, who normally seize on such events to vent their superlatives, would be moved to question whether Malcolm had gone too far.

In 1972, Malcolm's world conquest yielded Laucala Island in the Fijis, a South Pacific group of islands that had just won their independence from the British. The 3.5-mile-long Laucala fell to the increasingly voracious Forbes empire for $1 million. The previous owner was W. R. Carpenter Ltd., a trading company based in Canberra, Australia. The 3,000-acre island's main asset was three hundred residents and the production of copra, or dried coconut meat, from which coconut oil is extracted.

Like everything else Malcolm was buying, this was an investment not just in real estate but in his image. After all, who has his own South Pacific island? The superrich, the superstar, the dictator. But he wasn't about to own it simply as an image builder whose value would quietly appreciate. He wanted it to carry its own weight.

He intended to make copra output profitable and establish the island as an exclusive resort that would appeal to deep-sea fishermen and scuba divers. But ultimately, the resort function would dominate the activity on Laucala. "From coconuts to credit cards, all in one generation," Malcolm would boast later.

One of gossip columnist Liz Smith's lasting impressions of Malcolm was of him driving a small four-wheel vehicle past hordes of children and tossing them handfuls of hard candy.

It's not clear what the natives thought of having Malcolm's materialistic values and tastes imposed on them, but visitors would notice a somber attitude among the residents compared with that of their laid-back, neighboring islanders. And residents on those other islands would hear of vague misgivings among Laucalan parents about the influence of the rich, hedonistic Malcolm on their children. Erecting a church on the island would do little to dispel such misgivings.

Jim Christy and a friend would visit the island on Halloween, 1985. They saw a sharp contrast between Laucala and neighboring islands.

"We had been staying at the next island over, which was really the definition of unspoiled paradise," the friend says. They were staying at a modest resort on Gamea owned by a married couple from San Francisco—middle-class business people who had planned for years to run away to a South Sea paradise and actually did it. They had built a boat, sailed it across the Pacific, bought a piece of an island and built four or five bures—native huts—slightly modernized inside for tourists. They employed the locals but behaved as gracious guests, careful to be as noninvasive as possible. They kept a low profile, blending into the existing culture, and as a result were adopted by the natives as their own.

The Fijians would wander in and out of the Californians' modest resort, playing music—somewhat Hawaiian in flavor, but sexier—and sharing the local fare, including a mildly narcotic drink called tuak, made from kava, a root.

It was in the midst of enjoying this delightful resort imbued with Fijian culture that Christy and his companion were invited to visit Laucala.

They went over to Malcolm's place partly because their hosts were friendly with the Forbeses. They were picked up in a boat piloted by a young man who looked like he just stepped off a yacht from Connecticut—"a very blond guy probably two years out of college."

What they saw on Laucala was the result of a foreign culture that had successfully overrun the native one.

Forbes had moved the Fijians inland a few hundred yards away from the beaches, razed their bures—he called them "tin and wooden shacks"—and replaced them with parodies of suburban bungalows. A modest canteen that sold mostly canned goods had been erected, though the Fijians had little use for canned goods, living in a lush tropical paradise brimming with fresh produce. Among the new housing were concrete patios and a nautilus gym in a sort of community center.

It was as though Malcolm's main purpose was to establish his own country, domesticate the Fijians, and banish them inland.

The crowning insult to what otherwise was a beautiful island paradise was the New Jersey–style suburban ranch house Malcolm built on the topmost point of the island along with an Olympic-size pool whose sole decoration was a statue of a nude Greek boy. While this was no castle, the house had a commanding view of the entire island, like a fortress from which a king might be able to look down on the little people below.

"In the middle of this beautiful lush jungle, it seemed incongruous," the visitor said. "The house itself was remarkably unspecial. It was a conventional rancher. You wouldn't believe somebody wealthy lived there."

Later in the day, the young man in Topsiders, Jim Donohue, showed the couple the resort—a collection of generic luxury-resort-style cabins with cement patios. They returned to the rancher for dinner with the island's only other guest, an oil-company executive trying to get away from it all. Their host boasted of the kitchen and what it could produce and the wine collection, then served a totally American meal—mashed potatoes, a meat-loaf dish, lousy warm white wine, and Jell-O with something on it for dessert.

As if to epitomize in their minds the sharp contrast to the atmosphere in the paradise they'd come from, no wandering musicians casually dropped by to entertain and join in the fun. Instead, Dono-hue rounded up some employees with guitars and commanded them to play. When Donohue disappeared into the house, the natives would stop playing, resuming only when he stepped back outside, clapping his hands and barking at them in Fijian to play louder.

In the course of reporting a January 7, 1986, story about his Laucala visit for the *Toronto Globe and Mail,* Christy called Forbes Inc. offices in New York with questions on how and when the island's operations might become profitable. A Forbes official re-acted coolly.

"He might have glimpsed that I may have had a few negative impressions," Christy says. "Immediately after talking to him I started getting strange anonymous phone calls. In one conversation, a guy tells me, 'You know, nothing bad has ever been written about Forbes.' 'Why?' I ask. The guy says, 'Well, anybody who did want to write anything bad about him is dead.' "

(Nothing ever happened to suggest the comment was meant as a serious threat, and it wouldn't be Forbes's style to even try such a tactic.)

The *Globe* story mentioned how Forbes relocated the natives from their traditional homes and built new homes for them in a style ill-suited to their culture. For example, instead of duplicating the islands' traditional low doorways—a sort of symbolic deterrent against evil spirits—conventional Western-style doorways were in-stalled.

"When Mr. Forbes bought the island," Christy wrote in the *Globe and Mail,* "the natives lived by the water in their wooden and thatched homes called bures. He moved them. 'That's where Mr. Forbes wanted to put his paying guests,' Mr. Donohue says. Asked whether the natives had voiced any hesitation about their relocation, Mr. Donohue eyes his questioner suspiciously, 'No, why should they?' "

Says Christy, "It was a little, bad part of New Jersey stuck out there in the middle of Laucala. The people who are free in Fiji were free everywhere but there."

When asked if the Fijians had any say in the design of their new homes—which Christy describes as "cheap symbols of an old way of life"—Donohue is quoted as saying, "They worked for hourly wages if they wanted. Of course, people don't like to work around here. Look, just say Mr. Forbes built these people good, comfortable homes."

How did Mr. Donohue meet Forbes? "We were in the hospital together," he told Christy. "I had cancer and Mr. Forbes was in for a heart attack [actually a hernia operation, in 1983]. I was feeling sorry for myself. I didn't know who he was except that he was this cheerful old guy who used hip expressions and cheered me up. He said, 'If we ever recover from all this, let's ride motorcycles together or something,' He gave me the will to get better, and I did."

Malcolm was true to his word. After Donohue left the hospital, Malcolm called him and invited him to go motorcycling with him in France. Two days later, they were on their way. When asked why Forbes offered him the Laucala job, Donohue noted that Malcolm liked to be near young people. It was one of Malcolm's traits that some of the island's parents found worrisome.

Malcolm's eccentric whims would probably have been more disturbing if he spent more time on the island, but his far-flung interests wouldn't allow it. He did, however, throw an annual party on the island to entertain the local leaders. And he tried to throw a bit of his own weight around. He attempted to buy the local newspaper, the *Fiji Sun* from its Hong Kong owners, but was thwarted by the government, which had closed the paper in a military coup. Malcolm was embittered. Perhaps he felt cheated because he had agreed to feature Fiji in promotional material as a safe place to invest—despite the coup.

Along with Laucala, the chateau in France, and the Moroccan palace, Forbes bagged Old Battersea House, a rapidly deteriorating 1699 Christopher Wren mansion in London. He leased it for a peppercorn a year and subjected it to hundreds of thousands of dollars in renovations that took years to complete. It would eventually be the central repository of his son Kip's burgeoning collection of Victorian art, a special interest that emerged in college and flowered into a near obsession. (At one point Kip would take to wearing the turn-of-the-century Edwardian-style suits that symbolize that era's smug sense of materialistic wealth.) Today, the lavishly restored mansion in London houses the bulk of the nearly five hundred Victorian paintings Kip has amassed.

Kip's fascination with Victoriana was an interest he shared with Baroness Astrid. They were both members of an organization called the Victorian Society. Kip had divorced Sandy and married Astrid by 1975 when he and his longtime close friend Everett Fahy, chairman of the European paintings department at the Metropolitan Museum of Art in New York, collaborated on an exhibition of Victorian art at the Met.

While Malcolm was amassing a portfolio of exotic real estate—and a personal jetliner to get to it all—he discovered a sport that fit perfectly into his regimen of combining business and pleasure. Naturally he would go at it with the zeal of a religious convert. His interest in ballooning began with an ad in a local New Jersey newspaper advertising rides for $75 a person, $100 for two.

On a foggy July morning in 1972, Dennis Fleck, Malcolm's chauffeur, picked up his boss at the usual time, 6:30 A.M., for the ride into Manhattan. This time, however, Malcolm said, "We're going to take a little detour today," and directed Fleck to head for Princeton.

It wasn't until they pulled into an open field at Princeton Airport that Malcolm told Fleck what he was up to. They were there to meet Phil Hallstein of the Chelt Balloon Club. Hallstein showed up with his gear but told Malcolm it was too foggy to fly. Malcolm wasn't pleased.

"The boss being the kind of guy he was, he wanted something to happen," Fleck says.

"Can't you do something?" Malcolm asked Hallstein. "You know, inflate it so we can at least have a look at it?"

Hallstein agreed, and Fleck and Malcolm in his business suit crewed for him. They tied the balloon to a tree and rode it up and down.

"This is really neat," Malcolm kept saying.

Finally the fog cleared and they got their untethered ride. As they floated over the New Jersey countryside, Malcolm turned to Fleck and said, "Let's get one of these things. What do you think? We can put our name on it."

Both Malcolm and Fleck were absolutely hooked. Malcolm turned to Hallstein and asked him what it took to get a license. Hallstein filled him in on the details, adding that he was authorized as an instructor. With that, Malcolm said, "Can we start right now?" They did.

"It was the neatest damn thing that ever happened to me," Fleck says.

Three months later, they had their licenses, and two days after that, Malcolm took delivery of a green and gold balloon bearing the increasingly ubiquitous legend FORBES: CAPITALIST TOOL with the added tagline, "For High-ups in Business." It was Malcolm's version of the Goodyear blimp. "It's a Peter Pan thing," Malcolm liked to say in explaining the appeal, but the blimp factor gave it a legitimate business purpose. His approach was sufficiently aggressive that within a little over a year, he launched a cross-country balloon trip, something no one had ever done before in a single baloon, with all the attendant publicity normally associated with a coast-to-coast Michael Jackson tour.

At a 1973 preview of the $25,000 balloon he planned to use for the trip, he told reporters, "What in hell has this to do with a business magazine? The answer is, 'Nothing at all.' It's just for the fun-ness of it." But nothing Malcolm does was really just for fun, and he quickly added, "You people wouldn't be here today to write about the editor of Forbes magazine if it weren't for the balloon." Years later, the same sentence would work, substituting "Elizabeth Taylor" for "the balloon."

On November 6, 1973, just fifteen months after getting his license, Malcolm set the cross-country balloon flight record, making the trip in twenty-one days. On his way back East he used up lives number six and seven, crashing into high-voltage power lines in Virginia, and then ending the trip, with son Robert alongside him, by ditching in the Chesapeake Bay near Gwynn Island. Luckily, the water was shallow enough to stand in. (An Illinois farmer nearly shot them for Martians, but apparently people merely pointing guns at

Malcolm didn't count as close brushes with death; they actually had to be shooting.) Before he attempted the feat, Malcolm had logged just 33.5 hours in the air, yet he had suddenly forced himself to the center of the sport and was using it effectively to make Forbes a household name even among those who had no interest in business news. By the end of the transcontinental trip, it's safe to say that a great many Americans who had never heard of *Forbes* magazine now knew of the delightful millionaire Malcolm Forbes floating whimsically about like a real-life Phileas Fogg.

But there was nothing whimsical about Malcolm's purpose. The idea was to get attention, and an elaborate public relations effort—as sophisticated and thorough as any political campaign—kept the media's attention firmly focused on the trip every step of the way, with media kits, films, and promoters. It was a $120,000 image-building campaign. By the time it was over, *Sports Illustrated* noted, "Malcolm Forbes was almost as familiar to Americans as Evel Knievel. . . . The promotion was obvious, but the public loved it."

Some in the professional ballooning community bridled at Malcolm's tactics, noting that this headline-grabber weirdly clad in fur parka, red leather pants, and black calf-high boots had the support of dozens of people on the ground with a bus, cars, a motor home, and an airplane. But Malcolm was unapologetic: "The reason my flight succeeded and others failed can be summed up in one word: money."

Suddenly, though certainly not by accident, Malcolm had achieved celebrity status outside the world of financial journalism. He loved it and wanted to keep the ball rolling—and in a manner that would also increase his respectability. He decided the way to do it would be to become the first to cross the Atlantic Ocean in a balloon, something that had been tried twelve times before and had cost four lives, on a pseudoscientific mission. If it could be done, Malcolm's fame would expand greatly. To give it the necessary air of respectability, he focused the media's attention on the technological challenges the venture posed and the scientific experiments it would perform. This wasn't to be perceived as just another publicity stunt.

In September 1974, not even a year after finishing the transcontinental trip, Malcolm staged a news conference in a New York hotel room—the same one from which he launched the ill-fated *Nation's Heritage*—to announce the serious, scientific details of this grave transatlantic undertaking. The setup was similar to what one might expect for a national hero embarking on a dangerous mission to open up a new frontier. About the only reminders of the publicity purpose of the venture were the piles of Malcolm's poorly selling book *Fact and Comment* being given away and Malcolm's jockeying for proximity to the TV cameras filming the event.

Otherwise, every effort was made to give this undertaking the aura of a daring space shot by men risking their lives at the edge of the future for the good of all humanity. This was no publicity event. This was a mission. A cluster of helium balloons were to haul Malcolm and the project's prime contractor, onetime would-be astronaut Thomas Heinsheimer, in a 10-foot-diameter pod—dubbed Windborne—into the jet stream above forty thousand feet where they would be swept along at speeds of more than two hundred miles an hour. Along the way, tests would be done to see what could be learned about the jet stream.

Convincing the world that Malcolm Forbes was a scientist would prove more difficult than accomplishing other goals where spending enough money was all it took.

"The Atlantic balloon crossing looked like an elaborate suicide try," said a Forbes staffer. There were rumors that Malcolm thought he had cancer. (In fact, a few years later, he would discover he did have cancer and would undergo two years of painful treatments to cure himself.) Not all his family members—usually on hand for such events—showed up for this one. It was said that the entire elaborate system—the launching system, the helium balloons, and the landing routine—had flaws designed in to virtually guarantee disaster.

In Santa Ana, California, early Sunday, Jan. 5, 1975, Malcolm and Tom Heinsheimer crawled into the gondola. Leaving from the West Coast was supposed to give them about a day of flight during which they could abort the mission over land. Thirteen Mylar balloons full of helium were wheeled out attached to concrete-laden laundry carts that were supposed to release them gradually. But the carts weren't heavy enough to control the balloons as they shot up, yanking the carts off the ground, dragging them along the tarmac, and eventually jerking the gondola loose from its platform and bouncing it on the ground. As Roberta looked on horrified, along with TV camera crews and other media, Jean-Pierre Pommerau leaped on the careening gondola and managed to grab the baloon release on the first try. The balloons took off, leaving the aeronauts safe on the ground.

For Malcolm, it was life number 8 by his count. Not far downwind from the launch site, remnants of burst balloons were found indicating that only five of the thirteen survived the ascent. Eleven was the bare minimum required to keep the Windborne aloft. Had the launch succeeded, the gondola would have been taken up only high enough to ensure that when it came crashing down, its occupants surely would have been killed.

But in the same way that he garnered praise in the wake of his failed *Nation's Heritage* venture in the form of a Freedoms Foundation gold medal, Malcolm won the Harmon Trophy as Aeronaut of the Year in recognition of achieving the first coast-to-coast flight across the United States—despite his transatlantic failure.

Such feats—or near feats—were starting to generate interest in this unusual businessman. Who was this eccentric, daring millionaire? Harper & Row decided the world might want to know more about Malcolm and in 1977 published the semiauthorized biography by Arthur Jones. The book sold only five or six thousand copies out of a ten-thousand-copy printing, but this was before the corporate biography became a popular niche in the book publishing industry.

Says Hugh Van Dusen, who edited the Jones book, "We were hopeful that Malcolm at least would like it so much he'd buy several copies. I don't think he bought even one." Still, Malcolm must have sensed the public relations potential of books about himself.

The following year, in 1978, Harper & Row followed up by publishing *Sayings of Chairman Malcolm.* It sold much better—42,400 copies—but probably at a loss for Malcolm, who spent hundreds of thousands of dollars promoting the book and selling it himself by direct mail.

In 1986, Malcolm would publish *Further Sayings of Chairman Malcolm,* but sell only 17,700. As one book-publishing executive says, "He wasn't another Bennett Cerf. He had nothing particularly funny or acutely incisive to say. I don't understand why his own books sold so well."

It was Malcolm's practice to spend so much promoting his books that it would be hard for them to be profitable, but for him, profitability wasn't a simple matter of cash flow. Obvious benefits flowed through to the company's operations from books by Malcolm Forbes being prominently promoted and displayed. Soon there would be several more, all published by Simon & Schuster: *Around the World on Hot Air and Two Wheels,* 1985; *They Went That-a-way,* with Jeff Bloch, 1988; and *More Than I Dreamed,* 1989. At the time of his death, he had just completed work on another book again with Bloch, that took a look at what became of famous people's children.

Meanwhile, Malcolm was perfecting his ability to generate publicity via balloon and motorcycle. Abandoning the serious-scientific-adventure strategy, Malcolm set out to conquer the world one country at a time.

In the summer of 1979, after leaning on the industrialist Armand Hammer (Malcolm's friend, despite a *Forbes* story eight years earlier that suggested he was too old and frail to run his business) to pave the way, Malcolm, along with two of his children, two writers, and a photographer to record the event, rolled into Moscow on motorcycles. He handed the mayor's wife a tote bag emblazoned with the CAPITALIST TOOL logo—this when the Soviets were still rabidly anticapitalist. "The mayor was laughing. He also stopped laughing pretty fast," Malcolm said.

It was also in 1979 that Malcolm called his chauffeur, Dennis Fleck, to pick him up at home in Far Hills and take him to see his doctor. It was a Sunday morning. When Malcolm emerged from the doctor's office, he was catheterized and blood was slowly filling the bag attached to the catheter. The doctor told Fleck to rush Malcolm to New York University Hospital. By the time they arrived there—after speeding through every red light in New Jersey and being stopped only once, at the Holland Tunnel into Manhattan—Malcolm was unconscious and the bag was full to bursting. Apparently,

Malcolm was suffering from a rarely curable form of cancer that affects the urinary system.

The discovery must have been frightening. After all, it was bladder cancer that killed his brother Bruce. But after about two years of painful treatments, Fleck says, Malcolm would calmly tell him one day, "Well, I beat it." Recalls Fleck, "He said he drank some sort of solution, and that was it."

This brush with death would not be one of those he publicly counted among his nine lives, yet it probably did much to increase Malcolm's commitment to living life to the full.

Starting in 1982, Malcolm would begin a series of Friendship Tours that capitalized on the quirkiness of traveling in a pack of squeaky-clean motorcyclists followed by a collection of awesome hot-air balloons designed with particular destinations in mind and a gaggle of photographers, writers, and cameramen to record it all. (The film footage of these events tended to be dominated by scenes of Malcolm surrounded by his traveling companions and equipment and support vehicles.)

As one Forbes staffer would note after one particular trip, "Now I know what it's like to be a rock star." The PR machine that paved the way for these journeys often generated thousands of cheering locals eager to see what was then a rare form of entertainment that's hard to categorize. One thing was sure though: Whatever it was, these tours had much of the excitement one associates with a circus coming to town. The balloons were colossal. When the motorcycle gang roared in, all dressed in bright red and black leather, the local citizenry was ready for some pageantry, courtesy often of the country itself. Leaders presented medals to Malcolm and Malcolm presented them with numerous promotional objects from the Forbes storehouse of self-serving souvenirs. The climax: an amazing display of giant delights in an atmosphere of good-natured daredevilry.

The first of these journeys was to China. Perhaps the two most notable aspects of this initial attention-grabber were Malcolm's ability to use high-powered connections for personal gain and his willingness to flout local customs when the irresistible scent of publicity beckoned. After all, the fun of such travel would be hollow for

Malcolm if it failed to further his goal of putting and keeping Forbes in a prominent position in the lexicon of extreme wealth.

In the case of the China trip, he leaned on former President Richard Nixon, Henry Kissinger, and finally, once again, Armand Hammer to win permission to make the trip in a balloon proclaiming "*Forbes* salutes U.S.–China friendship" in Chinese. This was like the noisy parade that follows all conquering heroes, but in Malcolm's mind, *Forbes* was creating good will that didn't exist before he came on the scene. He called these trips unofficial diplomatic missions and reveled in the entree it gave him with local leaders.

The Chinese had insisted that all balloon flights be tethered for security reasons, but Malcolm was determined not to obey.

Timothy Forbes, Malcolm's fourth son, would say later that he tried to convince his father not to break the rule. "I said, 'No you can't'; he said, 'Yes I must.' "

The next morning, the balloon was launched on a tether. This time, however, the tether came loose from above and dropped to the ground, much to the horror of the group's Chinese escorts. The balloon floated free for twenty minutes, finally coming to rest in the middle of a military base. Soldiers rushed to meet them—with guns drawn (again, no shooting, so no close brush with death). "Pop and I spent some time in a room while they tried to decide what to do," Tim said. "Apparently they decided it never happened and returned us to our hotel."

At a farewell banquet, Malcolm noted that it wasn't his intention to be naughty but only to demonstrate that balloons aren't meant to be tied down. Neither was Malcolm—not by the Chinese, certainly not by his youngest son.

It was an exciting, death-defying moment—sufficiently controversial to get Forbes into plenty of headlines, thus making the trip pay for itself in valuable publicity. Malcolm seized on the formula.

A year after the China trip, Malcolm's CAPITALIST TOOL motorcycle gang and the Forbes Balloon Ascension Division—all team members dressed in brilliant yellow pants and red shirts—went to Pakistan with a balloon replica of the Minar freedom monument. Next was the trip to Egypt with the Sphinx balloon. The following year, it was Thailand, and an elephant balloon (documentary film narrated by Laurence Olivier); then off to Japan with a hot-air pagoda. In Germany, Malcolm launched a balloon shaped like a bust of Beethoven, supposedly tickling the fancy of officials sitting down to make some grave decision regarding the Western alliance, and later at the still-standing Berlin Wall to the delight of Germans on both sides. The next trip was to Turkey, with a towering likeness of Sulayman, the sixteenth-century sultan, followed by a trip to Spain with a likeness of the *Santa Maria* (documentary narrated by Placido Domingo).

In between these Friendship Tours Malcolm also took his gang on an annual motorcycle vacation. Bob Sipchen, a reporter with the *Los Angeles Times,* went on one of these trips—the 1989 ride from the Canadian border at International Falls, Minnesota, to New Orleans. What impressed Sipchen was that despite his age, Malcolm wasn't timid on a motorcycle. "We were doing ninety miles an hour in some places," Sipchen says. Everyone was always scrambling to keep up with him. Side trips were brief, and each stop ended with Malcolm firing up his Harley Electra Glide Sport in green and gold and heading out onto the highway, with the rest of the gang scurrying to fall in.

The whole balloon business would grow to the extent that he would set up a museum dedicated to the topic in a stable at his chateau in France. In a mind-boggling blend of the exotic and frivolous, a balloon was built as an exact likeness of the chateau itself. Other shapes—there would eventually be about fifteen—included a two-hundred-foot-long Harley-Davidson motorcycle and a Fabergé egg. Each year, Malcolm would stage an annual international balloon festival at the chateau, giving the world and his magazine "friends"—whose presence was a reminder that everything Malcolm did was meant to pay off—a chance to marvel at elegance in an atmosphere far removed from the usual snobbery and conventions of high society.

Did it sell ads? One Fortune 500 company executive says being treated to a ride in a balloon over the French countryside with Mick Jagger at your side can't help but influence an ad-placement decision.

"As a promotion device," *AdWeek* once noted, "it sure beats hosting a twenty-projector slide show/luncheon at a hotel ball-room."

And, best of all, many of these delightful "follies" were tax deductible.

7 | THE THIRD GENERATION

"To the casual observer," wrote Arthur Jones in his 1977 biography, "Malcolm's apparent domination of his wife and children looms as one of the least attractive elements of his very demanding personality. But behind the public glimpses is an esprit and organization quite familiar to those who know the lifestyle of, for example, the English upper class—most particularly those destined for or hoping for acceptance into the aristocracy."

Malcolm grew disenchanted with the political process partly because the demands of campaigning eliminated true family togetherness at the same time he was using the image of family togetherness as a vote getter. But he never lost sight of how important a public image of perfect family harmony is in business as well as politics. On the eve of the ill-fated Windborne fiasco, Malcolm during an interview with one of the television networks maneuvered Roberta into the picture to answer a few questions. He was well aware of how much she hated the glare of public attention, but far greater was

Malcolm's desire at that particular moment to seize the opportunity
to show the world that—like so many daring heroes before him—he
had a loyal woman at his side.

Roberta did not appreciate being so used, without warning, to fill
a role in Malcolm's image-building scenario. "Don't you ever do that
to me again," she told him later. Malcolm smiled. He had achieved
his goal: show the audience this was a man with a supportive family.
Of course, such actions ultimately would alienate his wife.

Roberta—whom Malcolm nicknamed "Bertie," coincidentally
his father's first name—was a perfect mate. She was a devoted
mother who never pursued a career of her own, despite being the
beneficiary of a blue-blood education good enough to serve as a
launching pad for almost any profession. In order to marry Roberta,
Malcolm, who formally renounced Catholicism while at Princeton,
joined the Episcopal church.

The youngest of five girls, Roberta got her name supposedly as a
consolation for her father, Robert Remsen Laidlaw, who had hoped
at last that his wife, Isabella Carter Onderdonk, would bear him a
son. Roberta, along with the rest of her sisters, was trained by her
mother to be the kind of woman who would support a husband in
his endeavors. She attended the prestigious Shipley School and then
Bryn Mawr College on the Main Line, Philadelphia's bastion of
old-money society. The Laidlaws owned Laidlaw & Company,
founded in 1854 by Henry Bell Laidlaw, whose father taught English
at Edinburgh University. When Roberta met Malcolm, she was
studying interior design in New York but never finished the course
"because I got married," she once said.

The apocryphal story about Roberta is that every Christmas, she
personally wrote out nearly a thousand greeting cards, which often
featured a photo or reproduction of a painting of the entire family.

It seemed that the more Malcolm pushed himself into the public
eye, the more Roberta gravitated to the private pleasures of family
and pets and life on the ranch out West. She was painfully shy. A
former *Forbes* writer recalls seeing her trembling on the podium
next to Malcolm in the days when he was campaigning for governor.
She clearly couldn't stand being in the public arena. "She sometimes

came off as being very standoffish," he says, "and that offended some people. But it was just shyness."

Increasingly, especially once the children were grown and on their own, she would spend more time on the ranch, returning only briefly for command performances at Malcolm's special events. An acquaintance recalls standing with Roberta at one such affair at Timberfield and marveling at the gaily uniformed team of handsome young men attending to Malcolm and his balloons. Roberta, drink in hand, shook her head in disgust and said, "Have you ever seen anything so goddamn ridiculous in all your life?"

Roberta was more interested in cattle and dogs and dressing comfortably in jeans and boots. One visitor to Far Hills—one who isn't fond of dogs—recalls how excited Roberta was that her enormous, 185-pound dog took a shine to him. "The dog would stand and put its paws on my shoulders and want to lick my face," he says. "Roberta kept saying, 'He just loves you! And you know he doesn't usually like men.' What an animal!"

Roberta was this "weather-beaten, outdoorsy Waspy lady who liked to wear blue jeans and sweaters," the visitor recalls. He was surprised that with all their money, Roberta cooked the dinner herself. "She was so much the opposite of Malcolm that you couldn't believe two people could be more different. She obviously hated all the attention and parties and uproar. She was a real lady."

Malcolm Stevenson Forbes, Jr., born in 1947, seems to have had but one aspiration: to fulfill his destiny as the oldest son and succeed his father. Nowhere is there any indication that Steve, as he is called, ever considered doing anything else with his life. He seemed to spend all of it studying unquestioningly for succession much the same as children of royalty prepare from birth to inherit a throne. Nor is there any indication that Malcolm needed to push Steve into the role of heir apparent. It came naturally.

Despite a less than stellar academic record in his youth—three times he attended summer school to get through grade school— Steve was able to follow in his father's footsteps to Princeton, as did Kip. As his father before him did, Steve founded his own college publication at Princeton: *Business Today,* a quarterly. This was a highly conservative, probusiness publication introduced in 1968 in sharp contrast to the trend toward intensely liberal social attitudes. Like many college campuses of the day, Princeton had its share of Black Panthers, anti–Vietnam War activists, and "heads"—students into pot and LSD. Against this tide swam Steve. His first editorial slammed Eugene McCarthy, the liberal U.S. senator whose pacifist views made him a counterculture hero and a serious opponent to Robert F. Kennedy for the Democratic presidential nomination.

Even in marriage, Steve followed the example of his father, marrying in 1971 the blue-blooded Sabina Beekman, daughter of the retired rector of St. Paul's American Episcopal Church in Rome. She shared Roberta's devotion to raising a family—Steve and Sabina would have five daughters—and enjoying life on a horse farm in Bedminster, New Jersey. (In 1976, the year Steve became an associate editor at Forbes, the company would buy the prestigious *Social Register* from Robert S. Beekman, a doctor related to Sabina.)

Steve graduated with honors from Princeton in 1970, spent a year in the New Jersey National Guard and went to work in 1971 for Forbes, where he'd previously spent time in the circulation department and the investment advisory division. Within just six years, Steve worked his way up through the editorial ranks, largely on the strength of his own talents, while at the same time getting increasingly involved in the company's financial matters, freeing Malcolm to spend more time generating press clippings with which to fill scrapbooks.

At the same time, Malcolm and Michaels had assembled a team of strong writers and were establishing an atmosphere more conducive to keeping talent from fleeing to better paying, more respected publications. One of the methods was the annual party for employees on the Monday or Friday closest to Malcolm's birthday, August 19. "I decided they should be happy working for Forbes at least one day a year," Forbes said. At first, some staffers were offended.

In later years, when it came to Malcolm's grandiose parties, "people just shrugged their shoulders and smiled," says former staffer Steve Quickel. "In the late sixties, though, people were taken aback by his aggressiveness. We weren't used to it. We had been ignored for so long, though, that we were thrilled to be getting some notice. Until then, when you had to call someone for an interview for a story, you'd have to explain to them what *Forbes* was. We weren't like *Business Week* or *Fortune* or the *Wall Street Journal.* By the mid-seventies, all that had changed due to Malcolm's public relations efforts."

Steve was there through this transformation into a magazine that prided itself on its willingness to stick its neck out with strongly worded—and preferably negative—pronouncements about businesses and their managers. It was during this time that *Forbes* was reaching its peak as an abrasive, tough-minded critic. With stories constructed like a prosecutor's final summation, *Forbes* attacked what it saw as the arrogant top executive who seemed to take the view that shareholders were cattle to be herded in whatever self-serving direction management chose.

"The magazine still retains much of its feistiness, though not to the degree that it used to be," Quickel says. "In the old days, we bent over backwards to be nasty. We sort of wanted to grab people by the lapels to get them to notice us. Anything positive was viewed as puffy, which was the reputation *Business Week* had. To do anything positive at *Forbes,* you had to struggle to get out of the mind-set of going for the jugular."

Michaels created this approach to reporting, writing, and editing. But doing it under the nose of an owner whose focus was on selling ads to many of the same people Michaels was trashing in the magazine was no easy trick. It was a juggling act. How do you keep your boss happy—in this case Malcolm—without alienating your staff? Michaels generally handled it well, though he would experience his share of awkward moments. He didn't mind cutting up Malcolm behind his back, Quickel suggests, perhaps to ingratiate himself with his writers and editors.

Michaels was not a great fan of publicity stuntman Malcolm, but that must have been more than offset by the freedom the owner gave him to run the magazine the way he saw fit. It was quickly becoming obvious that Michael's editorial freedom and Malcolm's promotional efforts were paying off financially.

It was also clear that Steve was learning more from Michaels than from his father. By the mid-1970s, Steve was already suggesting he could do without many of the trappings Malcolm used to call attention to *Forbes*. It was assumed that after Malcolm, Steve eventually would dispose of many of Malcolm's toys. "I will keep the yacht," he has said. "I see the value of the promotion."

But Steve also saw the value of Jim Michaels. After all, Michaels was *Forbes* magazine's greatest asset, the helmsman behind all those stories that formed the basis of so many great *Forbes* advertisements. It was Michaels who made sure the magazine delivered a level of quality that would grab and keep a high-quality readership. He was assignment editor, writer, rewrite man, personnel director, and coach. Michaels was the talent that set Forbes apart from its competitors. Steve seemed to recognize that and placed a great deal of importance on preparing for life after Michaels.

"At story meetings, Steve would trot out ten or twelve ideas, all of them winners, while the other guys would struggle for three ideas," Quickel says.

But Steve lacked his father's facility for turning on a natural warmth and charm as needed. "Whenever I would go into his office," Quickel says, "he'd stand up when I'd walk in and not sit down. And I could never get him to sit down in my office either, and I'd end up standing up. He's extremely bright. He could have succeeded somewhere else where the name didn't count." Some editors felt that Steve would have been a better manager if before Forbes he'd indeed worked someplace else where he had neither the benefit nor the stigma of being the boss's son.

Unlike Malcolm, Steve wasn't the type to let managers work without interference and second-guessing. He is a chronic buttinsky, a bad trait in a CEO, says Ray Yavneh, who shared a spot on Forbes Inc.'s board of directors with Steve.

As Michaels has said, Steve "takes part in all major decisions," whereas Malcolm delegated. With Malcolm, "I am pretty much left alone as long as I don't screw up," Michaels has said.

Steve also lacks a certain ability to show his appreciation for a job well done. When the IAI Weekly Report printer—Richard Koppel, CEO of Thomas A. Koppel & Son—sent Malcolm a bottle of champagne to congratulate him on the report's passing the 25,000 mark in subscriptions, Malcolm immediately sent it along to Yavneh with a note that said, "This is for you." Yavneh questions whether Steve would have seen any reason to pass it along.

When Yavneh left Forbes in 1969, the IAI Weekly Report had grown to 30,000 subscribers, books were selling at about 75,000 a year, the stock-market course had about 200,000 students, and Special Situations was going to about 5,000 subscribers at $300 each. But by 1971, without Yavneh or Wallace Forbes at the helm, IAI was becoming a basket case. At the same time, there was a growing fear that a conflict of interest would be perceived between the magazine's reporting function and IAI's investment focus. Would editorial judgment at the magazine be clouded by a desire to see IAI's projections fulfilled? It wasn't happening, but to eliminate the question—and a faltering operation—Malcolm shut it down one day in 1971, selling off the mailing list.

It was a typical Forbesian ax job. The IAI staff was informed on a Friday and told to immediately clean out their desks.

"They are ruthless closers," Yavneh says. "When Malcolm decided to do something in, he did it almost with a cruelness, a vindictiveness. They talk about the [corporate] Forbes family. That's hogwash. One day they're building you up, helping you in every way possible in, say, a relocation situation. If you didn't work out, you're dumped without any cushion."

The operational management theory at Forbes is that if you throw a big rock into a calm pool, it will cause big waves that emanate to the edges but eventually, very soon after the rock has hit bottom, the waves become tiny ripples that disappear and the pond is calm once again.

The Special Situations Survey, however, was retained. It couldn't lose. Through a constant stream of mailings to *Forbes* subscribers, it could maintain a healthy level of customers almost no matter how off the mark the surveys may have been. Nevertheless, Malcolm rehired Yavneh in 1972 in order to restore the luster Special Situations had previously enjoyed. He was named president of the division and joined the boards of Forbes Inc.'s thrift and pension funds.

Years later, in an incident with Yavneh, Steve showed how needlessly insensitive he could be in dealing with a valuable employee. Fearing the appearance of a conflict of interest, Steve asked Yavneh to quit the boards of two companies and membership on the advisory board of a third. He also asked him to quit his high-visibility consulting work.

Yavneh understood Steve's concern. Steve didn't want anyone to be able to suggest that the reports were being altered in any way to benefit Yavneh's other interests. But giving up those activities was painful because of the numerous contacts Yavneh was able to make through them—contacts who helped him develop sources of intelligence for the reports. "But I stopped because Steve asked me to."

That might have been the end of it for Yavneh, in terms of any unpleasantness, but there was no compensation for the income Steve had asked him to forfeit from his directorships and outside consulting. "There was absolutely no recognition that he'd taken something away from me," Yavneh says.

Steve may have been more intellectual than his father—four times he would win awards for being the most accurate forecaster of ten economic indicators a year in advance—but he lacked his father's common touch. He also lacked his father's tabloid appeal.

In the same month Steve Forbes made the cover of *Accounting Today*, a trade journal, for his comments on the economic future before a conference of internal auditors, Malcolm graced the front page of the *National Enquirer* for supposedly trying to break up Elizabeth Taylor's rumored plans to marry someone Malcolm allegedly didn't like.

Here was Malcolm cultivating a high-profile jet-set celebrity image that would make Huge Hefner look like a penny-pinching recluse, while Steve was quietly forming lasting friendships with and regularly matching wits with some of the world's most influential economists. One of his closest friends was Jude Wanniski, the former *Wall Street Journal* columnist who is generally credited with being among the most influential supply-side proponents in Ronald Reagan's constellation of preelection policymakers.

Steve was becoming an articulate, intelligent proponent of conservative economic views in his own right. And President Reagan would reward him with an appointment to the chairmanship of the board that supervises Radio Free Europe and Radio Liberty. He would use his share of Fact and Comment to make valuable contributions to the debates of the day in the economics forum—a sharp contrast to the generally shallow, not-so-insightful one-liners favored by his not-so-intellectual magpie father. "If all maidens stayed maidens," Malcolm wrote in one Fact and Comment, "soon there'd be nobody left." Pretty weak tea—not that the column wasn't liked for its minireviews of books, films, and epicurean delights as well as for its zingers on issues and public figures.

But in Fact and Comment II, Steve would make a forceful argument, for example, that the Federal Reserve Board chairman's monetary policy stood a good chance of sparking economic recession.

People took Steve seriously. About the only people who viewed Malcolm seriously on any level were those who competed with him in the magazine business, where his success was undeniable.

One leading financial columnist said of *Forbes* in *People* magazine, "It's a good read, and everyone on Wall Street sees it, but you take what it says with a grain of salt. As for Malcolm himself, you wouldn't cock your ear to hear what he says. If he didn't have that magazine, I don't think anyone would care what he said."

That was a perception Steve surely hoped someday not to have to contend with. Because the image of his father and the magazine were so closely linked, there was always a risk that the world would not take *Forbes* magazine any more seriously that it took Malcolm.

Former *Fortune* editor William Rukeyser, perhaps unconsciously, made the point crystal clear once in an interview for a *New York* magazine article. While noting that Malcolm was "a delightful fellow and a friend," he said, "I do not regard *Forbes* as a deeply reported, serious, authoritative magazine."

From his days at Princeton, it seems Steve has always been plotting a course to turn that image upside down. Steve—described by one associate as "a real straight arrow, rather shy, a solid citizen with some sense of humor"—probably would rather be known as the shy, retiring genius behind a highly respected publication than the ringleader of a media circus.

*   *   *

By the mid-1970s, Malcolm had already determined how the company's assets would be distributed in the wake of his death. Steve was to inherit just over 50 percent, with Kip, Robert, Timothy, and Moira dividing the rest. Malcolm already had decided his firstborn was best suited to see the magazine into the twenty-first century, and he didn't want to put Steve in the same position he was in at the time of B.C.'s death, when neither Bruce nor Malcolm inherited a clear leadership role.

Steve made the choice easy. He was the only son who showed the interest, talent, and inclination to operate *Forbes* in a conservative, probusiness, free-market tradition. Bobby, Kippie, and Timmy— born in that order after Steve in 1949, 1950, and 1953—were less interested. And Moira, the youngest, born in 1955, would later say she just wasn't that interested in business.

Robert L. Forbes, who graduated from the University of North Carolina in 1971 with a degree in Italian, worked for a time as a photographer for Forbes but wasn't considered a great talent. He was said to be the least aggressive intellectually of the brothers. On Malcolm's many tours, he was frequently at his father's side, appearing in the background of numerous photos featuring Malcolm being greeted by this or that dignitary on the yacht or on foreign soil.

Compared with his other brothers, Robert Forbes took longer to find his niche within the company, says Jay Gissen, a veteran of *Forbes* magazine and Malcolm's bike-and-balloon road shows. If Malcolm assigned Robert, a photographer, to help out on a project with Jay, "Malcolm would ask me if he was doing what needed to be done and apply a little pressure when necessary," Jay says.

Robert, who like his brothers attended St. Mark's School in Southborough, Massachusetts, went to work at Forbes as an executive trainee after graduating from college and produced a number of documentary films for the company. Four years later he left to become a professional photographer. During this time, he was the co-author of *Toy Boats 1870–1955: A Pictorial History,* published by Scribner's. He returned to Forbes in 1980, eventually settling in as vice president in charge of Forbes real estate operations in Colorado, Missouri, and London. He also oversees Forbes Trinchera, Fiji Forbes, and Forbes Europe. He married Lydia Appel Raurell-Soto in 1981, and lives with her and a stepson, Miguel, in Manhattan.

Says one acquaintance from the auction circuit who has dealt with the three older sons: "The one who struck me as most studious is Bobby, even though he has devoted a lot of time to toy ships. He's rather well-informed." Robert also "is not as hard-edged" as his brothers, he says.

While it may have taken some time for Robert to find his place in the empire, Kip carved out his niche early on as Forbes curator—a role clearly created more to accommodate Kip's interests than to fill any existing need at the company. Initially it was envisioned that Kip would eventually succeed Jim Dunn as head of advertising. That idea faded a little as Kip strutted around the office in Edwardian garb, pouring himself increasingly into the curator's role. It was a function that put him in regular contact with the flamboyant world of decorators, interior designers, and art professionals—people who helped design and build Forbes's various exhibits.

These include the toy-soldier display in the Tangier palace, featuring more than one hundred thousand examples; the Victorian paintings at Old Battersea House in London; the balloon museum at the chateau in France; and Forbes Galleries, the first-floor displays at the magazine's New York office, featuring the Fabergé egg collection, the toy-boat collection, the presidential papers, and fifty-nine collegiate mantles representing honorary degrees collected by Malcolm over the years.

One family member says Kip was a major proponent of Malcolm's bid for celebrity status and respectability in high society. It is said that it was Kip's idea that Forbes buy the *Social Register* in 1976. Kip himself certainly would accumulate all the right memberships; his 1990 biography would list twenty-five cultural affiliations, including associations focused on British and Victorian culture.

"Kip isn't shy, but he's not extremely outgoing either," says longtime acquaintance Randy Salewski, a commercial artist who has done some work on Forbes projects. "He's pleasant and easy to talk to and doesn't beat around the bush when it comes to business matters. The Forbeses are all very straightforward."

Like many people who are lucky enough to enjoy the benefits of the Forbes life-style, Salewski is reluctant to go into any detail about the family. Asked for a single anecdote that might illustrate his comments about Kip's personality, Salewski draws a blank and shifts the conversation to superficialities.

"Working for them involves some travel," he notes. "That's always been fun. They're always gracious hosts. I've been to the ranch in Colorado, the house in France. I remember the places, and they're neat places."

Kip married while he was still a student at Princeton. The wedding was December 4, 1970, the day before his twentieth birthday. The bride was Sondra Irene Simone, daughter of a French electronics businessman and granddaughter of a Pittsburgh ice cream company executive. The marriage lasted less than a year. A few years later, Kip, twenty-three, had met and married the baroness, Astrid, fifteen years his senior, and with her fathered a daughter, Charlotte.

Neither the baroness nor their daughter, with whom Kip lives on his father's estate in Far Hills, were with him at a thirty-sixth birthday party thrown for him in late 1986. It was at the Manhattan apartment of a male couple involved in designing Forbes exhibits.

Many of the other guests were gay men. The only women there were the author Fran Lebowitz and a friend. "Kip was kind of shy and retiring," one guest recalls. "He seemed a little bashful about being the center of attention." Even with all the uninhibited banter, the atmosphere was a little on the formal side, perhaps partly because of Kip's role as a major client of the hosts.

After a catered dinner of baked ziti and lasagna, the group was sitting in a circle finishing cake and listening to loud disco music when someone knocked on the door. The host opened it to discover a tall, beefy New York City police officer on the other side. As the cop and the host talked for a moment, everyone else began to realize there was a police officer standing there and was waiting expectantly to find out what was going on.

The host then turned and said, "Kip, would you come here a minute. This policeman wants to talk to you."

The officer then gently pushed Kip to a wall and tried to get him to put his hands on it to be frisked, but Kip wouldn't cooperate, refusing to assume the proper position for a search. Except for the blaring stereo, everyone sat silent and stunned, staring at what was going on.

Seconds later, the cop started gyrating, tossed off his cap, guided Kip into a chair next to Lebowitz, and started a strip act within inches of Kip, who blushed and giggled nervously. Lebowitz was deadpan throughout the performance. For his grand finale, the impostor cop pulled off his underwear and threw it in Kip's face. He continued his erotic dance for another minute or so, picked up his clothes, and disappeared into the bedroom to dress.

The party broke up about a half hour later without further incident. Because he seemed so reserved, it was hard to tell whether Kip had enjoyed himself.

Kip once said that he and his brothers were close, and that he, Tim, and Bob often dined together. Their closeness, he said, stemmed from their being forced to take bagpipe lessons as kids and attend church every Sunday in kilts. "It does bring you closer together when you're the only freaks in the place," he said. When they played bagpipes for guests, "family friends would sit there in awe— not of our talent, but of the sheer parental will it took to make us do it."

Timothy, who graduated from Brown University in 1976 and went on to study cinematography at the University of Southern California, initially pursued a career as a filmmaker. His wife, Anne Harrison, would eventually become development director for Martin Scorsese's film production company. Tim would make several films—including documentaries on *Forbes* the magazine, Forbes the collector, and Forbes the family. One of those films, heavily promoted by his father, was entitled, *Some Call It Greed—A History of Capitalism.* Another featured the Fabergé collection.

Early on it was assumed that Tim would be the maverick of the family. As late as 1984 he was quoted as saying, "I don't see where my interests and the magazine's best interests coincide." Apparently that view changed. After struggling to carve out a life of his own invention, he finally succumbed to the irresistible pull into Malcolm's orbit of lucrative enterprises. It became obvious that Tim was different from Kip and Robert, in that Tim actually had the necessary ambition and drive to consider challenging Steve for an active role in Forbes Inc.

In January 1986, the company bought American Heritage Publishing Company, then based in Rockefeller Center, for about $9 million, appointed Timothy, then thirty-two, president of the renamed American Heritage, Inc., named Malcolm chairman, and moved it to 60 Fifth Ave. Tim, who lives in Manhattan, said at the time he realized his chances of achieving a significant role at *Forbes* magazine were slim, considering that three older brothers already occupied executive positions in an empire known for its lack of room at the top. Nevertheless, it is said Tim didn't necessarily agree with Robert and Kip that Steve was the brightest and best suited of the brothers to run Forbes Inc. ("With us," Kip has said, "the oldest is clearly the most capable.")

"When I heard this opportunity was coming up," Tim said of the American Heritage buy, "I did what I could to lobby for it."

While he was generally considered bright enough to handle the job, it was nonetheless surprising to see him go for it.

"Tim," Jay Gissen said when he first visited him at the imposing Rockefeller Center office, "you look so out of place in this huge office." Tim was sort of a neoconservative hippie, says Gissen. The general consensus was that he took the job as a consolation prize, but would use it to prove he was smart enough to run a magazine.

The operation included the eight-times-a-year magazine, a thrice-a-year *American Heritage of Invention and Technology*, published for General Motors, and a book division. The challenge of finding subscribers for it in any form was formidable. At the time Forbes bought the company, the magazine was a bimonthly with circulation running about 150,000, down from a mid-1960s high of 350,000.

Tim projected it would reach its previous peak once again, theorizing that as a fixture in the baby-boomers' youth, it would be desirable as these same people begin to seek out such fixtures for exposure to their own children.

On one score Tim would upstage Steve—and the rest of his siblings. In 1989, he and Anne, who already had a daughter, would become the parents of Malcolm's first and only grandson and name him after Malcolm. (One of Steve's daughters once gave Malcolm an ashtray that bore this inscription: "There's nothing a man can do that a woman can't do better." It held a place of honor in Malcolm's office.)

Moira, the last of Malcolm's five children, would attend the University of Scotland in Aberdeen, near the ancestral home, and marry lawyer Kenneth B. Mumma, who graduated from Villanova law school in 1983. At one time she told the *Washington Post* she had no expectation of becoming a factor in the operations of Forbes Inc., though for a time she would run three suburban weeklies for the firm. "I'm not that interested in business, which would seem to be a prerequisite," she has said.

At one point she was working on a novel at her Devon, Pennsylvania, home where she lived with her husband, who is wheelchair bound by a spinal-cord injury suffered in an automobile accident after they met but before they married. She went on to do work with the disabled. While making the occasional appearance at family shindigs, she would remain—apparently happily—uninvolved in the family fortune, not unlike other relatives who marveled at Malcolm's successes but were pleased not to be caught up in his frenetic pace.

As it turned out, Roberta was one of those people who wanted little to do with Malcolm's life-style. Malcolm, she once noted, "loves to be photographed. I hate it." On Sept. 19, 1985, in Jackson, Wyoming, Malcolm and Roberta dissolved their marriage after thirty-nine years. Roberta preferred livestock and domestic pets to world leaders and the rich and famous.

"When our children were growing up, my wife and I were not great goer-outers," Malcolm once explained. "In more recent years I have had to do a great deal of entertaining and traveling, but Bertie remained an extremely private person. Public life was uncomfortable for her. She finally said she had enough of being told when and whom to entertain. It was not a case of a third party being involved on the part of either of us."

Malcolm would later brag that after Roberta moved into a house down the road from Timberfield, they would see more of each other than before. Still, after 1984, she ceased to appear—except for 1989—as one of the faces in the annual Christmas-card group photo of her children and grandchildren.

The similarities between the unions of Malcolm and Roberta and B.C. and Adelaide are hard to ignore. Both Malcolm and B.C. were comfortable with their wives taking the roles of social sidekicks and caretakers of small children—not that the two men weren't deeply involved in the formation of their children's values and goals. Both couples had five children. Both wives eventually would conclude they could no longer stand to subordinate themselves to these domineering men and their relentless business activities.

8 | THE RICH LIST

In the magazine business there is probably no more coveted annual feature than the Fortune 500 compilation of America's biggest publicly held companies. The list is widely consulted. It is an adjective denoting considerable size and respectability. And it is a promoter's dream—to have a vehicle that puts your product's name into the everyday vocabulary of the common man.

Malcolm hated it. He hated it because somehow *Fortune* had made its list the authoritative ranking system for corporate America, much to the detriment of the Forbes 500. With relish, Malcolm attacked the Fortune 500 list—launched in July 1955—in its advertising, but to little avail.

Forbes got into the list business back in 1948 when Malcolm first suggested that his father rate companies for a special January 1 issue. From that grew the Forbes 500 lists, in which roughly 800 companies were ranked five ways: by sales, profits, assets, stock market value, and number of employees. Malcolm believed this was a much more useful corporate ranking system than the Fortune 500, which looked at companies only by sales. But more important, Forbes felt, was that *Fortune*'s list was only of industrial concerns, leaving out retailers, utilities, banks, insurance companies, financial firms, and transportation companies.

Using advertising, Malcolm tried to chip away at the rock-solid reputation of the Fortune 500. Forbes frequently advertised the Forbes 500 issue against the Fortune 500 with headlines like "What the Forbes 500 has that the other 500 hasn't." An ad in 1979 asked, "What makes the May 14th annual directory from *Forbes* so much more valuable than Fortune-telling? Only *Forbes* measures the actual top 500 American companies." Perhaps the most memorable of these ads asked, "Why didn't AT&T, Sears or Bank America make the Fortune 500?"

Still, *Forbes* couldn't erase "Fortune 500" from the language of business. It was a coup when Dow Jones News Retrieval, the electronic data-base service, decided to feature the *Forbes* list over *Fortune*'s for all the reasons raised in *Forbes*'s ads. Yet *Fortune* continued to get most of the publicity every year when its updated list was released. (Not that *Fortune* wasn't upset by Dow Jones's decision; soon afterward it announced a companion list to the industrials—the Fortune 500 service companies—to include the banks and phone companies.)

Practically every newspaper in the country would report which companies had risen to the top of the *Fortune* list and which had been displaced. It was the kind of high-quality publicity Malcolm lusted for—a gimmick that increases name recognition while simultaneously bolstering that name's air of authority. Even though the Forbes 500 issue was an annual multimillion-dollar ad magnet, Malcolm wanted something with the cachet of the *Fortune* list.

Against this backdrop Malcolm seized on an idea that was as brilliant a marketing ploy as it would be controversial—the Forbes 400 richest Americans. Why 400? In the nineteenth century, "the Four Hundred" was the definition of New York high society; after all, that was the capacity of Mrs. Vanderbilt's ballroom.

Malcolm Forbes, editor in chief of *Forbes* magazine. *The Bettmann Archive, Inc.*

Left: Malcolm and his young family in 1957:
(*left to right*) Steve, wife Roberta, Moira,
Christopher, Robert, and Tim. *AP/Wide World
Photos*

Below: Roberta Forbes in 1957: Malcolm's wife
for thirty-nine years, until their divorce in 1985.
AP/Wide World Photos

Gubernatorial candidate Malcolm Forbes in a campaign stop in Hampton Lakes, New Jersey. A publicity stunt that did little to help his chances in the election. *AP/Wide World Photos*

Malcolm Forbes voting for himself on the eve of his loss in a landslide to incumbent Democrat Governor Robert B. Meyner. *AP/Wide World Photos*

Malcolm Forbes and sons: (*left to right*) Robert, Christopher, and Steve (Tim not pictured) in the Oval Office with President Eisenhower, whose candidacy Malcolm had strongly supported. *AP/Wide World Photos*

AIDS policy activists protest outside *Forbes* offices on Fifth Avenue, angered by an article in the magazine in 1989 that suggested the AIDS threat may be overblown. *Keith Meyers,* The New York Times

Malcolm and one of his biggest
toys, the 151-foot *Highlander* V,
scene of frequent parties for
advertisers to mix with the
fashionable, rich, and powerful.
Dennis Brack/Black Star

Malcolm Forbes and Elizabeth
Taylor posing for the media at
Forbes's Moroccan palace at the
start of Malcolm's seventieth
birthday bash. *Mario Suriani/
Photoreporters*

Above: The Forbes hot-air balloon replica of the family's French Chateau Balleroy in Normandy.
P. Bourseiller/Sygma

Left: Malcolm sporting the jacket that served as part of the uniform for his Capitalist Tool club of motorcyclists and balloonists.
Osamu Hashimoto/Sygma

Another one of Malcolm's dozen
balloons, floating above the real
Chateau Balleroy. A. *Davis/
Stills/Retna Ltd.*

Opposite, top: The Forbes corporate jet, a Boeing 727 valued at about $8.5 million, is dubbed—like many of Malcolm's visible trappings of wealth—"Capitalist Tool," the magazine's ubiquitous tagline. *Pat/Stills/Retna Ltd.*

Opposite, bottom: Malcolm eschews the limo in favor of his transportation of choice, one of his beloved Harley-Davidsons. *Stephen Allen/Globe Photos*

Above: Malcolm on the deck of the *Highlander* V yacht next to the Bell JetRanger helicopter, *Highland Fling,* one of the yacht's many accessories. *Abolafia-Liaison/Gamma*

Some of the scores of motorcycles Malcolm collected over
the years, in a garage at his Far
Hills, New Jersey, home, Timberfield. *Gamma/Liaison*

Malcolm and Elizabeth Taylor show off novelty skull rings they exchanged on a motorcycle run in New Jersey in September 1987. *Ricki Rosen/Picture Group*

Malcolm Forbes aboard the *Highlander* V. *Yvonne Hemsey/Gamma Liaison*

Jonathan Greenberg, who started at Forbes in 1980 as a research assistant, was asked in June 1981 if he would volunteer to work on a Rich List, as the project came to be known internally. From the beginning, it was clear this was Malcolm's brainchild.

Malcolm had told Michaels, who hated the idea ("I was hung up on the risk, he on the opportunity," Michaels would write later), to figure out how it could be done. Michaels kicked it over to Zalaznick, who also initially wasn't thrilled. To begin with, no one believed it was possible to do such a list; that was the major criticism. It's not like ranking publicly traded companies whose financial information is disclosed in accordance with federal Securities and Exchange Commission laws. Tax returns for private individuals are proprietary. How could Forbes uncover the necessary information to confidently say such a list was authoritative?

Because Michaels viewed the project with such disdain, the staff generally saw any related assignment as punishment—certainly not a good sign for one's career.

Michaels and Zalaznick could think of many obstacles that would make the job impossible, but they could not alter the most important fact of all: this was the boss's idea. Greenberg was paired with assistant managing editor Jim Flanigan, now a Los Angeles *Times* business columnist, for a two-month stint to get started.

Greenberg's initial function was to call the 500 biggest companies to determine who owned them. Meanwhile, the bureaus—Houston, Los Angeles, Chicago, and Washington—were told to accumulate local rich lists and related information and relay it all to Flanigan. Like Michaels and Zalaznick, the bureaus also perceived this as an odious, impossible job and thus did the bare minimum. The fact that everyone detected Michael's lack of commitment to the project didn't help.

"What they sent Flanigan amounted to nothing more than a few newspaper clippings," Greenberg says. "Clearly this wasn't a high priority."

By mid-August, it was clear that the job was far from done. Zalaznick was convinced the job couldn't be done. The next step was merely to go back to Malcolm with the proof that the idea was impractical. Says Greenberg, "We tried to do it and failed. This was the message that Michaels and Shelly then took back to Malcolm."

Zalaznick had sent a memo to Malcolm telling him why he opposed the project. First, it would require a huge commitment of reporters' time when the staff already was stretched to the limit. Second, Zalaznick didn't believe there was a way the job of identifying the 400 richest Americans could be done accurately. Thus, once it came out, "there would be four hundred people in this country who would know with certainty that Forbes was full of shit," Zalaznick says.

Malcolm responded quickly to both criticisms. First of all, he was willing to commit whatever resources would be necessary to get the job done. "I don't care what it takes; I want it done." Second, Malcolm conceded that the first rich list might be riddled with inaccuracies, but experience would lead to improvements and greater reliability.

Zalaznick may not have been entirely convinced, but it wasn't the kind of issue one puts one's job on the line for. And the Rich List would go on to become an excellent training ground for reporters; it required a lot of travel, a lot of interviewing, and a lot of delving into public records to root out information that private citizens fight to keep secret.

For Malcolm, money was no object in getting the necessary resources to surmount the obstacles. Even time initially wasn't important. Whatever it took, Malcolm was committed to the concept. He was convinced this was a hot idea.

"That embodied the nature of Malcolm's leadership ability," Greenberg says. "Very rarely did he pull rank in a way that has left such an impression on the magazine. It wasn't just money." It wasn't just that this would be a great ad-sales vehicle. "It was fame. The Fortune 500 had always been such a barometer, and it clearly irked him that nobody quoted the Forbes 500."

This was Malcolm's answer. He knew he would be achieving what no one else had done on quite this scale. He wanted something that people would talk about the way they talk about the Fortune 500 or the Dow Jones averages.

Now the effort got under way in earnest. The appointment of a senior editor, Harry Seneker, to work on the project full time put the effort on a higher level of importance. A number of publications that had done local rich lists—*Texas Monthly, Minneapolis* magazine, *New Jersey Monthly, Philadelphia* magazine—were studied for ideas about how to gather and assess information.

The entire effort caused something of a split in the editorial office: between people pulled away to work on Malcolm's new project and everyone else lined up behind Michaels in the belief that Forbes ultimately would be embarrassed by the effort.

Michaels, for example, clearly wasn't pleased when it was decided to assign Greenberg to the project for an entire year. Greenberg, for his part, felt caught in the middle. The project fascinated him, but "if Michaels doesn't like something that Malcolm wants to do, being assigned to it automatically puts you on Michaels's shit list," Greenberg says. (Still, Michaels ultimately would heap praise on Greenberg when he left the magazine in August 1983 with an editorial note headlined A BEAUTIFUL SWAN SONG, a reference to Greenberg's final story.)

By spring 1982, Seneker's Rich List crew had grown to include a host of talented reporters—including John Dorfman, who later went on to write for the *Wall Street Journal*, and Jay Gissen, later a founding editor of *Manhattan, inc.* The strategy was to send reporters to spend a week in each of several major cities. Greenberg alone went to San Francisco, Los Angeles, Denver, Minneapolis, Chicago, Cleveland, Columbus, Pittsburg, Philadelphia, Atlanta, Miami, and Tulsa. Jay Gissen concentrated on the Oil Patch.

Gissen, one of the few who didn't view the assignment as a booby prize, volunteered for it. He was fascinated by the prospect of developing a snapshot of personal wealth in America. Who had it? Where did they come from? How did they earn it? In the beginning no one had any idea how much money it would take for inclusion among the 400 richest Americans. Would the cut off be $10 million, $100 million, more? It became readily apparent early on that it took about $10 million just to have the visible trappings of great wealth—a private jet, a tremendous house, expensive cars, frequent appearances at luxurious resorts.

The instructions were to keep the purpose of the digging a secret.

The fear was that someone might try to stop the process with a lawsuit charging invasion of privacy. Many of the targets weren't public figures. In fact "reclusive" is probably the most commonly used adjective with the words "millionaire" and "billionaire." Forrest E. Mars of the Mars, Inc. candy company in Hackettstown, New Jersey, was a perfect example; worth billions of dollars, he'd done everything he could to avoid the kind of publicity that definitely would flow from the Rich List.

A man like Mars may spend his life trying to avoid the spotlight, but as the owner of a major corporation, he can't hide his wealth completely. But what about truly hidden wealth? How do you track down the very discreet rich?

This turned out not to be too hard. It was easy to go into a particular town and find out through the local newspapers who had the most amount of financial clout. But nailing down precise figures wasn't so easy. A number of factors had to be considered, not the least of which was an individual's debt load.

"We'd go into a city," Gissen says, "and talk to the local newspaper's business editor. We'd talk to local bankers in confidence. Most wouldn't tell us anything, but some would."

The Forbes researchers found that wealth generally came in the form of company stock, oil and gas holdings, real estate, media properties, and inheritance, which included all of the above. Soon, Forbes reporters with expertise and sources in these various areas began to contribute valuable information. Greenberg, for example, became particularly interested in the enormous value of Manhattan real estate. About 10 percent of the original 400 were on the list because of New York real estate holdings.

"Granted, a list like this has to be based on a pile of absurd assumptions," says Gissen, later editor of the *Cable Guide*. "The value of stock and oil in the ground, for example, isn't real until you sell it."

While debt was perhaps the biggest unknown factor, the hidden role of silent partners also clouded the picture. Nevertheless, it became apparent that the cutoff for inclusion on the first list was going to be about $100 million.

Maintaining secrecy about the project would be no easy task. Forbes reporters were talking to local-newspaper business editors, society columnists, fund-raisers, politicians, and the semirich. Making such inquiries without tipping one's hand about one's purpose isn't easy. A newspaper in Columbus, Ohio, ran a story in the winter of 1981 reporting that Forbes had come to town in search of candidates for a list of America's richest. Ultimately, it did no harm.

Meanwhile, roughly eighty people threatened to sue Forbes if they appeared on a Rich List. The main fear among potential subjects was that the Internal Revenue Service would scrutinize the list for income not listed on returns. An IRS agent in the New York office, however, once told Gissen the agency had taken a look at the list but didn't see anything worth investigating.

Also, there was protest over Malcolm's insistence that the list include names of nonadult children, which was perceived as a sort of potential shopping list for kidnappers and terrorists. In fact, Gissen and Greenberg both implored Malcolm not to include children's names, but Malcolm insisted they be included (perhaps he saw the value of establishing a data base of rich heirs).

An equally important reason for secrecy was to keep the news from leaking out to archrival *Fortune* for as long as possible. Presumably, since *Fortune* had done a similar list—of private companies and who owned them—it was conceivable that it could develop a competing rich list on relatively short notice and steal Malcolm's thunder.

One area full of reclusives was the field of New York real estate investment. Greenberg spent the last three months of his research on it, managing to identify and rank the big players. The sources turned out to be less impenetrable than he expected. To begin with, he had the advantage of relatives close to the business. A grandfather was an accountant to many of the biggest New York real estate investors of the 1930s and 1940s, and that helped open doors to some of the heirs of these investors. And his brother in the real estate business in New York helped him identify the major individuals in Manhattan's biggest land deals.

But the most useful sources were the subjects themselves. While they were reluctant to discuss their own holdings, they talked freely about everyone else's. Usually they were accurate. Everyone seemed well informed about who owned what. By playing one against the other, Greenberg was able to nail down a fairly accurate accounting.

Many candidates for the list tried different tactics to avoid inclusion. William Randolph Hearst, Jr., of the publishing fortune, for example, tried to convince Malcolm to keep his name off the list. Hearst had a legitimate reason for fearing public attention to his wealth; even without a published rundown of it, the Symbionese Liberation Army correctly determined how much it could expect the Hearsts to be able to put their hands on in an attempt to get back his kidnapped niece, Patricia. Still, Malcolm wouldn't be moved. "Tell you what, Bill," Malcolm told him. "You shut down *Town and Country* magazine and I'll cancel the Rich List."

One day a real estate baron came into Seneker's office, obviously agitated about the prospect of getting on the rich list.

"Harry immediately called me in," Greenberg recalls. "He didn't want to spend one second alone with this guy. He was very nervous."

Greenberg walked in. The man was just standing there sweating profusely. "I want to talk to Harry Seneker," he said. Seneker refused to ask Greenberg to leave them alone. "Can we close the door?" Again, Seneker refused. He said he wanted off the list. He said he wasn't worth it. Besides, he was embroiled with relatives in a dispute over his assets. Having them detailed in *Forbes* could hurt. He kept looking at Seneker and Greenberg. He didn't have anything further to say.

After a long, uncomfortable silence, he said, "Don't you think you could do something here?"

It was apparent the visitor was willing to do almost anything—perhaps even pay—to avoid the publicity. He was shown the door.

At one point there was even a rumor that someone was selling people on the promise that for the right amount of money, he could get your name off the list. A host of petty bribes were offered by individuals wanting off—from free football tickets to barrels of popcorn to, in one case, $50,000 for two reporters.

Several Rich List candidates who wanted off made powerful arguments, appealing to the reporters' personal morality. How would you feel if you'd worked hard all your life to amass a fortune and keep it secure? The prospect of gaining wide publicity for it might threaten that security.

"People said, 'It's on your head,' " Greenberg says. "It was hard, particularly when you felt they were entitled to their privacy."

But once you were on the list, a new set of concerns arose. One secretive New York developer who made the first list, much to his displeasure, came back as the second annual list was being compiled and told Greenberg, "You put me on this list. If you take me off, it'll make me look bad. I got no choice but to stay on this fucking list."

The process of ranking the other real estate tycoons in New York was helped by Greenberg's practice of sitting down with each subject with a preliminary list in front of him. The subject wanted to see who stood where. Greenberg's list had thirty or forty names paired with the addresses of the properties they held, what they paid for them, what their liabilities were, and who their partners were. It was all on one page.

"They were fascinated to see how they were placed," Greenberg says. "For all of them, this was probably the first time they'd ever seen such a list. And they all wanted to move themselves up on the list or at least push others down. They were extremely competitive. As a result, you'd learn everything about everyone else. They'd say, 'So-and-so doesn't own that all by himself' and proceed to tell you who the other partners were. Then there were the people you never heard of, but they'd tell you about them because they envied their holdings."

Part of what made this process of eliciting information work so well was Greenberg's refusal to tell anyone else what others said about them. That way, a subject could feel more comfortable about being a source.

Donald Trump was one of those who insisted he was worth more than Forbes thought. In interviews with Greenberg, he aggressively deconstructed the wealth of everyone above him. He wanted to be on top.

In addition to those who feared inclusion on the list, there were those who were desperate to be members of this exclusive club. One public relations person was told by his client that if he didn't get him on the Rich List, he'd be fired.

An insurance man from Chicago whose business card proclaimed himself one of the wealthiest men in America felt left out when the first list ignored him.

Then there were the Wayne Newton types—the ones who insisted they were worth more than the research suggested. "Newton's business manager made a pathetic attempt to prove he was worth $125 million," Greenberg said. "You could understand why. It would have been good to get on the list; it might calm down your creditors."

When the first list was ready for publication in a September 1982 issue, one last attempt was made to get confirmations of asset value from the subjects.

"We called the lawyer for the late Lila Wallace, who owned the *Reader's Digest,*" Gissen recalled, "and told him we put a value of $500 million on the magazine. He said it was more like $200 million."

When Gissen told Malcolm this tale, Malcolm said, "Call him back and offer him $250 million."

Wallace's lawyer wasn't amused; he was one of those who threatened to sue. The list used the $500 million valuation.

In the end, no one sued, and no one got kidnapped for ransom. The issue was such a sensational success, it was decided to make it a separate, additional issue for the following year.

Early on, the question came up, Where does Malcolm go on the list? At first, he insisted that he not be included at all—for the same reason cited by many of the subjects who threatened to sue if they appeared on it. "Malcolm's argument was that the IRS might take a look at this list and assume that he had provided us with the exact number," Gissen said. Somehow, Malcolm found that threatening. "But we argued that Malcolm would have to be on the list for the sake of credibility."

The compromise was that Malcolm would be at the bottom of the list—number 400—but without a valuation. Still, a halfhearted attempt was made by the staff to put a number on his worth. In 1982, the magazine itself was valued at about $250 million, giving a total of about $400 million, including real estate and collections. In fact, after the second 400 list came out a year later and Gissen moved on to *Manhattan, inc.*, Gissen mentioned the $400 million number in a short item about the Forbes list, and Malcolm indirectly picked it up for use in later 400 editions, as in "Published reports have put Malcolm Forbes's net worth at . . ." But the mention didn't constitute a confirmation.

The first list, published in September 1982, was a resounding success both in the amount of advertising it attracted and in the amount of media attention it won. Once again, Malcolm's marketing instincts were proved right. But the jury was still out on just how accurate the list was, and that was why it was decided not to assign an actual number to each entry but simply stack them in descending order, starting with the highest rollers.

"We had a dart board in our office, which we played in between calculating people's net worth," says one former staffer. "Sometimes the symbolism was more than just symbolism."

Robert Teitelman, now a senior editor at *Financial World* magazine, was among the first Rich List hirees. "It was like Vietnam," he says. "There was an electricity in that place."

The second year, the list included an explanation of who came off and why—usually it was the result of death or the discovery of huge debts. One individual with ties to the Dorrance family came off the list because it turned out he had only two shares—not two million— of Campbell's Soup Company. "Do you have anything to do with Campbell's Soup?" Forbes asked him. "I eat the product," he said.

From the first Rich List to the second in 1983, seventy-five names changed as a result of fine-tuning the search-and-evaluation process. The threshold for inclusion moved up to about $125 million from $100 million. Most important of all, the second list, rather than being simply a cover, became a separate special issue—an added edition that meant added advertising revenue. It was shepherded mainly by Zalaznick with staffers like Gissen, Richard Behar (later a *Time* magazine writer), and Greenberg doing much of the reporting and Seneker overseeing it as senior editor. Gissen met with

Malcolm once a week to let him know how the project was proceeding, but Malcolm's interest wasn't meddlesome. Even though it was his pet project, Malcolm, as was typical, left the staff to handle it, except for an occasional suggestion that usually was helpful but didn't take the form of a directive.

Once it was clear the Rich List was a success and not a source of embarrassment, Zalaznick became a convert. One writer recalls that in an interview for a job on the Rich List staff, Zalaznick told him the 1983 edition would be the vehicle for the best and the brightest to advance at Forbes. ("It turned out to be just words," recalls this writer, who found it impossible to advance despite numerous reporting coups.)

For Zalaznick, the project was a natural, with its focus on the glitz and glamour that go with big money. Zalaznick's background was not business journalism. Before Forbes, he was at *New York* magazine where he and Clay Felker perfected an irreverent, sophisticated, urbane feistiness that specialized in exposing the underbelly of high society. That orientation served him well in determining the proper editorial spin for the rich list.

The editors at Forbes quickly realized how powerful the list was. Being on it might actually influence whether someone got credit in certain business situations. It became increasingly important that the list be accurate. Guesstimates were no longer acceptable.

Bob Hope was among those who felt wronged by Forbes. In 1984, he told reporter Richard Behar, "If my estate is worth over $50 million, I'll kiss your ass. I mean that." Behar put Hope at $115 million. *Forbes* ran Behar's story in the October 1, 1984, issue explaining how the magazine arrived at the number, knocking Hope off the list from a year earlier when the estimate was $200 million. The story led with Hope's ass-kissing promise and concluded: "You're off the list, Bob, but you're not off the hook. Isn't there something you owe us?" Hope turned the experience into a gag: "If I was as rich as you said I was, I wouldn't have gone to Vietnam; I would have sent for it."

"We knew the first list was very inaccurate, though we always tried to be conservative in our estimates," Gissen says. The second time around, though, the cooperation level improved vastly. "A lot more people got on the phone with us. They seemed to decide that as long as we were going to do this, we might as well get it right. And a lot of people called to let us know who we missed the first time."

One of the strangest experiences in the early days of the second 400 list started with receipt of a letter from an outfit that said it might be able to assist in the evaluation process of individuals' assets. It was signed by Wallace Forbes, then of Standard Research Consultants, a firm that specialized in evaluating private companies.

No one could believe that one of Malcolm's little brothers—whom he'd bought out of the family business seventeen years earlier—was now offering his services to the magazine. It must be a different Wallace Forbes, Gissen thought.

It wasn't. The question was cleared up immediately when Jay Gissen and Rich Behar showed up at Wallace's office to have lunch with him. Wallace immediately handed them a box—about the shape of a shoe box but a little smaller—and said, "Here's a little something to give my brother when you get back to your office."

The "little something" was ticking, Gissen says. (Wallace says he doesn't remember what was in the box.)

Gissen and Behar then proceeded to watch Wally drink and grow increasingly frank. He seemed bitter that he hadn't kept his interest in the family business, Gissen says. There was precious little talk about the premise for the meeting—to offer help in evaluating assets—despite Gissen and Behar's efforts to steer the conversation in that direction.

Both Gissen and Behar were thankful that Wallace never got to the point of criticizing Malcolm. They were nervous enough as it was being cast as Malcolm's proxies.

By the end of the lunch, Wally had worked himself into such a state that when the bill came he insisted that Forbes pick up the tab. Malcolm certainly could afford it, he said.

Gissen and Behar were dumbfounded and puzzled about what to do with this ticking box for Malcolm, considering the agitated state Wally was in by the time they parted company. They discussed deep-sixing it. They didn't want to be linked to this family thing if they could possibly avoid it. They toyed with the idea of sending the package to Malcolm anonymously through the interoffice mail, but finally decided they'd better just hand it over to Malcolm's secretary, Mary Ann Danner. She laughed it off, and that was the last Gissen and Behar ever heard of it.

Wallace laughs at Gissen's version of the meeting, which he recalls only vaguely. In any case, he says he felt no animosity toward Malcolm. Selling out to Malcolm "wasn't a wise business decision," he says, "but you can't cry over spilled milk."

As the Rich List matured, the priorities of its subjects began to change. This was a direct reflection of its success. Just as the Fortune 500 had become a yardstick of corporate success, the Forbes 400 was becoming the measure of individual success. As a result of its increasing acceptance as such, the people who were on it—or close to being on it—became less concerned with how to get off it.

After the first year, a Florida real estate developer told a reporter, "I didn't work this hard all my life to be put on the paupers' end of your list." At the time, the "paupers" were worth at least $100 million. The developer sent in documentation—including disclosure of vast land holdings in Orlando, Florida—in a successful attempt to win a higher ranking.

The superrich who managed to escape attention may have breathed a sigh of relief that they weren't on the Rich List the first year, but as time passed and year after year they never appeared on it, they faced a new dilemma. Their friends began to wonder, If they're so rich, how come they're never on the Forbes 400? "Then it becomes a matter of wanting to get on it to prove you're as rich as they think you are," says one staffer.

The fascination of the Rich List is closely related to that of pornography. It was the last American taboo, and Malcolm violated it in as public a manner as possible. The rest of the media were drawn to it like vultures to fresh carrion. Local newspapers reprinted the information, but added their own number ranking, which Forbes had deliberately omitted. Malcolm had struck a nerve. He was answering the most basic question in financial journalism: Who's got the most and how did they get it?

In polite blue-blood society, what could be more crass than to focus the spotlight on personal wealth and turn it into a contest? Not the sort of thing you'd expect to be discussed at a gathering of *Social Register* types. Actually, only five of the fifty-one billionaires in the Forbes 400 had a sufficiently elite lineage to qualify for the 1989 edition of the Forbes-owned *Social Register.*

9 | CAPITALIST RULE: COMPETITION

During the late 1970s and early 1980s, *Forbes* magazine hit its stride, with the Rich List as probably the most obvious example of how Malcolm's marketing genius had contributed to its success. Meanwhile, Michaels had established the magazine's mission—first to amuse and entertain, then to inform—and there were numerous reporting coups to make the competition envy *Forbes*'s reporting staff. At the same time, Sheldon Zalaznick had overseen the physical transformation of the publication, giving it a slick, almost *Gentleman's Quarterly* look.

It was Jefferson Grigsby, however, who figured out how to get the magazine printed on time every two weeks without the entire organization getting apoplectic.

Grigsby, raised in Denver, started his journalism career at United Press International's bureau there, became Cheyenne bureau chief, moved to the Dallas bureau, covered the early stages of the space program in Houston, then went to San Francisco, and finally landed in New York where he eventually became UPI's managing editor of news. In July 1975, Grigsby quit over a personnel-related dispute.

By January 1976, "I was getting desperate," Grigsby says. "About that time I read an interview in the *New York Times* with publisher Jim Dunn talking about *Forbes*'s success. I had no business-writing experience, but I sent a résumé anyway. Until then I had never heard of *Forbes*."

In March, Dero Saunders called Grigsby in for an interview.

"I met with Dero, who was so relaxed that there would be these long moments of silence. You'd wonder, 'Is the interview over?' " Grigsby says.

Then Saunders said, "I'd like you to meet Jim Michaels."

Michaels walked in, looked over Grigsby's résumé, and said, "It looks like you never got stuck." Getting stuck at UPI wasn't hard to do.

"Do you know anything about business?" Michaels asked.

"Oh, a smattering," Grigsby replied. In fact, he knew the difference between a stock and a bond, but that was about it.

Michaels then said, "I have two stories here that I'm not very happy with; see what you can do to salvage them."

One was about atomic energy, the other about the Federal Reserve system. Grigsby was given about a week to work on them. He contacted the appropriate federal agencies in each case and got them to send him everything they had on the subjects. "I got tons of information and put it all together." He was told they were able to use both stories as a result.

Michaels then said to him in his officious manner, "I'd like to make a proposal to you. I don't know if you can be a financial writer and neither do you. Why don't you try it for three months and find out?"

Michaels then asked him how much salary he'd want. "At that time, a managing editor at UPI made less than a researcher at *Fortune*," Grigsby says. "I'd been out on the street so long, I decided, what the hell, and asked for a ridiculous amount of money, and I got it."

At the end of three months, Michaels named him an associate

editor. That way, Michaels reasoned, if it didn't work out, at least Grigsby could say he had a title, as he had at UPI.

In short order, Grigsby found he didn't have to worry about things working out. He was promoted to senior editor, then executive editor. He started working with researchers who yearned to write and helped them get ahead. The list included Lawrence Minard, who would later succeed Zalaznick as managing editor and become Michael's first-choice successor.

But Grigsby's lasting contribution to Forbes was a production system that, to this day, is known as the Grigsby.

"I was lucky to start at Forbes at a time when the magazine was just taking off," he said. "When I started, a seventy-four page book was big. But suddenly we were doing two hundred-page books, with a hundred pages of ads. We liked to maintain a fifty-fifty ratio. That's a lot of editorial to fill with a small staff and get it all out on time. It was just killing us. We'd work all night to get the pages out and then come in the next morning and find all these errors. Everyone was very scared. I was helping Dero when I developed the Grigsby. It was a schedule for closing pages. The key to getting the pages out on time was get them done the day before they had to be transmitted to the plant instead of doing it that day."

The expansion of Forbes had outgrown the existing haphazard system to the extent, for example, that a color photo of an executive had to be shot so that, if need be, it could be used in one of two layout options—across three columns or cropped to one column. "That meant in the three-column version you had a picture of an executive with a head about the size of a dime lost in a huge office."

The solution? "We had to pretend Wednesday was Thursday," Grigsby says. "For a while, people would be asking, 'Is this a real close?' But after six months, it all started to work."

Soon people were asking for copies of the Grigsby—his continuously updated 8½-by-11 sheet listing in three columns of stacked boxes all the pages and stories and when they were to close—to keep track of what was expected of them and when.

"It got so that when Dero retired," he says, "we had the tools to take over in an operational crisis."

At one town house lunch, when an executive began relating a

major problem his company was having, Malcolm turned to Grigsby and said, "So, Jeff, tell them how you solved our operational problems."

Says Grigsby, "He was really very good about showing his appreciation."

In 1986, Grigsby would leave after an argument with Michaels over the editor's last-minute decision to kill a story, forcing the magazine to miss a crucial deadline. It wasn't the first time Grigsby felt Michaels had thrown a monkey wrench into the machinery by wading in on deadline to make last-minute alterations.

Grigsby eventually landed at *Financial World*, the repository of numerous Forbes veterans. What attracted him to the biweekly was that editor Geoffrey Smith, one of those veterans, was committed to doing what Forbes seemed incapable of doing consistently— aggressively covering companies with market capitalizations in the $1 billion–plus range.

By 1983, Forbes had peaked. Between the Rich List and steadily growing ad revenue, Malcolm's business was prospering, and Malcolm was reveling in what it was doing for him—freeing him to pursue his quirky mix of business and pleasure. In its fifth annual magazine rankings of the top ten hottest magazines for 1983, *Ad-Week* ranked *Forbes* eighth—fourth hottest for the five years. "The question is," *AdWeek* said, "how long Malcolm Forbes, . . . Publisher of the Year for 1983, can keep up this remarkable momentum. In the five years we've been tracking the hottest, *Forbes* has nearly tripled its ad revenues. It probably won't end until Yuppies turn back into Yippies."

Whether young urban professionals would ever turn back into flower children was debatable, but in 1983 all of financial journalism was basking in the warm, lucrative glow of a roaring, year-old bull market that would last many more years. The Reagan '80s were coming into focus as a time of unapologetic greed. Following the crippling economic effects of oil embargos and double-digit inflation in the 1970s, it had become socially acceptable—maybe even fashionable—to get rich quick. Takeover speculators were starting to make overnight fortunes, and small investors were developing an appetite for stocks that hadn't been seen for years.

Against this background, Malcolm was beginning to garner yards of positive publicity as the publishing genius who could do no wrong. But 1984 would prove, in some respects, to be a plateau year for Forbes, mainly because *Business Week* editor Lou Young quit and was succeeded by former *Newsweek* senior editor Stephen Shepard, whose mission was to stop the erosion of market share by *Forbes.*

It would not be long before *Business Week* would start beating *Forbes* at its own editorial game. Malcolm, however, would not stand quietly by as this happened.

Paul Sturm, a highly prized assistant managing editor under Michaels, left for *Business Week* at the end of 1984. Probably nothing rankled Michaels more—and perhaps Malcolm as well—than to lose top talent to competition.

When one writer entered Michaels's office to inform him he was leaving for the *Wall Street Journal* to cover a particular beat, Michael stood up and began pacing. He told him, "The *Wall Street Journal* doesn't know shit about [that topic]. And it doesn't matter if you write well or not—they won't know the difference. In the land of the blind, the one-eyed man is king."

And in Sturm's case, the competition he was going to was especially threatening. *Business Week* and *Forbes* were head-to-head rivals going after the same readers and advertisers. Between jobs, Sturm went on vacation in Australia. It was there that he learned about a *Forbes* ad in the *New York Times* in February 1985 featuring this headline: "We want to make Business Week more like Forbes." The ad attributed the comment to Shepard as his explanation for hiring Sturm and asked how many readers would want to read something that aspired to be like Forbes "when they can have the real thing."

Sturm felt betrayed. *Business Week* editor Shepard was livid. Shepard had already begun to take steps to improve the magazine, which had steadily been losing market share to *Forbes* for about ten years. Shepard had moved to improve the look of the magazine and the writing as well as make it easier to get more last-minute news into it. He was also going for the feistiness more commonly associated with *Forbes.* The cover of the first issue under Shepard featured the headline OOPS, referring to a story about all the troubles at many of the companies praised in Tom Peters's management bible *In Search of Excellence.*

Shepard had mixed emotions over the *Forbes* ad. "First of all I was angry because it was a lie. My second reaction was, it was a stupid ad because what it said to people was that we hired away one of their best people."

Did Malcolm mind being called a liar? Not in the least. "I'm more than satisfied that he said it," Malcolm said at the time. Besides, Malcolm was getting great mileage out of the controversy he knew this ad would generate. Forget that *Business Week* was actually starting to make headway against *Forbes* in the three-way race of financial magazines.

"We viewed this as getting down into the gutter," says one former *Business Week* staffer. "It reinforced for me that Malcolm's view is everything is secondary to making money for Malcolm." Forbes viewed this kind of competition as a big game, and it was. But this ad took it to a personal level that initially made life difficult for Sturm because it affected his credibility, and that's a criticism Malcolm probably would have accepted cheerfully.

The ad itself was pure Malcolm. For this one, its ad agency, Doremus and Company, simply executed orders. It was cooked up by Malcolm and his own in-house PR staff. But Malcolm was always the guiding spirit in all the magazine's advertising.

Curtis R. Troeger, chairman of Doremus, says, "Malcolm had a real knack and love for advertising. He really did understand it, and he used it brilliantly. He'd say occasionally, 'I have the seed of an idea,' then he'd let people do their job. He could say, 'Here is a research report,' or 'Here is something that has potential' and we'd work at it and come back with three different approaches. He would say which approach he wanted us to develop, and we'd get more of his thinking."

Malcolm's willingness to take risks—the "feistiness reflex," Troeger calls it—was a function of the freedom he had as the sole owner of the company. This wasn't the head of a public empire with numerous constituencies—including a stable of lawyers—to be consulted before finally deciding to go with some bland consensus.

"Frequently he would run an ad concept through a lawyer,"

Troeger says, "and I've heard it come back that it's too risky, but that wouldn't stop him. . . . I've never known any individual who had better instincts."

In ad meetings with family members, Jim Dunn, and the agency, Malcolm was shrewd in eliciting people's true feelings. He'd often throw out a negative remark to see who would pick up on it. "He tested the waters like that to get people to say what they thought," Troeger says. "He himself wouldn't give a clue as to what he thought—like 'This is embarrassing' or 'This is tasteless.'" In this way Malcolm was in total control of such meetings, in that he was able to prevent people from telling him what they thought he wanted to hear.

The ad about *Business Week* luring away Sturm wouldn't be the last time Malcolm would treat his larger rival to a good-natured lambasting. In a Fact and Comment in June 1989, Malcolm wrote, "Well, now for five hundred bucks a year . . . Business Week itself will 'leak' early copies to a 'select group of executives who want the very latest news at the earliest possible time.'" *Business Week,* still smarting from a couple of scandals involving leaks of inside information, demanded that Malcolm retract the item. Malcolm responded by reprinting the item *Business Week* wanted retracted and adding, "We did not say nor did we imply that it's illegal for them to attempt to hijack $500 extra from a 'select group of executives' to buy their Business Week ahead of the other subscribers who will have to continue to get Second Class treatment."

A wicked sense of humor was often at the center of Malcolm's perspective. New York TV journalist Jack Cafferty remembers being on the *Highlander* in July 1986 for the Statue of Liberty Centennial when Malcolm told five Russian journalists on board, "You know, everyone in America has a boat just like this, but we have to take turns on this river or it would be much too crowded." The journalists didn't laugh and Malcolm left them there to ponder the awesomeness of every American being able to afford a $10 million, 151-foot yacht, complete with lecture hall, motorcycles, speedboats, a Bell Jet Ranger helicopter, floors of teak and holly, seats and ceiling done in padded gray leather, fourteen bathrooms, double-size whirlpool, sauna, four staterooms, a master stateroom, six "saloons," and separate quarters for a crew of thirteen.

Forbes may have been losing some of its momentum and some of its edge, with Michaels increasingly less able to massage every bit of copy because of the sheer volume of it and Steve nudging the editorial bias in the direction of his right-wing political views. But there were qualities in Malcolm's leadership that kept the business vibrant. He had made himself a hero of the wealthy, flaunting a lavish life-style while seeming not to take it seriously.

"Malcolm could laugh at himself," says Ray Brady, of CBS.

Of all the flamboyant people in the world, Malcolm certainly was among the most harmless. "The most attractive thing about Malcolm was his absolute indifference to grudge-holding and score-keeping," says Sheldon Zalaznick. There would never be any smoldering resentments with Malcolm. That was a very valuable part of his mind. "It enabled strong people to continue doing business with him. It was a new blackboard every day."

Just how much did Malcolm rely on instinct? Not much, necessarily. Perhaps it's more appropriate to say that he had the necessary self-confidence to stand by his decisions. In editorial matters, certainly, he always had clearly well-thought-out reasons behind his decisions. "The notion that Malcolm had a short attention span in such matters was bullshit," Zalaznick says. "I never left his office feeling he didn't listen to me."

Another important quality that helped maintain Forbes's excitement level was Malcolm's willingness to give young people more responsibility than they'd be likely to get elsewhere. Chris Miles, a former Forbes staffer, says Malcolm "gave young, bright people an arena not only to learn in but to really show their stuff in." Miles was only twenty-four years old when she was promoted to run a department of ten researchers. To turn that job over to someone her age, with full responsibility for hiring and firing and overseeing the operation, would never happen at *Fortune* or *Business Week,* she speculates. "As big as the place had gotten, it was still a family-run place, and the top guy still cared about giving new people a chance," says Miles, who went on to become a founding editor of *Manhattan, inc.* "That was Malcolm's greatest gift: creating an organization where people had the freedom to do what they could do." The flip side was that a lot was demanded. "It was never a place where you could let up for a minute."

In his own self-appointed role as spokesman for the downtrodden rich, Malcolm was indefatigable. He restored a certain respectability to extreme wealth, as UPI's Frederick M. Winship put it in a 1987 feature, "by daring to take delight in being a money-maker. This obvious enjoyment has caught the imagination of millions of Americans who have cringed at the meanness of millionaires ever since the original John D. Rockefeller doled out dimes."

But the delight was tempered by the intensity of the competition in financial journalism, which didn't exist for years after B. C. Forbes invented the business magazine. By the mid-1980s, it was a crowded field of rivals vying for the limited amount of time their audience had to read such publications. Aside from *Fortune* and *Business Week*, competition for *Forbes* came from the *New York Times*'s national edition; the *Wall Street Journal*, with an ever increasing emphasis on features; a slew of specialized national and regional business publications like *Inc.*, *Manhattan, inc.*, *Financial World* and *Crain's*; a growing number of excellent trade journals; and expanded local-newspaper business sections.

Just as the reader's time was being spread more thinly across several excellent publications, so were the advertiser's dollars—a reality that would hit especially hard when the October 1987 stock market crash practically erased financial advertising.

But even before the crash, some *Forbes* staffers had started to sense a decline in the magazine's quality—a decline that seemed to be tracking a drop in Michaels's own energy level. It was growing increasingly difficult to excite him. After thirty-five years, "fresh" doesn't look so fresh anymore. Kinky and off-the-wall started to look fresh, and nonbusiness kinky and off-the-wall ideas were being taken seriously as candidates for space in *Forbes.* It was starting to get beaten at its own game—the feisty, investigative exposé of executives betraying shareholders' trust.

In July 1986, for example, *Business Week* would run a cover story on junk bond wunderkind Michael Milken comparing him to J. P. Morgan just as *Forbes* was about to run its own piece on Milken making the same comparison. "We thought we owned the Milken story," Michaels said at the time. Normally under such circumstances, the *Forbes* response would be to simply kill the story. If *Forbes* can't be first, its policy is not to bother. But in this case, the magazine lacked a sufficient backlog of good cover stories to run something in its place. Instead, they ran it anyway, changing the focus somewhat to make it look at least superficially like a repudiation of the *Business Week* angle, dropping the Morgan comparison and scolding *Business Week* in an editor's letter for making such a grand comparison.

It was about this time that *Business Week* had begun to halt the erosion of circulation it had been experiencing against *Forbes* for a decade.

In 1986, *Business Week* was projecting that by 1987, circulation would rise 15,000, to 790,000. *Forbes,* at 730,000, hadn't seen much change in its circulation for three years. *Fortune,* which went from monthly to biweekly in 1978 in response to *Forbes*'s passing it in circulation, was running about 640,000.

For *Forbes,* it was the end of an era of rapid growth. Since 1970, it had gone from carrying 18 percent of the ads in the Big Three to 33 percent, all at the expense of *Business Week.* Still, at a time when all national advertising was on the decline, *Forbes* continued to look better than its rivals, with only a 7.8 percent decline in ad pages, compared with *Business Week*'s 11.9 percent downturn and *Fortune*'s 15.8 percent drop.

The Milken piece was just one of several examples in which *Forbes* came in second. In August 1986, *Business Week* ran a hard-hitting story about Allegheny International Inc., the Pittsburgh appliance maker, and its chairman and chief executive, Robert J. Buckley. Shareholders sued Buckley, who quit soon after, and Buckley would later sue *Business Week* for libel. (In 1990, the libel suit was unresolved; the shareholder suit had been settled, with Buckley paying nothing and admitting no liability.)

On October 19, 1986, the *Los Angeles Times* ran a story praising *Business Week* under the headline, FORBES HAS THE YACHT, FOR-

TUNE HAS THE PRESTIGE, BUT SPUNKY BUSINESS WEEK IS COMING ON. Included in the story was a quote from one *"Forbes* veteran" referring to the Allegheny piece as "the kind of story we used to do."

What made the comment particularly painful for *Forbes* staffers was that before the *Business Week* story hit, Matthew Schifrin had written a similar story about Allegheny that never ran. In fact, at the same time *Business Week* was asking its toughest questions regarding Allegheny, *Forbes* was asking the same questions. "I always wondered," said one associate of Buckley's, "why *Forbes* never ran the story." The rumor mill ascribed the story's death to Buckley's friendship with Malcolm. It may be, as some staffers believed, that Malcolm killed the story, overruling Michaels, but a legitimate editorial problem—though never identified—could just as easily have been the reason.

Adding insult to injury was a quote by Shelly Zalaznick in the *L. A. Times* story saying, "I'm impressed; they're doing the right thing." He conceded that *Forbes* was having to kill more stories because its rivals were beating it into print with them.

Says one former staffer, "That's when people quit."

With the shift to the right inspired by Malcolm's heir, Steve, with Michaels winding down, and the magazine growing too big for one editor to handle anyway, with Malcolm focusing his energy on promoting his playboy image, with increasingly aggressive competitors, and with national advertisers spending less, Forbes was beginning to look as if it had reached full maturity.

10 | SYMBOL OF CAPITALIST MACHISMO

"Malcolm Forbes—capitalism's flamboyant macho man"
—photo caption in *The Record,* Hackensack, New Jersey

On the question of Malcolm's sexuality, an acquaintance once said, "The only thing that stimulates Malcolm is two pages of color." Ads, that is.

The question was inevitable. Usually it would surface without coaching within the first five minutes of an interview. Was this book going to mention Malcolm's alleged appetite for young men? "You can't do a serious book about him without at least acknowledging the rumors, they're so widespread," one fellow journalist said.

It didn't take a lot of digging to uncover evidence to back up the rumors. This was largely because he sometimes approached young men on the job he'd never met before, a careless thing to do if you're truly trying to be discreet—especially where journalists are involved.

Forbes Inc.'s chief spokesman, Don Garson, concedes that rumors about Malcolm may have been widespread, but that shouldn't be surprising for someone who spent so much time in the company of young men—bodyguards, motorcyclists, the balloon crew. But as for any substance behind the rumors, Garson says, "There could have been some other explanation. I'm sure you can find people who are willing to say anything, as Father Bruce Ritter has learned."

Garson was referring to the Catholic priest who became the subject of press reports about alleged sex liaisons with young men. The scandal ultimately forced Father Ritter to step down as head of Covenant House, the highly acclaimed Times Square shelter for runaways.

Indeed for the last eighteen years of his life, Malcolm Forbes was, as former Forbes staffer Michael Cieply put it in a January 1990 feature on Malcolm, "the very symbol of capitalist machismo when he is aloft in one of his balloons or is swathed in leather astride a Harley-Davidson."

When one seventeen-year Forbes veteran learned of Malcolm's in-office dalliances, he found it hard to believe. "That's suicidal," he said. Yet in the context of Malcolm's instinct for "driving right to the edge," such risk taking wouldn't be out of character, he added.

But why would anyone care to expose Malcolm's sexual orientation? He wasn't a Father Ritter, entrusted with the protection of young people often trying to escape prostitution. Nor was he a Gary Hart preparing for the presidency. He was a private person. What irked the people who worked for Malcolm was that he felt compelled from time to time to impose his sexual advances on young, potentially vulnerable employees. Not only did it smack of sex harassment, it also seemed hypocritical in light of the virtuous family-man image Malcolm tried to project.

It is this second point that some elements of the gay community itself found so galling. Increasingly gay writers and publications were taking the more militant stand that gay public people and celebrities who actively portray themselves as straight are actually promoting homophobia.

To attempt to counteract this, *Outweek,* a fledgling gay publication in New York, wrote, among other things, about public figures who are openly gay and teased those—including Malcolm—who the magazine believed were gay and who pretended not to be. The latter group, says features editor Michelangelo Signorile, were "only reinforcing the notion that it's bad and must be hidden."

For a time, Malcolm's moves on young men at the magazine, usually new employees, were so common that some supervisors actually found it necessary at times to warn newcomers on how to deal with the boss's unwanted sexual advances.

Some men who weren't warned let Malcolm have his way with them for fear they might otherwise forfeit their jobs. And gay men who acquiesced were sometimes handed an unexpected $100 at the end. Those who were warned still resented being put in the uncomfortable position of having to refuse their employer's seemingly harmless dinner invitation. And there were those who weren't warned and didn't give in.

One such employee was an artist who worked at Forbes in the late 1970s and early 1980s. His story was well known at the magazine and served in the following years as a warning to others.

At the time, *Forbes* was being remade into one of the slickest-looking magazines going. It was attracting top talent and its looks further fueled the magazine's challenge to *Fortune* and *Business Week.* Internally, the competitive environment was intense; the pressure to produce consistently fresh content was relentless. One's job depended on it. Staffers put in long hours without complaining. Jim Michaels used praise on writers like a highly addictive drug meant to generate an ever-improving product.

It was in this environment in the summer of 1978 that Malcolm asked the young artist to join him for dinner. "At the time, I had no idea Malcolm was gay," he recalls. People knew about it, but no one talked about it. "Of course, since then, a couple of the gay guys at work told me they spotted him at gay bars in New York and were practically shell-shocked to see him there, apparently unconcerned about being seen, though he did get a little nervous when he saw a couple of employees there."

The artist didn't fit the description of the blond-haired young male Malcolm typically sought out for companionship. Malcolm asked the artist into his office and said, "I'm having a dinner at the town house. Would you like to come?"

The way the invitation was phrased, the artist assumed other employees would be there. Besides, why would Malcolm want to meet just with the artist, a relatively low-level employee? If Malcolm wanted some input on what was going on in the art department, there were plenty of higher-ups who could provide a broader view. The artist asked around, but no one else seemed to be aware of the town house dinner.

"I couldn't find anyone else who said they were going," he says.

At the end of the work day, he went into the bathroom to spruce up and ran into Steve Forbes.

"Steve," he said. "Guess where I'm going to dinner?"

He figured at least Steve would know about this town house dinner.

"Where?" Steve asked.

"The town house," he said. "Malcolm invited me. Aren't you going?"

Steve kind of stopped in his tracks. His face darkened with disgust. He entered one of the stalls without a word and slammed the door. "It seemed like an odd reaction," the artist recalls. "I didn't understand why he would get angry."

The artist rang the bell at the door between the office and the town house. Malcolm appeared in a smoking jacket. He thought, This is an odd way to dress for a dinner with all these people.

He walked in. No one else was there. Malcolm strode over to a kind of fake-waterfall construction, pressed a button, and a panel opened, exposing an audio system.

"What kind of music do you like?" Malcolm asked.

Thinking it wasn't appropriate to rock out with the boss, he said, "Oh, I like classical music."

With that, Malcolm punched up Led Zeppelin. The artist was puzzled, but he still hadn't figured out what Malcolm was up to. Soon it would become all too clear. The two men squeezed into a tiny elevator that had only two floors marked on it. Inside the elevator was a huge Victorian-style painting that you couldn't get more than six inches away from to look at. Malcolm stopped the car at what appeared to be between floors.

The artist thought, We're not on the first floor. We're not at the second floor. Where are we?

The door opened to a wrought-iron staircase leading a few steps up to a doorway. It was the entrance to living quarters. As he walked through the doors, the first thing the artist saw was an enormous, beautifully painted oil of four men with erections whipping a fifth lashed to a table as he gazes wistfully into the distance. It was one of many high-quality, realistic paintings Malcolm had commissioned from well-known artists. Some of these canvases run to 10-by-10 feet. They all featured very strong, blond, Aryan-looking men.

Any doubts the artist had at that point about what Malcolm was up to vanished. He thought, Oh my God, we're in for an interesting evening here.

They went into a living-room area. Malcolm made the artist a vodka and tonic in a large tumbler with just a splash of tonic. The room was filled with pornographic art—all involving men. The subject in one was masturbating. In between these paintings were photos of Malcolm's kids when they were children playing with trucks and other toys. The contrast was jarring.

The artist sat on a couch and Malcolm flopped down beside him and snuggled up.

"Well, then, tell me all about yourself," Malcolm said.

The artist figured this was a good time to tell him about his imminent plans to marry the woman he was living with. The artist assumed this would be enough to indicate his complete lack of interest in homosexual intimacy. It wasn't. After all, the fact that Malcolm was still married to Roberta wasn't inhibiting Malcolm.

After a brief chat, Malcolm said, "Let me take you on a tour of the apartment," which meant heading straight for the bedroom. More male-oriented pornographic art. The only female nude in the whole place was in the bathroom off the bedroom, a gold-fixture decorated affair.

Malcolm sprawled out on the bed, letting his smoking jacket fall open and squirming around in an apparent effort to be sexy. The artist sat on a footstool at the end of the bed. Malcolm, fondling himself, invited the young man to join him on the bed.

"I'll sit here," the artist said, declining. "What about this dinner we were going to have?"

"Well, you know, I review all these restaurants," Malcolm said, "so I thought we might try this nice French restaurant at Sixty-first Street."

He said he wanted to wash up first, and said to the artist, "Why don't you go upstairs and get cleaned up?"

The artist headed upstairs and spotted the steam bath. Thinking he'd successfully dispelled any hope Malcolm might have had of sleeping with him, he decided it was safe to indulge in a steam bath. He undressed, wrapped a towel around himself, and sat down. Ten seconds later, Malcolm cruised in, sat down next him, and started to put his hand up the towel the artist was wearing.

"Give me a break," the artist said. "Get your hands off me."

Malcolm wasn't grabbing him. He was being very forward but not obnoxiously aggressive. Even if Malcolm did get more aggressive, the artist figured he needn't worry. "I figure this guy is sixty. Sure, he's in good shape for his age, but if worse comes to worse, I can deck the guy and get out of there."

Malcolm clearly had had a fair quantity of liquor at that point. In the course of two hours, he'd consumed the better part of a fifth of scotch. He said, "I won't bother you anymore, but would you mind if I relieve myself?"

"I don't care," said the artist, annoyed. "Do whatever you want."

Malcolm then proceeded to masturbate in full view of the artist.

At the conclusion, the artist said, "Look, let's get out of here and go to dinner." By this time, the artist assumed this episode might cost him his job, so he decided he wasn't going to let the evening conclude without at least getting a decent meal.

Together they climbed into a cab at Fifth Avenue and Twelfth Street, and headed uptown. The fare was about $2.65. Malcolm handed the driver, an elderly Italian man, $3 and asked for 15 cents change.

"I can't believe this," the artist said, amazed that Malcolm was asking for change. "With all your millions, you're demanding fifteen cents back?"

Malcolm was clearly a little insulted, but he chuckled and took the change anyway.

(The public Malcolm would later tell a reporter for *Newsday*, "I've found nobody gets mad at being overtipped. If you can afford to be generous, it's kind of chintzy not to be.")

The restaurant staff knew Malcolm was coming. They were all standing at attention when he arrived. They drank $150-a-bottle wine—"the best wine I ever had in my life," the artist says.

By now, the two were boisterous and getting louder and more argumentative, despite the presence of staid-looking elderly patrons at the four or five other tables being served.

At one point Malcolm said, "You know, my average night consists of going back to the town house by myself, drinking a fifth of scotch, and jacking off."

The conversation continued in the manner of a debate, with the artist trying to steer it away from the topic of sex.

"Well, what about your wife?" the artist asked. "I mean, you just go out and fuck anything that moves while she's marooned on a ranch in Montana. How would you feel if she was getting laid by all those cowboys on the ranch?"

This struck a chord. Malcolm slammed his fist on the table and thundered, "God damn it, she'd better not be, or I'll have her hide!"

"Malcolm, you ought to be ashamed of yourself," the artist said. "You're supposed to be this fine example of the virtuous family-man millionaire having a wonderful time spending your money. Hell, you're just a hypocrite."

Malcolm was no hypocrite, he insisted. "I think it's every man's duty to have orgasms in whatever manner possible—with a woman, a man, an animal. It doesn't matter."

Even as the two argued, the artist was still reeling from the revelation that the public Malcolm Forbes—one of high society's most beloved, charming hosts, whose guest lists included the world's most powerful leaders in business and government—privately pursued homosexual interests apparently without concern for the possible damage such behavior might cause to his reputation. It was a side of Malcolm the artist wasn't prepared for. "The whole thing completely threw me," he says. "It was like being with some lecherous old grandfather. He kept trying to get me to cooperate.

"It's almost as if Malcolm would try to see how far he could go and how outrageous he could get and still maintain this image of the perfect family man, father of financial journalism.

"It was just kind of a game, a lark" for Malcolm, the artist speculates. "It seemed that it didn't mean much to him. He had a good time anyway, even though he lost his temper. He went on about how lonely he was, that he was just glad to have the companionship."

The two left the restaurant around two or three A.M. The younger man was hoping Malcolm would send him home to Brooklyn in a cab; instead he put him out at a subway station.

"I felt like death warmed over," the artist says. "I thought, there goes my job. Malcolm's going to see me in the morning at work and I'm going to get fired on the spot."

His fears proved to be unfounded.

"The amazing thing is that Malcolm was always extremely friendly," he says. "Even after this whole ridiculous evening I spent with him, he acted as if nothing ever happened. The next day was closing. I was so hung over, I was sick. But I had to be there for closing. Malcolm was the second person I saw when I arrived in the morning. He was as bright-eyed and refreshed as ever—as though he'd somehow gotten eight hours of sleep. He didn't look the least bit hung over. It was like: 'Good morning! How're you doing? Time to get another issue out, huh?' "

Remembering Steve Forbes's reaction in the bathroom on the artist's way to the town house the night before, the artist concluded that Steve must have been aware of what his father was up to, perhaps based on past knowledge.

Malcolm never said a word about the evening to the artist, and the episode never affected his career. In fact, a year later Malcolm granted him a leave of absence from the magazine, during which he paid him to do a photography project for Forbes on Laucala—including free room and board for the month he spent on the idyllic South Sea island.

Still, what astounded the artist was the contrast between the public Malcolm and the private Malcolm. The public persona was a delightful millionaire, down to earth yet whimsical, family-oriented yet macho, rich but not miserly, a firm believer that wealth is useless unless it serves to increase the pleasure of living. The private Malcolm came off at times as an awkward, hard-drinking, lonely man whose sexual encounters often seemed to lack emotional depth.

Another widely known story inside *Forbes* is that of Georg Osterman, now playwright in residence at the Ridiculous Theater Company, who worked at Forbes from the summer of 1981 to the spring of 1984 as Forbes's communications manager.

In the winter of 1981, Osterman, about twenty-seven years old at the time, says he became aware that from time to time Malcolm was following him in the halls as Osterman made his rounds delivering copy to editors.

"I decided one day to let him catch me," Osterman says, conceding he was a little intrigued with the idea of sleeping with a billionaire.

Malcolm knew his name. He invited him into the town house for drinks—strawberry daiquiris. Malcolm seemed impressed that Osterman was familiar with many of the artists whose work adorned the walls. He asked Osterman questions but didn't really seem interested in his answers, often cutting him off in midsentence to ask another. Mostly, Malcolm talked about himself, asking whether Osterman had seen this or that bit of news about Malcolm in the media.

"It was odd," Osterman says. "He was being pretty charming, but I felt in a way he was this really lonesome person. It's hard to explain. It seemed money couldn't buy him what he wanted. I never felt comfortable around him. He seemed self-conscious, unable to relax really."

After chatting pleasantly for about twenty minutes, Malcolm said, "Would you like to see more of this art collection?" and led the way to the bedroom decorated with erotic sculpture.

There the two men undressed, hugged and kissed a little, and had sex by rubbing against each other. "It was like little-kid sex," Osterman says. "It was boring. It made it even sadder that this guy seemed to be retarded sexually."

When Osterman left, Malcolm dug out $100 from his jogging suit and handed it to him. It seemed Malcolm simply wanted to do something nice; there was no implication that the money was payment for anything.

A few months passed before Malcolm again invited Osterman in for drinks at the town house. This time they watched a muscleman pornography video and masturbated. Shortly afterward, Malcolm came to see Osterman perform in *Secret Lives of the Sexists*. Malcolm left about halfway through. Osterman speculated that Malcolm wasn't comfortable seeing Osterman and others perform in drag.

Their third and final encounter was the oddest of all. Malcolm called the copy desk and asked to speak to Osterman. People on the copy desk were amazed. What did the chairman want with a communications manager? Osterman went to his office.

"Oh, yes," said Malcolm's secretary. "Mr. Forbes would like to see you."

Osterman walked in leaving the door wide open between Malcolm's and his secretary's offices.

"Come, sit down," Malcolm said. "How are you doing?"

Malcolm started to explain that he needed an address for a friend of Osterman's who used to work at *Forbes*. The funny thing was that while he was asking this question, Malcolm was opening Osterman's fly and starting to perform oral sex on him. Osterman says he was in shock.

"This conversation about wanting my friend's address was to sort of cover what was really going on," Osterman says. "Every once in a while he'd come up for air and ask another question to keep the conversation going. It was so bizarre."

This went on for only a few minutes with neither man climaxing. "It was almost just like a naughty-boy thing he wanted to do," Osterman says. About the only thing Malcolm ever said to indicate what attracted him to Osterman was that he thought he had "a nice butt."

"Have a Merry Christmas," Malcolm said as Osterman was leaving, then added with a sly grin, "That oughta keep me going through the holidays." As with the previous two encounters, Malcolm stuffed $100 into his pocket and said goodbye.

"He was kind of a sad character," Osterman says. "He was really trying to be hip and use slang. It was kind of embarrassing, because he didn't need to do that."

What amazed Osterman about all this was the obvious: "Propositioning people at work is such an uncool thing to do," he says. "If you want to keep something a secret, that's not the way to go about it. He must have known it would eventually come to the forefront."

The public image was one that Malcolm spent millions developing and maintaining, yet he was reckless with it. What could be more careless—at least in American high society—than propositioning an employee who had had virtually no prior personal contact with the boss?

Did Malcolm want to be found out? Probably not.

Says one relative who had known Malcolm all his life, "This one invented the closet."

In fact, Malcolm in later years seemed to vacillate between carelessness and caution. Perhaps he wanted to move freely in the gay community, but without the whole world finding out. In short, he wanted it both ways.

On April 5, 1989, for example, the whole world—or at least the millions of readers of the national daily *USA Today*—would learn how Malcolm, decked out all in leather, arrived by motorcycle at a night spot in Manhattan called Mars, only to be turned away for being too old. *USA Today* didn't say whether this was a Sunday, which is gay night at Mars. On Sundays, proclaims an ad for the club, "The QUEER NATION Rules Mars!"

Probably not. It is said that on one Sunday Malcolm arrived at the door of the same bar and decided not to enter upon learning it was gay night. How would it play if word got out that Malcolm liked to cavort with the gay crowd? Would corporate America notice and wonder whether Malcolm was the Liberace of financial journalism? Would they care?

Malcolm must have thought so. There was speculation, for example, that fear of discovery helped determine Malcolm's response to a ruckus in 1989 over a story by then *Forbes* staffer Joe Queenan.

Queenan came to *Forbes* from *Barron's* in March that year. Magazine editors—including Jim Michaels—admired Queenan's satirical wit. His pieces had appeared in *New Republic, Rolling Stone* and *Spy* as well as *Barron's,* where he'd been on the staff for a little over a year. His writing had the unique quality of being simultaneously hilarious, arrogant, merciless, accurate, and often right—qualities much admired by Jim Michaels.

It was Michaels who approached Queenan about the job, perhaps anxious to recapture some of the sharp-edged writing at *Forbes* that seemed to be vanishing with the steady exodus of older talented writers and editors. Perhaps in recognition of his exceptional skills, Queenan was hired as a senior editor, which is as high as one can go at *Forbes* without stepping into the three or four jobs that might put one in line to succeed Michaels.

Queenan had done numerous amusing stories for *Forbes* by the end of June, but perhaps his strongest piece would be a serious critique, co-authored with Tatiana Pouschine, of Peter Cohen, then top executive at American Express's Shearson Lehman Hutton unit. It would fully illuminate why Cohen would be sacked six months later. But two weeks before the Shearson story ran, the magazine carried a short piece by Queenan that caused a storm of controversy in the gay community and came within a hair's breadth of exposing Malcolm. Were it not for Malcolm's unusual response to the crisis, it might well have worked that way.

The story was a short feature on the trials and tribulations of Michael Fumento, an AIDS specialist at the U.S. Commission on Civil Rights who lost his job for promoting the politically unpopular idea that AIDS wasn't as big a deal as everyone was making it out to be—especially for heterosexuals.

Michaels edited it—no one else was editing Queenan at *Forbes*—making minor changes. He did make one major change. He added the opening line: "It doesn't pay to be the bearer of good news." He also deleted a quote by Fumento that likened the AIDS hysteria to a drive in the 1890s to get more federal money to build whaling ships: The money was there but the whales weren't. The headline was STRAIGHT TALK ABOUT AIDS, a cute but perhaps insensitive way to advertise the story's focus on the AIDS threat to heterosexuals.

The story came out on Saturday, June 17, in the issue dated June 26. The following Monday, Queenan learned that a proofreader, Al Weisel, had initially refused to proofread it because of the implication that AIDS wasn't as serious a threat as everyone says it is.

A few days later, Queenan was standing by the soda machine talking to another staffer when the proofreader approached Queenan.

"Are you Joe Queenan?" the proofreader asked.

Queenan said yes.

"I just wanted you to know that I think that story was despicable, racist, and homophobic."

Queenan asked him who he was and what he did at *Forbes.*

"I'm a proofreader," he said.

"Are you a good proofreader?" Queenan asked.

"Yes."

"Well, then, why don't you go back and do it?" Queenan suggested, adding that he wasn't interested in talking to him.

The discussion deteriorated further, ending with Queenan calling Weisel a fucking asshole.

Queenan related the story to Zalaznick, saying it didn't seem right that he should have to take such crap from an underling.

Zalaznick's response puzzled Queenan: "You have to take the heat." That would have seemed an appropriate response if the harassment were coming from higher-ups or competition or sources or targets. But this was harassment from a lower-level employee. In a normal environment, such an employee might be at least warned about his behavior, Queenan thought.

A few days later, Fumento called Queenan.

"Did you get much feedback from the story?" he asked.

"Not too much," Queenan told him. "Just a few calls. But other than that, not much reaction."

During the conversation, someone popped into Queenan's office and said, "Now you've done it. There's two hundred of them out there demonstrating."

This was June 20, shortly after the issue was published.

ACT UP, which stands for AIDS Coalition to Unleash Power, noticed, and had mobilized some demonstrators—actually only about 40 of them—for the protest in front of Forbes headquarters. This was in the week leading up to the twentieth annual Gay Pride Day. The group was outraged at the callousness of printing a story packaged to give the impression that Forbes agreed with Fumento. Clearly, Queenan hadn't set out to participate in the debate between Fumento and his detractors. This was simply a report on what happened to Fumento and why. But the headline and the first line of the story definitely implied that the magazine found Fumento's assessment at least plausible.

Jay Blotcher, a media coordinator for ACT UP, admitted there was a certain irony in AIDS activists attacking Malcolm Forbes, who gave Elizabeth Taylor a $1 million check for AIDS research at what was then the megabash of the century—the magazine's seventieth anniversary party at Malcolm's Far Hills estate. One of the protest placards read, "What would Liz say?"

Another read, "Hey Malcolm! At least get your facts straight!"

This was a deliberate attempt to tease Malcolm about his unstraight sexual reputation, Blotcher admitted.

"We're not trying to drag anyone out of the closet," Blotcher said. "It was really a denunciation of someone with such a high profile who should know better."

About eight members of the group—including Blotcher—entered the building and went straight to Michaels's office. It was clear the group knew their way around the building.

They were milling around in front of the office, blocking a busy part of the hallway when Zalaznick approached them. He invited them into his office to discuss their problem. They talked at Zalaznick about their objection to the Queenan story and demanded equal time.

"We will not make such an undertaking, but we will consider it," Zalaznick told them. "Only the editors can decide."

Meanwhile, Queenan called Michaels and asked if he wanted him to talk to the protesters. Michaels said no.

At the same time, Malcolm was headed toward Michaels's office on an unrelated matter when he spotted the commotion. Soon after, Queenan saw Malcolm heading down the hall toward Zalaznick's office with Michaels a few steps behind. "I thought that story was off the wall," Malcolm told Michaels.

Malcolm then invited the group into his own office. There they presented their statement to him. The headline read, "The Capitalist Tool is a shovel. How many AIDS graves will *Forbes* dig?"

Malcolm's immediate response to the group's anger was that he had been out of town at the time the magazine was put to bed. (Staffers insisted he wasn't away at the time; one of them, Ian Hersey, who also was an ACT UP supporter, had photocopied Queenan's story a day or so before closing and delivered it to Malcolm's office attached to a letter urging that the story be killed.) Malcolm agreed to print a retraction of the story and a slightly rewritten version of the group's statement in the next issue in his Fact and Comment column.

"He was gracious in agreeing to print a retraction," Blotcher says.

Queenan later told Michaels, "Look, Jim, if you're caught in the middle of all this, I'll resign."

"No," Michaels said.

Queenan's willingness to quit stemmed from his disgust with the strange atmosphere at *Forbes*. At *Barron's*, it was simple: Either the boss liked you, or he didn't, in which case you were in trouble. Those were the only two choices. At *Forbes*, some staffers' animosity toward Malcolm complicated things. It wasn't a simple matter of whether Michaels liked you. It wasn't even a simple matter of whether Malcolm liked you. If Michaels liked you, that was fine, unless of course you did something that Malcolm liked but Michaels didn't, or you did something Michaels liked but Malcolm didn't. Then there was the added complication of how the rest of the staff negotiated these constantly shifting shallows of loyalty. This tension between Michaels and Malcolm left staffers often in uncomfortable positions—like that of Jonathan Greenberg when Malcolm was promoting the Rich List against Michaels's will.

One way the staff dealt with such murkiness was to wage battles by proxy through third parties like Queenan when someone got caught in the middle.

"I was sick of the whole thing," Queenan said. "It seemed they all were against me—the staff, the gays, Malcolm. Fuck this. I'll go work for someone else. I'd been hired to do these kinds of stories, yet here I was getting blasted for it."

The retraction, in the July 10 issue, ran under the headline "Why did *Forbes* run Fumento's fulminations on AIDS?" followed immediately by the line "Because I was traveling, I didn't see it in time to kill it." He then explained that Fumento's views in his forthcoming book, *The Myth of Heterosexual AIDS*, were "asinine." "Because Forbes gave him space, some unknowledgeable or unthinking readers may give his opinions credence they don't deserve." Under Malcolm's excuse, he ran ACT UP's manifesto in full, criticizing Queenan for presenting a contrary view of the AIDS issue without a "however" element. Indeed, the story made no attempt to present both sides of the issue, but only to tell how Fumento brought heat on himself.

Patrick J. Buchanan, the syndicated conservative columnist, ran a column July 5 that basically said he agreed with Fumento's basic thesis. He led it with this line: "This is a story of a journalistic capitulation, of how the great motorcycling capitalist, Malcolm Forbes, caved in to the Red Guards of gay rights." It called Queenan "one of the gutsier young journalists writing today."

Why was Malcolm so uninhibited in his attempt to wash his hands of the story and suggest that Michaels and Queenan were to be faulted for exercising lousy news judgment behind the boss's back? If it had been up to Michaels to respond to the protesters, perhaps it would have been a simple "Write a letter to the editor."

(In fact, Michaels's response in similar situations in the past has been a bit more colorful. When *Financial World*, a competing weekly edited by *Forbes* alumnus Geoffrey N. Smith, wrote Michaels to point out a *Forbes* headline that closely matched that of an earlier story in *FW*, Michaels wrote back to *FW* publisher Douglas McIntyre: "Sir: You are a pitiful jerk and your rag shows it. You may quote me.")

The most mealymouthed thing an editor in Michaels's position might have done in the Queenan case would have been to tell the protesters he'd consider revisiting the topic at another time and at that time air their point of view. But that's not necessarily Michaels's style, nor is it the style of most self-respecting journalists in the face of criticism that amounts to little more than a difference of opinion. When ACT UP entered the offices of Helen Gurley Brown at *Cosmopolitan,* for example, to protest an article that suggested straight women weren't that vulnerable to AIDS, Brown ordered them out and called the police to have them thrown out when they failed to respond quickly enough.

Nine days after the ACT UP protest, the *New York Times* ran an editorial headlined "Why Make AIDS Worse Than It Is?" It criticized the General Accounting Office for playing a numbers game that could lead only to more hysteria. That day, Michaels and Zalaznick called Queenan in and implored him not to quit. Michaels mentioned the *Times* editorial, about which he seemed jubilant. After all, Michaels once again had been stabbed in the back editorially by Malcolm. Nothing would make Michaels happier than to see Malcolm's apology made even more puzzling by the fact that someone besides Michaels and Queenan—a respected newspaper, no less—thought the AIDS machinery was worth taking a second look at.

Malcolm's response to this incident was so extreme, journalists privately questioned his motivation. Was it simply that he, as a financial supporter of AIDS research, didn't want to see anything in his magazine suggesting the need for such research was overblown? That was plausible. If Jerry Lewis were the owner, he probably would be equally mortified if the magazine ran a piece downplaying the threat of muscular dystrophy. But in this case, the main question was, Had Malcolm capitulated for fear that an angry gay community might try to expose him? Some journalists actually toyed with the idea of exploring that question in print, but didn't. The issue faded away rapidly without further scrutiny.

A brief item in *Newsday* about Malcolm's controversial response to ACT UP seemed to sum up the media's simplistic view of things: "It's the least you'd expect from a guy who dates noted AIDS activist Elizabeth Taylor." A guy who dates Elizabeth Taylor: Malcolm must have chortled when he saw that line.

Zalaznick defended Malcolm's decision to print the ACT UP press release: Fact and Comment was Malcolm's four pages to use as he saw fit. It was not part of the rest of the editorial staff's domain. In fact, back in 1976 when Zalaznick was developing proposals to redesign the magazine, he sent a memo to Malcolm with suggestions on how Fact and Comment could be repackaged. Malcolm replied with a brief note to "stay out of it." Those four pages were exclusively Malcolm's; no other editor was permitted to get involved.

"When you own the magazine," Malcolm once said, "editors can't say 'This is silly' or 'You've got to rewrite that.' I can say what I want to say and express the opinions that I want to and it doesn't affect the articles in the rest of the magazine. Everyone knows it's the old man's opinion."

The comment is much like one B.C. made in the 1940s when Malcolm criticized as "unprofessional" some words of praise about someone in one of B.C.'s columns. B.C.'s response: "One of the pleasures of being the owner as well as the editor is that I can say what I damn please—whether or not some smart young fellow thinks it's corny or not."

Of course, as the ACT UP incident demonstrated, the casual reader doesn't see such lines of demarcation, with Malcolm on one side and the rest of the magazine on the other. In the view of the outside world, it was *Forbes* that printed the story and *Forbes* that apologized for it. At best, it made it look like Queenan and his editor had slipped one by the boss and were publicly rebuked for it.

Apparently, the ACT UP incident didn't raise any eyebrows in the mass media. Just as the flap was resolving itself in New York, the American public was treated to this July 4 *National Enquirer* front-page screamer: "Keep Your Hands Off My Liz! Fiancé Fights Malcolm Forbes' Bid to Stop Wedding." Obviously, the fictional romance of Elizabeth and Malcolm was alive and well.

ACT UP, which counted among its members a few Forbes employees, was grateful for Malcolm's swift retribution against his own staffers and quietly went away to focus its noisy attention on bigger targets—including disrupting Mass at St. Patrick's Cathedral.

The clincher that pushed to the back burner the whole question of why Malcolm gave ACT UP nearly a page and a half—about the same amount of space Queenan's original story occupied—was a classic Forbes PR juggernaut. It already had begun to surge through the media like a tidal wave. It was distributing tantalizing tidbits about the party of the century—Malcolm's seventieth birthday party at the palace in Morocco, an all-expenses-paid junket. This was going to be even bigger than the $2 million bash in New Jersey two years earlier. And this time, everybody would fly free—including the press.

11 | THE LIZ FACTOR

The association between Elizabeth Taylor and Malcolm Forbes began as a business relationship, and as much as the tabloids would view it otherwise, it stayed that way for the most part. Both of them, however, milked the speculation of a romance for all the publicity it was worth.

Taylor started it by contacting Malcolm for help promoting her fledgling Passion perfume. The launch date was January 14, 1987, at the Helmsley Palace Hotel in New York, and Taylor invited Malcolm to be master of ceremonies for the event. The idea was to have a high-profile classy big-bucks type to help establish the perfume's image. This was a product for sexy, classy ladies who wanted to appeal to sexy, classy, respectable millionaires. Malcolm seemed to fit that description, and he had sufficient name recognition after years of pounding it into the public consciousness as a synonym for happy-go-lucky macho rich guy.

But the public's awareness of Malcolm was nothing compared

with its adulation of Taylor. At the hotel where the introduction was being staged, Malcolm was sort of standing off to the side not being noticed by anyone when one of the television reporters spotted him.

"Malcolm! What are you doing here?" she asked.

It turned out he hadn't even met Taylor yet. The reporter introduced the two, and Taylor took him literally by the hand and led him onto the dais to begin what would turn out to be for Malcolm a publicity gift from heaven. What better role to be cast in, and what better co-star to be cast with—even if only for a brief new-product introduction. The opportunist in Malcolm must have jumped for joy. His wife had already dumped him, so he was free to shift from the family-man mode into that of eligible bachelor alongside the then single Taylor. For Malcolm, playing emcee to Taylor was like putting money in the bank. Even though the media barely noticed him in the glare of attention to Liz, he would soon accept repayment in a level of publicity that's hard to achieve outside of Hollywood.

"What I do, I do to enjoy life and promote my business," Malcolm once said, conceding that squiring Taylor around served both purposes.

And as often as Malcolm would be quoted saying he and Taylor had no interest in marrying, he'd do things and make public comments to feed the rumors that they might.

Of course, the idea that they were a couple was reinforced by the May 1987 bash in Far Hills at which Malcolm handed her the $1 million. That was quickly followed by a gift to Taylor that September of a purple Harley decorated with her Passion perfume logo— "Purple Passion," Malcolm called the bike. Then at a biker outing in New Jersey, they exchanged novelty rings. (The magazine *Outlaw Biker* proudly ran a cover photo of Malcolm modeling his ring with Taylor cropped out of it, so all you saw was a grinning Malcolm giving the photographer the finger.)

"I think bikers are great," Taylor said. "I want to become one. Malcolm is making me a biker. I'm working on my tattoos." She had temporary ones applied to her forearms for the occasion.

As always, they denied marriage plans, when asked. "We're good friends," Malcolm added. "Why complicate things with marriage?" Liz nodded in agreement. This kind of comment, however, seemed almost intended to invite speculation of a romance. After all, "friends" don't talk about marriage complicating things at all, unless of course they're lovers.

In myriad other little ways Malcolm fed the romance myth. At one point in Chicago, for example, at a "Toys for Tots" charity run by bikers in 1987, Malcolm was confronted by a female biker enthusiast who stripped to the waist for a souvenir snapshot of her with her arm around the grinning, leather-clad millionaire. The woman, a tattoo artist, was covered with samples of her craft. After her friend took the picture, Malcolm laughed and said, "Well, I'm not going to send that one to Elizabeth." The implication of the comment, of course, was that "Elizabeth" was a girlfriend who would become jealous on seeing Malcolm with a strange, half-naked woman.

Of course, later in the same *Newsday* feature in which David Firestone mentions this anecdote, Malcolm characterized as "crap" the tabloid rumors about his supposed marriage proposal to Taylor. That's okay. He still hadn't debunked the fiction that they could be having some sort of romance.

At the time, Firestone was well aware of the rumors about Malcolm being gay, though he had no direct evidence of it. He planned to ask him directly about his sexual orientation but chickened out. "I felt a little silly having ridden on his bike holding onto his back," Firestone says, "and there I was on his plane at thirty thousand feet thinking, My God, am I really going to ask him this question? There was a level of uncomfortability that wouldn't have been as intense if I'd been in his office and asked the question. Then I could leave immediately after getting him angry. On the plane, I essentially owed him the rest of my transportation to New York."

Firestone's experience is a perfect example of how Malcolm, intentionally or not, got the media to be nice to him. Perpetuating the Taylor-romance myth was one of those fictions the press seemed most willing to support.

In fact, months later in the July 1988 issue of the now defunct *Hollywood Reporter Magazine,* Malcolm was gushing about Taylor to writer Leonora Langley in a manner that seemed clearly intended to feed the marriage rumor.

"We laughed till we hurt last night," he said of their date, during which they took in the Broadway show *Phantom of the Opera*. He went on like a smitten fan: "She has such a sense of humor, such an element of common sense, and she's so attractive and wonderful. . . . She's fun to be with and I look forward to spending time with her. I have no idea what she sees in me, but so far, I'm glad she sees something in me rather than through me, by me or past me."

And on the prospect of marrying Liz: "As for Elizabeth and me, we talk about marriage once in a while, but we don't see why we have to complicate our lives. We're having a happy time together without being married. There's a lot of people who practice rather than tie the knot. Trying to take possession of or fence Elizabeth in would be wrong. She isn't the type."

Clearly little effort was made to steer Langley and her readers too far away from the idea of a romance between Malcolm and Elizabeth Taylor. Perhaps it was done unconsciously. Malcolm often operated on instinct, and combining business and pleasure was one of those instincts. It was second nature for him. He wasn't much interested in activities that didn't somehow serve both needs, though there is every indication that he was indeed fond of the superstar.

Langley herself says she never believed that Malcolm actually had a love affair going with Taylor, but the writer, now West Coast editor for *Elle* magazine, was beguiled by Malcolm. "He struck me as very individual and very American with a very, very childlike quality—an ability to view everything with a certain naiveté. I actually found him physically quite frail, though he was a big man."

As far as the Taylor thing goes, in June 1988 Liz Smith in the *New York Daily News* noted that in the same week, the *Star* was quoting Taylor on the marriage question as saying, "Good Lord, no—we'll never get married," while the *Enquirer* was predicting a quiet family wedding in New York in September.

Of course, no such wedding took place, but the business purpose of the friendship was growing increasingly useful. Malcolm had invested time and money in Elizabeth Taylor and her causes. Now he was ready to get it all back with interest. She would figure prominently in Malcolm's seventieth birthday party at Palais de Mendoub, his Moroccan palace overlooking the Strait of Gibraltar.

At that party Taylor was cast in the role of gracious hostess and guest of honor, but it was really a cameo role. Malcolm may have been borrowing her fame, but at the same time, he was degrading its value by using it so blatantly. Knowingly or not, she was a prop for a decadent monarch hosting a hedonistic celebration of excess complete with "slaves" and belly dancers. It was the kind of choreographed, ostentatious display that Roberta hated but was expected to endure with grace and smiling demeanor.

As an actress, Taylor was perfectly suited for the job. After all, if there is one element that stood out in all of the Forbes shindigs, it was the distinct sense that this was *theater* and everyone was there to play a role, whether it be gracious host, respected government official, society matron, Hollywood celebrity, obsequious servant, or devoted family member. Malcolm's strength as director was his ability to charm so many people into willingly playing these roles. Of course, being called on repeatedly to do so must wear thin, as it did for Roberta. (As someone back in Scotland once said, having observed two generations of Forbeses, "Forbes men are hard on their wives.")

One of the people who rode regularly with the motorcycle gang, for example, said he and his girlfriend finally dropped out, because they grew tired of the lack of freedom. Everything was so tightly planned, it left little room for spontaneity.

The party in Morocco became a study in this phenomenon. The press seized on it, and for the first time a Malcolm production drew public complaints from guests who usually quietly accepted their role in exchange for the opportunity to rub shoulders with the rest of the rich, powerful, and famous while enjoying great food and extravagant entertainment in an opulent setting.

About eight hundred people—many of them media people—were invited to the party, with all transportation expenses to be paid by *Forbes*. Not everyone in the media felt comfortable with this arrangement. The *New York Times* decided not to go at all. *New York Newsday*, for example, wanted to cover the event—including the free flight over—but didn't want to take the free ride, insisting on paying *Forbes* the equivalent of what it would have cost to fly there and stay in a hotel.

Newsday's regular society columnist, Jim Revson, had been invited but couldn't make it. The newspaper asked if it could send Ellis Henican instead, who was actually more desirable because the paper was more interested in taking a jaundiced view of the event than it was likely to get from a society columnist. At first, Don Garson, *Forbes* public relations director, balked but eventually acceded once he realized Revson wouldn't make it.

Garson also balked at *Newsday*'s insistence that it pay all of Henican's travel costs. He refused to provide an estimate of the costs, so *Newsday* priced it through a travel agent and sent a check for the amount to *Forbes*. Then off to the party.

Newsday, however, apparently was in the minority of journalists who insisted on paying their way. "It surprised me the number of people who seemed to be taking it as a freebie," Henican says. Liz Smith, the New York *Daily News* gossip columnist, took the free ride and defended her decision to do so. It's not surprising. Many journalists had allowed Malcolm to pay their way on numerous junkets, to France, for example, for the annual balloon festival, which perhaps explains why Malcolm was constantly mentioned in gossip columns and almost never in a negative context.

This time, however, Liz Smith did not hesitate to complain in print, writing, "Some of it was like taking an un-air-conditioned bus trip with 700 people to Ardmore, Okla., over the dog days." The hotel rooms "smelled of fish and new paint . . . [and] the water taps were often empty."

At *Newsday*, however, the view was that if the party was important enough to cover, it was important enough to pay for.

What Henican found so amazing was just how uncritical the press was during opportunities to interview Malcolm and Taylor. It was as though most journalists went with the preconception that they were there primarily to catalogue the vulgarity—to "keep track of every shrimp stuck into every mouth," as Henican says. "It says something that the world is comfortable with this kind of news."

Perhaps the toughest question posed to Malcolm had to do with the tax treatment of the supposed $2 million cost of the party. Would it be tax deductible as a business expense, as was presumably the case with the 1987 party at Timberfield? The answer was yes, though a subsequent furor led to a quick public reversal. (Who would ever know the truth? Because Forbes Inc. is privately held, it would be no one's business beyond the IRS's to know whether Forbes would take the deduction.)

By and large, the questions focused on the statistics of excess or were otherwise soft.

"Most of the press was extremely fawning," Henican says, and that was a lot of reporters—110 members of the working press. One news conference lasted an hour, and if there were a hundred questions, probably ninety-five of them were focused on such things as what Taylor got Malcolm for his birthday, what would Malcolm do for his seventy-fifth birthday, and so on. Very few journalists were inclined to seek his response to the criticism that this was an overwhelming display of excess and ego.

Yet for all the homespun, self-effacing humor and wisdom, Malcolm displayed his worst side as well—a nastiness with underlings on the payroll—and no one seemed to notice, at least not in print.

"He was not very nice to people who worked there," Henican says. "He snapped at them. 'Get me this, get me that.' "

Henican wrote one of the most provocative leads of the scores of features written about the party:

> As is his way, Malcolm Forbes brushed aside the question with a self-deprecating quip.
> "Is this a business expense?" the seventy-year-old publishing mogul said, repeating the inevitable query. "I wish it was entirely. Some of it is a business expense."
> Forbes' accountants are already at work trying to figure out precisely how much of the bill for his $2 million weekend birthday bash can be forwarded to Uncle Sam. Not an easy calculation, to be sure. In Forbes' ever-public style of operation, the lines between business and pleasure are drawn in just two shades of ink: faint and invisible.

This was probably the only story angle that had any near impact. One angry congressman, Democrat Fortney Stark of California, wrote the IRS, warning it not to allow the deduction—not that such a letter would make much difference in an IRS decision. "The public's support of the tax system is destroyed by reports of tax-deductible birthday bashes by belly-dancing billionaires," Representative Stark wrote.

Malcolm said Stark was simply trying to appeal to voters. But Malcolm quickly changed his tune and called a news conference immediately after the party to let the world know it. "I would say ninety-five percent—it's business related," he said. "But the question is are we using it as a business deduction? It was never intended to be and not a penny of it is. But certainly a case can be made when seventy-five percent of your guests are your biggest customers." He went on to defend the party as truly beneficial to the business of *Forbes* and its constituents. He claimed that the party opened the door to *Forbes* publishing editions in Germany and possibly Italy, Japan, and Spain—all practically cost-free ventures that amount to simply licensing others to reproduce translated versions of the magazine in those countries.

Clearly, Malcolm wanted to erase the negative impact by suggesting he would deduct "not a penny," but at the same time, he wanted to make it clear, probably for the benefit of potential auditors, that he certainly would feel justified in writing off at least a portion of the party. After all, there's nothing in the IRS rules that says you can't tell people you don't plan to take some particular deduction and then, in the privacy of your own office, go ahead and do it anyway.

Bringing all these people to Tangier seemed to the more savvy observers to be another case of Malcolm letting his sexual preferences rise to just a hairbreadth beneath the surface. Julie Baumgold kind of danced around it in her feature on the party in *New York* magazine: Tangier, she noted, is described in guides as "the world's most famous gay center," famous for brothels and pedophiles. "All in all, not a totally inappropriate selection of site," she wrote, without elaborating.

Meanwhile, Malcolm deflected criticism of excess with this defense: "We all do things in our life where we could have given the money to charity. It's hard to argue with that. It's just that the scale is more visible here. So you don't defend it in the abstract. I don't. On the other hand, I don't feel guilty about it. I feel grateful that we can do it."

Earlier he said, "You could point out we give several million dollars a year to philanthropies and worthy causes."

But even when he's giving away millions, it's not really in the tradition of the Rockefeller or Ford foundations where staffs search for the most effective ways to spend money for the betterment of humanity. It was Rockefeller money invested in research, for example, that ultimately eradicated several diseases. The Forbeses, however, are less focused on social issues. Giving money to find a cure for AIDS is noble, but would Malcolm have thought of doing it if it didn't simultaneously provide an opportunity to bask in the instant worldwide media attention accorded Elizabeth Taylor?

He was proud of his 1985 gift to his alma mater, Princeton University, creating a residential college designed to make life easier for incoming freshmen. He even named it after his son Steve, but at the dedication he felt compelled to respond to criticism about his choice of charities. Some ungrateful student had asked Malcolm how he could justify giving millions to a university already as richly endowed as Princeton when the world is so full of truly needy people.

"Money can do a lot—but basically, a few million bucks would have no lasting impression on all these vastly greater problems of our society," Malcolm said in his dedication speech. "The solution for these problems will have to come from minds that have been stimulated, opened, broadened—minds with the capacity to resolve, better than past generations have been able, problems of this magnitude. The kinds of minds, in other words, developed in a place like this."

Of course, Forbes College was established with none of this in mind, really. And a student's remarks at the dedication drove home what really matters in the minds of the people such a bequest is meant to benefit.

The student, Karl Beinkampen, class of 1987, started his speech by explaining how he'd gone to a professor to find out what he should talk about. The professor told him, "Talk about what you think is important." "Well," Karl told the crowd, "as a true capitalist tool,

I decided I might ask Mr. Forbes for a job. Upon further consideration, however, I thought it might not be appropriate at this ceremony."

He went on to extol the virtues of a separate residential college
to nurture the younger students. No focus there on doing anything
about closing the gap between rich and poor, between those who
starve and those whose table scraps would be a life-saving bounty.
Of course, it wouldn't look good for the Capitalist Tool to suggest
anything that might be construed as support for redistributing the
wealth.

When it comes to philanthropy, Malcolm seemed to have
weighed his decisions on the basis of what was in it for him. Giving
money to AIDS research meant acquiring a new level of fame.
Creating a Forbes College at Princeton immortalized the name in
a prestigious institution that probably wouldn't do so without such
a bequest. It also guaranteed, as Mr. Beinkampen's remark indicated, that an annual new crop of the nation's brightest youth who
might not otherwise have thought of it would offer their services to
the magazine.

One of Malcolm's favorite charitable activities was giving of his
time—and some money—to colleges and universities offering
unearned honorary diplomas, which he loved to accumulate, along
with commencement address invitations.

But charity was not the mission in Morocco. In three days, the
Forbeses would manage to spend $2 million to create a media circus
of immense proportions—a bargain when compared with the 1987
event at Timberfield. That earlier production also supposedly cost
$2 million, but Malcolm literally got more bang for his buck in
Morocco than in Far Hills. While the 1987 party featured 121
pipers and drummers, the Tangier affair included appearances by
600 drummers, acrobats, and belly dancers; 300 turbaned Berber
horsemen fired muskets, and 20 women showered guests with rose
petals. Most of the "extras" were provided free of charge on orders
by King Hassan of Morocco.

After all, the king was also acutely aware of the public relations
opportunity the party posed. In fact, the country put together promotional kits for top executives—a free Moroccan leather briefcase

filled with detailed information about the financing, tax, and labor benefits of investing in Morocco. One hotel-industry executive says he was heavily lobbied at the party by Moroccan officials to consider developing lodging there—and they were convincing.

The prospect of making important business contacts was a major drawing card for many of the guests in Morocco. If this was really only a birthday party, then why did only twelve people show up with birthday presents? Apparently gifts were discouraged, but Lee Iacocca made a comment that summed up the main point of the whole event: "Maybe I could give him a few more Chrysler ads."

Thomas Fey, president of Godiva, a *Forbes* advertiser, told *Newsday*'s Henican at the party that he attended to two important business relationships during the party not related to Forbes. "These are big potential customers for us," Fey said.

Hisashi Ito, chairman of Japan's Nikko hotel chain, said, "I created many new friends here. I hope I will do business with many of them."

These are the people Malcolm really aimed to please. It wouldn't be cost-effective to throw, for example, a truly Hollywood-type party. That might provide lots of publicity, but would it generate business for *Forbes?* Elizabeth Taylor supplied as much of that kind of celebrity as he needed. Dina Merrill was the only other actress there. After Taylor, virtually all the guests were, as Henican puts it, second-string celebrities—including hundreds of chief executives who themselves weren't well known but whose companies' names were household words.

After the non-Hollywood celebrity types—like Barbara Walters, Henry Kissinger, Beverly Sills (who led the crowd in singing "Happy Birthday"), Walter Cronkite, Pauline Phillips (Abigail Van Buren) and twin sister Eppie Lederer (Ann Landers), William F. Buckley, Calvin Klein, Oscar de la Renta, Lee Iacocca and governors of several states—and the billionaires—including Gordon Getty of the oil-rich family, John Kluge of Metromedia, Robert Maxwell of the British publishing empire, Sir James Goldsmith, the British corporate raider, Leonard Stern of Hartz Mountain and the *Village Voice,* and Gianni Agnelli of Fiat—there were the true guests of honor, the bread and butter of Forbes publications:

Merv Adelson (Mr. Barbara Walters) of Lorimar, Carter Bacot of Bank of New York, James Bryan, Jr., of Airbus, Rodney Canlon of Compaq Computer, Daniel Davison of U.S. Trust, Barry Diller of 20th Century Fox, James Emshoff of Citicorp Diners Club, William Esrey of U.S. Sprint, Charles Exley of NCR, Keith Garrity of Fansteel, John Georges of International Paper, William Gladstone of Arthur Young, Alan Greenberg of Bear Stearns, Marshall Hahn of Georgia-Pacific, John Gutfreund of Salomon Brothers, Alex Hart of MasterCard, Pascal Henault of Peugeot, William Hulett of Stouffer Hotels, Sadahei Kusumoto of Minolta, John Marous of Westinghouse, Donald Marron of PaineWebber, John McGillicuddy of Manufacturers Hanover, Masaaki Morita of Sony, Denis Mullane of Connecticut Mutual Life, Dean O'Hare of Chubb Group, Jerry Pearlman of Zenith, Ronald Perelman of Revlon, Harold Polling of Ford, Thomas Pritzker of Hyatt, John Roach of Tandy, James Robinson of American Express, Charles Sanford of Bankers Trust, C. J. Silas of Phillips Petroleum, Frederick Smith of Federal Express, Roger Smith of General Motors, Dellbert Staley of NYNEX, John Teets of Greyhound, Yukiyasu Togo of Toyota, and Joseph Vittoria of Avis.

As a group they represented one of Malcolm's most prized collections. And like his inanimate collections, this one included some fine examples picked up before their true values were generally known. "Malcolm recognized me before anyone else, which is something I will always appreciate," Kissinger once said. He was merely a Harvard professor when he met Malcolm.

Malcolm had chartered a Concorde, a 747, and a DC-8 to get them all there at his expense.

Were all eight hundred guests close personal friends? Malcolm was asked. "Yes," he said, "in the sense that eight hundred people can be close, personal friends. And some of them have proved it by the business they've brought to the magazine."

James Risher, president of Exide Electronics and a *Forbes* advertiser, said: "Their whole approach is really very effective. They have you up to the magazine for lunch. It's all very casual. They show you all around. They take you down to where they actually put together the magazine each issue. They take you into their world. They make you feel like a part of this interesting, vibrant culture. It's very seductive. Events like this, that's the icing."

A major difference between the New Jersey party and the Morocco event was the tone of the press attention each generated. It was not all positive, as in the 1987 party. There wasn't even a charitable donation to AIDS research, for example, to give the occasion "more significance than just a social event." This time, the press was practically invited to focus on the party's business purpose. Malcolm encouraged the media to consider his birthday as merely an excuse for an event to focus the attention of the press and advertisers on *Forbes*. Thus, the dishing began.

Baumgold's report in *New York* magazine contained this quote attributed to an unidentified society figure: "Malcolm uses people for props. He throws them to the wolves. Anyone who was in New Jersey with the 2,000 Forbes advertisers should have known better." Baumgold hammered away at the point. Some of the guests "began to feel like props. Names on a list. Press food." Another ungrateful cynic is quoted as saying, "You must participate in each event so you feel thoroughly worked over and taken advantage of."

Much was made of the lack of air conditioning at the Hotel Solazur in Tangier, which Malcolm had taken over for his guests for the occasion, forcing the eviction of more than a handful of ordinary tourists. Numerous publications delighted in reporting how the superrich Henry Kravises of the leveraged-buyout fortune bought electric fans. Then there were the lines. It took an hour, some complained, to get through the reception line and get seated for dinner. Martha Sherrill of the *Washington Post* confirmed that at one point, they ran out of ice. But the accommodations were what they complained about most.

"What did they expect?" Malcolm said later. "That I should build them a hotel?"

Privately, Malcolm might well have wanted to say to these complainers what he said to Jay Gissen back in 1984. Gissen was complaining about the lack of hot water and towels in their hotel during the Egypt Friendship Tour. Malcolm turned and snapped, "If you wanted the comforts of home, you should have fucking stayed there."

Then came the complaints at the end that all these rich and famous people were left on their own at Kennedy Airport back in New York to grope about in the dark for their luggage on the tarmac where it had been dumped.

Still Malcolm made it hard to be critical, he was so blatant about his purpose. *Newsweek*'s report on the party showed how tough it was, starting with the headline: "Forbes's Publicity Machine/A gift for the man who has everything: ink"—including the two-page spread of it *Newsweek* devoted to the affair, complete with six photos featuring mainly celebrities. The piece included this self-effacing sentence regarding the practice of schmearing advertisers: "Forbes's parties are just splashier versions of the country-club outings sponsored by most publications, including *Newsweek.*" End of hard-hitting criticism.

Newsweek did make note of the apparent double standard of Forbes not wanting the press to pay its own way, yet conceding that *Forbes* magazine prohibits its own writers from accepting such junkets. Also to *Newsweek*'s credit, it refused to play along with the rest of the media in their insistence on treating the Taylor-Forbes relationship as a romance, which "reporters believe is fake but print anyway."

Executives from all walks of journalism were taken along for the junket, including James Hoge, publisher of the New York *Daily News.* When editor Gil Spencer quit, the rumor was that it was over Hoge's decision to take the free ride. Spencer later denied this, saying, "I thought it bizarre, but it wasn't a big deal and it would never have occurred to me to leave over that."

Perhaps the harshest criticism came in a column in Leonard Stern's own *Village Voice* a month after the event. In it Gary Indiana bemoaned "the nearly uniform ickiness of the magazine and newspaper pictures it generated." He went on to describe photos showing "the curiously drab Forbes offspring baring their congenital overbites." Robert Maxwell looked like a "clown." Then there was "the malignant visage of Henry Kissinger creased in a rictus of vile enjoyment." Liz Smith "resembled a skittish, jowly bovine on its way to the slaughterhouse." William Buckley's wife, Pat, "looked as if she'd been forcibly face-lifted from the buttocks up, while her husband's head and neck suggested a carelessly sculpted pile of Philadelphia Brand cream cheese in full melt."

But Indiana's sharpest jabs were aimed at the host, the host country—a nation run by a dictator with little regard for civil rights—and the relationship between the two:

> . . . the fact that *anything* can be bought in Morocco is what attracts people like Forbes there in the first place. A Latin American writer who lives in Tangier told me, "If he wants to rent the whole Hotel Solazur, that's his right. He could do that anywhere, though . . . the rest of it he could only get away with here."
>
> By "the rest of it," my friend did not mean the jokes about Malcolm Forbes ubiquitous in Tangier, jokes that lend a certain piquancy to Forbes's "romance" with Liz Taylor. . . . Rather, he meant (among other things) the widespread suspicion about why dozens of beggars, deformed and/or crippled and/or "touched" street people were yanked off the streets and thrown in jail for the party weekend.

This was about as close as anyone had come in print to discussing the irony of Malcolm Forbes, the rumored homosexual, luring all his straight friends to Sodom to help perpetuate the attention-getting myth of his "affair" with Cleopatra.

At the other end of the spectrum—the spectrum viewed by the vast majority of the public—were the supermarket tabloids and *People* magazine. Anyone casually scanning the mass-market coverage without reading the words could easily have gotten the impression—as they could have at the 1987 party—that the celebration was actually a wedding reception and that Taylor and Malcolm had gotten married. The *Star*'s headline supported this concept: "The Arabian Nights of Queen Liz & King Malcolm." The two-page spread that began *People*'s six-page feature was dominated by a closeup of Malcolm and Taylor kissing. Taylor was described as the guest of honor. At the end of the piece, Malcolm was quoted as denying any plan to marry, while being careful not to preclude the possibility that the two were romantically involved. "You don't have to marry somebody before you have fun together," he said.

The *National Enquirer,* which also featured the kiss and had the look of wedding coverage, bent over backward to suggest Malcolm was interested in marrying Taylor. Its headline read: "At His $3 Million Birthday Bash, Malcolm Forbes Begs Liz: Don't Marry That Penniless Bum!" a reference to Taylor's reported boyfriend, Larry Fortensky.

USA Today was also shameless in its willingness to feed the public impression of a romance. Its party story led with this observation: "Like prom night kids, multimillionaire Malcolm Forbes and super-star Elizabeth Taylor—who left . . . beau Larry Fortensky at home— were virtually inseparable this weekend at Forbes' $2 million 70th birthday bash in Morocco."

This was just the sort of publicity for which Malcolm would gladly pay $2 million—or even $3 million. Of course, this would be only a secondary purpose, the first being to earn advertisers' continued support and loyalty.

"This party wasn't done for ego or to show opulence," Malcolm told Julie Baumgold. It was staged to attract several hundred chief executives who "would not go to another night at the Waldorf while we pat ourselves on the back."

"Meek children shall inherit the magazine," Steve Forbes said during toasts after dinner. "How can we top this party? We'll try, Pop. Again and again and again." (Ralph Ingersoll of Ingersoll Publications would later implore Steve to reconsider making such an effort.)

And for all the jaded remarks, no one could deny that the event was spectacular. The food—pigeon pie and grilled lamb—was excel-lent. The entertainment was exotic, with horsemen charging the domed tents, stopping just short of them and then firing their muskets. ("I don't know what happened," guest Denis Mullane told Martha Sherrill of the *Washington Post,* "but after the last charge someone was carried away in an ambulance.")

Newsday's Henican was one reporter who expected to hear more at least off-the-record sarcasm about the party's excesses and Forbes's business purpose in having it. "But I didn't detect any cynicism about the overkill," he says. "No one saw it as the work of some pathological mind or the last gasp of the Reagan eighties or the start of a new round of extragavance. I found it very hard to get people to be thoughtful about it at all."

Somehow Malcolm cast a spell over everyone. Just as *Newsday*'s David Firestone had expected to be more critical in a feature about Malcolm a year earlier and ended up admiring him as engaging and disarmingly nice, Henican was thwarted in his effort to find cynics among Malcolm's guests. After all, for all the excesses, nothing looked chintzy or gaudy or tacky. Even the most jaded found this party of "rich mammals on camels," as some dubbed it, tasteful if slightly mismanaged at times.

"Forbes co-opts the press in a very sophisticated way," the *Washington Post*'s Martha Sherrill told *Newsweek*. "The attitude isn't 'We're so glad you're covering it,' it's 'We're so glad *you* are here.' It's seductive."

Final score in Morocco: more than twenty thousand press clippings. Who cares if Carl Jensen, Sonoma State University communications studies professor, ranked the party among the top ten junk-news stories of 1989—right up there with Zsa Zsa Gabor's traffic-ticket trial?

Meanwhile, the Malcolm-Taylor thing was starting to draw criticism, even in the context of raising money for AIDS research. The *Village Voice* questioned whether it was useful for people the world doesn't take seriously to promote serious causes. At issue was the way the *New York Times* covered a social event called "A Day Without Art" meant to demonstrate the impact AIDS had had on the arts community. The *Times* story said, "It was *La Cage aux Folles* meets the Fortune 500," and the *Voice* described the story as featuring a "three-column photo that amply displayed the considerable cleavage of the evening's co-chair, Liz Taylor, as she posed with the inevitable Malcolm Forbes and Mr. and Mrs. John Kluge."

Was Taylor sensitive to such cynical treatment? Maybe not. But when it came time a month after the Morocco affair to promote her "Passion for Men," her first scent for men, she apparently didn't need Malcolm. This time the high-profile rich guy was Saudi financier Adnan Khashoggi. At least, second to Taylor, he was the celebrity who attracted the most attention to the introduction party, given on the floor of the New York Stock Exchange.

Not that Malcolm was incapable of getting media attention without standing next to Taylor. His name continued to appear almost daily in one or more of the gossip columns in the New York dailies. In fact, on one day, October 10, 1989, the *New York Post* alone would mention Forbes on three consecutive pages—on page 6 to compare Malcolm with another balloon adventurer; then a full page on the just released Forbes 400 Rich List; and a mention in Aileen "Suzy" Mehle's society column of Malcolm's being honored by the New-York Historical Society.

12 | ONE-MAN SHOW

Toward the end of 1989, writer Joe Queenan would quietly leave Forbes after less than a year, having concluded he would never be comfortable there. He could never forgive his editors for failing to stand by him and his story. And he could never write the controversial stories he was hired to write, because he could never be sure that his editors wouldn't once again publicly flog him to appease some angry reader.

"I hated the place," he says. "I couldn't even write about it, I hated it so much." Queenan says the ACT UP incident was about 70 percent of the reason he decided to leave.

Michaels, who liked Queenan, asked him what his other reasons for leaving were. Queenan explained that unless he came in extremely early or stayed late into the night when no one else was around, it was impossible to get any work done.

Michaels asked why.

"Because my office is filled with people always telling me how much they hate working here but don't know how to get out of the place," Queenan told him.

"But you know as well as I do that journalists are chronic complainers and malingerers and hate their jobs," Michaels said. Wasn't that the case at other publications?

"Sure."

"Then what's different about it at Forbes?" Michaels said.

"Here they *really* hate it," Queenan said.

One of the timeless conflicts at every publication is the struggle between ad and editorial departments. At *Forbes* perhaps more than at other national publications, some had the feeling that editorial values were compromised to protect other interests. Editorial staffers sometimes felt their self-respect as journalists was jeopardized, caught in the dilemma of upholding professional values and staying employed.

Forbes made a name by bravely criticizing high-powered executives who could hurt the magazine financially, but critics say that boldness had ebbed.

"While small companies (and the government, of course) continue to be attacked," *Newsweek* once noted, "large firms with large ad budgets tend to get off. 'It's not as fearless as it used to be because it has more to lose,' says Allan Sloan." One of *Forbes*'s best, most aggressive writers, Sloan was a senior editor when he left in 1988 for *Newsday.*

But fear of offending big companies wasn't the reason *Forbes* focused so much attention on small fry. The more likely reason was that it simply was harder for its reporters to cover big companies because of the magazine's reputation for going for the jugular and little else. And big companies tend to be much more effective than small ones at deflecting nosey journalists.

One of the most regularly compromising positions Malcolm put his writers in was the town house lunch. "They would call me to come to these town house luncheons," says Queenan. "I would say I'm a journalist, not a circus performer. I don't sell ad. That's whoring yourself. The people who agree to do that, they're not self-respecting, and a large number of them do. It's a real masochistic environment."

In fact, no journalist at Forbes was really asked to sell ads, but that was a major purpose of the luncheon—to impress the CEO guest of honor with performances by bright journalists (the product) and follow up immediately with an order request. It has been estimated that 10 percent of the magazine's ad sales—300 to 400 pages a year at $40,000 a color page—occurred in this setting.

"It's a constant moral compromise," Queenan says.

These lunches would occur a couple of times a week, usually with one particular executive as the main guest. Sometimes, it would also include a prestigious economist or politician. Malcolm always made the same joke about a Raphael painting of a nude who looked like she was slipping off a couch, saying she couldn't fall off because "she's screwed on." For Steve, the often repeated gag was that once you'd had enough to drink, the David Hockney collage of a nude would come into focus.

Malcolm—who used fine epicurean delights the way a call girl might wear the world's most expensive perfume and lingerie to attract a well-heeled john—often would conclude lunch with an honored guest at *Forbes*'s executive dining room by presenting him with a bottle of wine for the year of the guest's birth. Chrysler chairman Lee Iacocca got a bottle of 1924 Chateau Margaux. John F. Welch, Jr., chairman of General Electric, got a 1935.

Honored guests would get a silver stirrup cup with a stag's head from the Forbes crest and their name engraved on it. One chief executive, upset by a negative story about his company, angrily returned his souvenir goblet. Malcolm, never wasteful, had the engraving erased so the cup could be reused.

Many reporters actually found these off-the-record gatherings helpful. Executive-laden trips on the *Highlander* around Manhattan served a similar purpose, which was to provide the opportunity for informal meetings that might help open doors later when a writer was working on a story. But other journalists were uncomfortable about the link between such meetings and ad-sales efforts. One of the Forbes family would always give the signal that the editorial part of the meeting was over—by offering cigars—and that the ad-sales part was about to begin. The editorial types were then supposed to excuse themselves, noting they had a magazine to put out.

On one occasion, Arthur Jones, who worked for *Forbes* for five years until 1974, refused to cooperate. "I'll stay," he said. "I'm all caught up on my work." And remained to watch "the arm-twisting for next year's ad schedule." When he returned to the office, he remarked, "They do it very poorly."

This close relationship between editorial and ad functions as exemplified by the town house lunch was an intentional tactic of persuasion on Malcolm's part. He alluded to it in a 1989 interview with *Personal Selling Power* magazine. In it, he suggested that *Forbes* advertisers weren't just buying ads in a desirable place to be seen; they were making themselves accessible to the editorial staff to protect themselves perhaps from unbalanced reporting.

"Entree," Malcolm said in the interview, "means being able to have these people level with your writers and editors. . . . We have got to establish rapport. And it goes both ways. The scenario of power is constantly changing. And in our appraisal of how they are doing with that power, it does a lot to determine whether they continue to be people with power. So it's not a one-way street where the customer is doing you a favor."

But if times get tough, the balance of power can shift to the advertiser when it comes to coverage by a magazine that believes "it's not a one-way street." This makes it trickier to maintain a high level of editorial integrity, if writers and advertisers both sense that the boss views his editorial clout as a sort of bargaining chip in ad sales. When advertising weakens, for example, because of economic conditions or increased competition, advertising executives at any publication can gain more clout under pressure than the guardians of editorial content.

At *Forbes*, these interests were pretty much represented by one man. Malcolm was not a dispassionate owner who let these two sides coexist, maintaining a separation of influence. This separation at other publications is intended to keep advertisers from getting the idea that they can effectively censor a publication by threatening to cancel ads to protest stories they don't approve of. This is a problem at every publication, from the small-town weekly to the biggest of national publications.

In 1954, for example, the *Wall Street Journal* lost $250,000 worth of advertising from General Motors and its subsidiaries, as well as editorial access, because *Journal* reporter John Williams got advance information about the auto companies' new-car-model plans and wrote about them. In an editorial, the *Journal* wrote that "when a newspaper begins to suppress news, whether at the behest of its advertisers or on pleas from special segments of business, it will soon cease to be of any service to its advertisers or to business because it will cease to have readers." Before the year was out, GM quietly ended its boycott.

In that case, no threat was issued in advance of the story. It was a simple act of retaliation, and it turned into a PR disaster for General Motors. But if a threat had been issued, how would the *Journal* have responded? The managing editor would have considered it sacrilege for an advertising executive to even suggest that a story be altered or killed to save an ad account. And that would certainly be the case at *Forbes*.

But the difference at Forbes was that the owner was both the top ad man and the top editorial man, with hands-on authority in both roles. So how would editor Jim Michaels know whether an editorial order from Malcolm was motivated by pure news considerations or by concerns for an ad account or a friend? It might not always be easy. For one thing, there probably were at least as many examples of Malcolm not caving in to pressure from an advertiser or friend as there were of Malcolm subordinating editorial values for other considerations. Further complicating the issue was Michaels's way of dealing with directives from the boss.

While Dero Saunders was "a very graceful editor," former staffer Jeff Grigsby says, Michaels was heavy-handed. "If he gets mad, he can rip the shit out of a story." But editorially Michaels always took the heat from above. "He's eccentric," Grigsby says. "If he does something crazy, you have no way of knowing whether he just went crazy or if Malcolm was behind it. It's Faustian."

But as former *Forbes* writer Frank Lalli saw it, Malcolm may have imposed his editorial will from time to time to protect some noneditorial personal interest, but it happened no more frequently than it does at other publications. And it is hard to find any corporate executives willing to say they felt they were either punished or rewarded editorially according to the amount they spent on ads in *Forbes*.

Still a few writers left *Forbes* over editorial decisions by Malcolm that they felt violated journalistic ideals. Lalli, who eventually left for Time Inc.'s *Money* magazine, was not one of them, though he came close at times. His career at Forbes embodies many of the elements that led to the love-hate relationship writers often formed with the magazine. A lot of that has to do with the personality of Jim Michaels.

"Jim Michaels is the smartest person you'll ever meet in any category," Lalli says. "That's what makes him so hard to work with. He gets bored very easily. You've got to keep him interested all the time. But it's almost inevitable that eventually you're going to bore him."

Lalli came to *Forbes* in 1970. He had done a freelance piece for the magazine and was offered a job. At the time he was making about $12,000. Asked what he wanted, he told Michaels that if he figured he was worth having on his staff, he'd be worth about $18,000. Michaels told him he'd have no way of knowing what he was worth until he'd been there for a while. He started Lalli at $14,000. Within a couple of months, Michaels increased Lalli's salary to more than $18,000, noting that he now knew he was worth what Lalli had asked.

"That was the amazing thing about *Forbes* back then," Lalli says. "You kind of figured that if you were worth it, you'd get a raise before you had to ask."

On his first day, Lalli was led down a hall, then down another, and another, and so on through a rabbit warren until he was shown a room near an exit sign. Inside was a telephone, a desk, a typewriter, some pencils and paper. That was it. He was wished good luck. No one asked him to do anything. He was on his own to produce. He had no beat, no assignment. Just produce.

"I remember at one point I had a story idea," Lalli recalls. "Michaels was out of town, so I just got started on it. Finally I called him from Tokyo and said, 'Jim, I think I've got a story idea that's a cover.' We discussed it and he said fine. I never had to ask anyone if it was all right to head to Tokyo for a possible idea. I just went."

That was the beauty of *Forbes:* total freedom, no limitations. As long as you were producing fresh ideas, you could do anything you wanted. But the minute that freshness vanished, watch out. Michaels knew how to fire people.

With regard to Malcolm's influence, Lalli believed it was minimal.

"I never had a problem over an advertiser with Malcolm," Lalli said. "With friends, perhaps, but never with an advertiser. In fact, I remember in one instance I had done a story on Sears, a cover. It was one of the first that suggested Sears wasn't going anywhere. Malcolm told me it wasn't tough enough, and it wasn't. I should have been much tougher."

In another case, Lalli had done a piece on John Kluge and Metromedia. It was an embarrassing story for Kluge. Before the piece ran, "I remember seeing Malcolm walking Kluge out of the office with his arm around his shoulder, yet I was never asked to change anything in the story. Malcolm simply had him in to warn him that a tough story on him was about to run so he could prepare himself."

In the early 1970s, Lalli did a scathing piece on corporate entertaining at the Superbowl. It was a satirical look at how fans are squeezed out by the corporate junketeers. It was loaded with juicy facts and anecdotes. "Michaels hardly touched it in the editing process," Lalli says. "A day or so later, Jim said, 'We've got big problems with the story.' "

The problem was that Malcolm, the last of the big-time spenders when it comes to corporate entertaining, didn't think it would be appropriate for *Forbes* to seem critical of others who do such lavish entertaining.

Michaels gave Lalli two choices. He handed him an edited version of the story and said, "We can run it like this"—a much shorter version with every other paragraph X-ed out and lots of art—"or we can kill it."

Lalli told him to kill it, but added that he would take it and sell it elsewhere. Jim said, "Okay, but I can't promise to protect you from whatever might happen as a result."

In retrospect, Lalli believes he was wrong to sell it elsewhere (eventually *Rolling Stone* ran the story). "I should have been fired," he says. "If one of our writers did that to us now, I'd fire him. But at the time I was determined: You're not going to keep this story out of print."

Michaels later would defend the decision to kill the piece, noting that at the time, it was the only story in twenty years that Malcolm ever killed. Another of particular note would come later.

Malcolm and Lalli eventually had a face-off over the Superbowl story. "Malcolm dislikes confrontations," Lalli says, "but he had to face me in this case."

"I hope nothing like this ever happens again," Malcolm said. He was visibly angry. He was shaking.

"I hope so too," Lalli replied.

That was the end of it. Lalli says it wasn't a factor in his decision to leave, but it clearly was a case of an editorial decision driven by a concern for not offending *Forbes*'s friends and supporters. Equally as clear was that it showed a weakness in Michaels's editorial spine; in head-to-head confrontations, Malcolm was bound to win some of the time.

Generally in those days, Lalli says, *Forbes* backed its writers. And it did so in the case of Lalli's story on the Gallo brothers of wine-making fame. It would portray Ernest Gallo in harsh terms—a man beneath whose "crusty exterior . . . sits a heart of stone." Soon after Lalli interviewed Ernest for the stroy, Lalli had a late dinner with his wife and Jim Michaels at a restaurant in Los Angeles. "I didn't know it at the time," Lalli says, "but these four friends of Gallo managed to get themselves seated right next to us at the restaurant, despite the fact that no one else was eating there."

During the course of the meal Lalli talked about how the story was developing. Based on this intelligence, Ernest wrote a letter to Malcolm saying how awful it was that one of his staffers would sit in a restaurant with an attractive woman and a balding man and talk loudly in disparaging terms about a company. The letter made it clear that he assumed Malcolm would want to fire Lalli immediately. Malcolm rejected Ernest's suggestion and wrote back telling him so.

Malcolm's power in editorial matters derived not only from his ownership role but also from his reputation for an ability to make brilliant editorial decisions.

"I won a national magazine award for a story that was Malcolm's one-line idea," Lalli says. "He wrote it down on a piece of paper and handed it to Michaels and Michaels handed it to me: 'Who owns New York?' It took me months, but it was a great story."

And Michaels himself had always had the freedom to make his own brilliant decisions.

Lalli was working on a feature on *Playboy* when the company let it slip that they were about to go public. "I called Michaels and told him I had to get back to New York to write the story."

"Now wait a minute," Michaels said. "What's the story you were working on before you found this out?"

Lalli explained how he'd learned how Hugh Hefner actually lived the life-style that the magazine promoted—that he lived in his pajamas in a big round bed.

"Stay and write that story," Michaels said. "Don't worry about the news."

As it turned out, *Forbes* got to do both: write the feature and break the news.

For Lalli, working at *Forbes* was an ideal situation. You had a full-time researcher to use in whatever way you needed, an unlimited budget and resources, time, a national magazine, and an intelligent editing job at the end by someone who would drop in philosophical hand grenades to sharply focus the story. Not that life was easy. Staffers would get fired regularly, but the rules were clear. If your freshness was gone, you were gone. It was Jim's way of keeping the magazine vibrant.

"You were expected to produce at least one feature and one short per cycle," Lalli says. "That's twenty stories a year. Your output was actually measured in inches. They actually kept a string." You could take time on something long, but you'd be in trouble if the long piece didn't work out.

For Paul Blustein, working in the uneasy balance between Malcolm Forbes and Jim Michaels was intolerable. At the center of his problem was this question, as he posed it in a letter to Malcolm: "At what point does a publisher's 'superior insight' become a matter of altering the truth merely to protect the sensibilities of the publisher's friend?"

At issue was a 1979 story on Itel Corporation, a San Francisco leasing company founded in 1967 by Peter S. Redfield, a friend of Malcolm's and a *Forbes* advertiser.

The story, as edited by then L.A. bureau chief Norman Pearlstine, was highly critical of Redfield and his practice of spending lavishly to impress customers. It talked about the company's "exquisitely furnished headquarters" and "its dazzling secretaries." Entertainment for customers was "decidedly lavish." The dignified Redfield underneath was "a yeller." Marketing people "adopt a 'fast buck' approach." And Itel took "almost indecent advantage" of Lloyd's of London's willingness to insure against the technological obsolescence of the IBM computers Itel was leasing. Itel, "already known as a slick operator," looked "a little too clever in the way it shucked its exposure off on Lloyd's" when, in fact, the computers were quickly rendered obsolete by new models. Itel had "characteristically managed to irritate a lot of people" it did business with.

Michaels liked the story, but after Malcolm saw it, the spicy characterizations fell by the wayside. Itel's "driven, almost abrasive hunger for business" became a "lean, intense hunger." A "sugar-coating of polished charm" became "a great deal of polished charm." A borrowing "binge" became a borrowing "program." A unit would have posted a loss "had not an accounting change papered over the loss"; this was revised to read that the loss was "offset by a switch to flow-through accounting," whatever that is. "Decidedly lavish" entertaining of clients became "first-class" entertaining.

Taking "almost indecent advantage" of Lloyd's became simply "asked Lloyd's to write insurance." The whole paragraph about being slick and too clever was gone. And a section saying that the real story was about Itel's management style dropped a phrase that said that style was "almost entirely attributable to Peter Redfield." A paragraph illustrating how overly aggressive Itel was in brokering deals that weren't necessarily sound had this sentence added: "Similar things could, of course, be said about other aggressive companies."

And some of the most negative proofs of Itel's overly aggressive tactics were omitted. One supported the "fast buck" comment—which was deleted—illustrating how Itel hard-sold small-town banks on leases that more sophisticated institutions would shun.

Blustein's conclusion was hard-hitting. It suggested that Redfield was less capable running a billion-dollar company than one that was one tenth the size. "Does that mean that Itel's profits will slow or even crash, as they have before? Perhaps. But then, considering the sort of manager Peter Redfield is, it is hardly surprising that Itel is facing some reversals. It is the price he pays for taking a mere twelve years to build a [big] company. . . ."

Michaels's version concludes: "But does a billion-dollar company have to behave differently from a $100 million company? . . . Keep tuning in for the answers." Possibly the lamest of all possible conclusions.

It appeared Michaels was taking his instructions on this story from Malcolm. The toning-down process was highly uncharacteristic; the hand grenades were coming *out*, not going in. Another unusual twist in the editing process was that it continued mysteriously even after the last set of editing eyes had seen it at press time.

"That was the most aggressive interference—and not the only one—that I saw the man engage in," says one former *Forbes* editor, adding that last-minute changes in the Itel story were deliberately made behind the usual editors' backs.

While Blustein protested, he was resigned to a certain amount of editing. He knew that Redfield and Malcolm were friends, but what came out in print went too far in softening the blow to Redfield. Blustein was enraged. He decided he no longer could work for *Forbes*. Like Queenan, he felt the magazine lacked the necessary courage to stand by its writers.

Malcolm's excuse for all the meddling was that he knew Redfield better than Blustein and therefore had the authority to make changes. Also, Malcolm objected to Blustein's heavy reliance on unidentified sources.

In his letter of resignation, Blustein pointed out that reliance on unnamed sources had seldom been a reason to alter a story before at *Forbes.* Second, Blustein argued, Malcolm's knowledge was based on his friendship with Redfield, while Blustein's was based on extensive interviews with dozens of well-placed sources. "I hardly think that your perception of Itel—based as it is on social contact with Mr. Redfield—could be as thoroughly informed as mine," Blustein wrote.

He noted that Malcolm invited him to ask the magazine's libel lawyer whether Malcolm was justified in deleting many of the negative references to Itel's aggressive marketing tactics. Blustein did so. The lawyer, he reported, "tells me that he had ample time to review the story, and that he would have called me had there been any legal problem with the portions in question."

Blustein told Malcolm that the experience threatened his self-respect as a journalist, and he quit. In his face-to-face meeting with Malcolm, in which he was asked not to leave, Blustein discovered a man far different from the tough-minded, confident war hero the public knew.

"It was a very strange confrontation," Blustein recalls. "To my surprise, this real ebullient, strong personality became sort of emotional. He kind of rambled incoherently. I never saw him like that. He always seemed so in control of things socially. It wasn't that he was being apologetic. Suddenly he was totally ineffectual."

In other words, Malcolm was unable to rebut Blustein's assertion that Malcolm lacked sound journalistic reasons for gutting the story. Malcolm's strongest defense seemed to be that Redfield didn't seem the sort of person who'd be capable of the kinds of marketing practices Blustein's story documented.

Michaels was obviously upset over this, Blustein says. "He thought I was making too much of this. He agreed what Malcolm did was terrible, but this was simply the dark side of what makes the magazine so great."

Michaels told Blustein, "You've got to pick your battles." This one wasn't worth quitting over, Michaels said.

Two months later, in July 1979, Blustein followed Pearlstine to the *Wall Street Journal.*

A month later, Redfield's aggressive tactics caught up with him.

He was ousted as president and chief executive officer. And five months after that, Itel filed for bankruptcy court protection from creditors and operated that way for two years before it got back on its feet.

"I liked the original story," Michaels once said of the Itel story. "I like any tough story. And [Blustein] was right."

For Malcolm and Michaels, the Itel story was embarrassing. But more important, it was an example of the inevitable clashes of owner and editor. What is hard to determine in these situations is true motivation. Was it simply a case of Malcolm going to bat for someone he felt he knew better than the reporter? Or did Michaels have second thoughts about whether the story was sufficiently reported anyway, and, not wanting to appear indecisive, let Malcolm be the bad guy? As Steve Quickel says, "Jim never operated on just one level."

In 1986, Malcolm essentially killed a hard-hitting story by Allan Sloan suggesting that Malcolm's friend Rupert Murdoch was taking too many risks in order to finance News Corporation's aggressive acquisition campaign. Sloan was cleared eventually to sell the story elsewhere, but Malcolm felt fully vindicated on his gut decision not to run it in *Forbes*. Of the journalists "out to hatchet and slaughter" Murdoch, Malcolm said, "They've turned out, in terms of the bottom line, to be absolutely dead wrong."

In November 1987, *Forbes* ran stories by Richard Behar focusing on the rocky marriage of two companies that included details of alleged IRS corruption. When Behar proposed a third story that focused more on the IRS, Michaels said, "Save your ammunition." With that, he informed Behar he was promoting him to associate editor, a move intended perhaps as a vote of confidence coupled with instructions to take an additional four or five weeks to continue researching a story about mid-level corruption within the IRS.

In January 1988, Behar delivered the results. The story was accorded a higher-than-usual level of importance, with three top editors working on it before Michaels himself ran it through his typewriter.

As the story neared publication, Michaels got a call from Malcolm. Another editor was in Michaels's office, so the phone conversation was brief.

"That was Malcolm," Michaels said, after hanging up. "He's killing the IRS story."

The rumor mill had it that Lawrence Gibbs, the IRS commissioner at the time, had asked Malcolm to kill the story. Both Gibbs and Malcolm denied they ever talked. It was then suggested that then Secretary of the Treasury James Baker, an acquaintance of Malcolm's, had made the request.

Michaels and Steve Lawrence were stunned.

The two editors then met with Zalaznick and Behar in Zalaznick's office to see if they could find a way to salvage the story. While it lacked any smoking gun, they felt the story was worth running, because it showed a pattern of the IRS not doing what a well-intentioned public servant would be expected to do. Still, this wasn't a story about a crime for which someone had to hang. Exactly what Malcolm's objections to it were never made clear to Zalaznick, but it was clear Malcolm felt it wasn't good enough.

Word of this event—including the rumor of government intervention—spread fast. Laura Landro, a reporter for the *Wall Street Journal*, apparently closed the rumor loop, contacting Malcolm for confirmation. Malcolm called Chris Byron, Behar, and Michaels into his office for what amounted to a "let's get the story straight" meeting.

"I realize there's considerable staff discontent over this decision," Malcolm said, adding, however, that there never was any call from the commissioner. "I'm killing the story because I just don't have faith in it."

Then he asked, "How did this rumor get started in the first place?"

Michaels looked at Behar, and Behar said, "I heard it from you, Jim."

The meeting ended. As they walked down the hall, Michaels kept shaking his head, asking rhetorically, "Did I hear that? Where did I hear it? My memory must be failing me."

Within hours, the story was widely known in the office. Behar instantly acquired the nickname Rich "I heard it from you, Jim" Behar.

A few days later, after the *Journal* and the *New York Post* had run stories on the incident, Behar met with Malcolm and other editors to argue his case for running the article.

"He listened, but he didn't listen," Behar recalled. At the end of the presentation, Malcolm said no.

"In no way does this affect my feelings for you guys," Malcolm said, "but I won't run the story."

Behar then went to see Michaels a few days after. He apologized for the mess, but Michaels assured him he had nothing to be sorry about. He wasn't at fault.

Behar said, "Jim, I'd like approval to publish the story elsewhere."

Michaels was obviously agitated. "You'll have to go see Malcolm about it. He owns the magazine. I wash my hands of it."

Behar took Michaels's advice. Noting all the press coverage the flap had garnered, Malcolm congratulated Behar on being an instant celebrity. Behar then sat down with him and asked for permission to publish it elsewhere.

"No. I own it," Malcolm said. "You've already been paid for your work on it."

"I'll give you whatever I get paid for it," Behar said.

Malcolm was adamant. "If you worked for *Time* and this happened, you wouldn't go to *Newsweek* to sell it, would you?"

"I want one more chance," Behar said. "If you firmly believe the story can't stand on its own, give us two more weeks to improve it."

Malcolm's face turned red. "What did Jim say?"

Behar told him.

"I feel the same way," Malcolm said. "I wash my hands of it."

At one point, Malcolm said, "With the new tax bill, everybody is upset and angry with the IRS. We don't need to do any more to hurt the public's confidence in the IRS."

It was a diplomat's—not a journalist's—response. It wasn't as if the story were exposing widespread corruption involving top officials. Behar's article was simply a tale of what happens when a self-policing agency discovers such a problem—it tries to cover it up. This wasn't going to paralyze the agency, somehow forcing it into a mire of indictments and legal entanglements that would bring the nation's ability to collect taxes to a screeching halt.

But even before the confrontation with Malcolm, Michaels in conversations with other editors had indicated he had his own doubts about whether the article went far enough past Behar's previous ones to justify running it.

Five days after the *Journal* broke the story about the IRS story Malcolm killed, Congress launched an investigation of alleged misconduct and mismanagement of the IRS's Criminal Investigation Division, the subject of Behar's pieces.

Eventually, the story Behar had hoped to run in *Forbes* did find its way into print—in *Time* magazine where Behar went to work in April 1989—just as congressional hearings on the issue were about to get under way.

"As painful as it was," Behar says, "I wasn't sour grapes. To the contrary I've always had immense respect for Jim and Malcolm. Forbes runs with more hard-hitting stories than most magazines will even consider publishing. You've got to keep it in perspective; nine out of every ten tough stories I submitted were published without interference."

Still, the IRS story was another classic example of a staffer getting squashed between the machinations that were a unique feature of the symbiotic relationship of Malcolm and Michaels—two brilliant men with slightly different agendas.

Former *Forbes* staffer Jonathan Clements remembers one encounter that illustrates Malcolm's priorities. Clements in 1987 had done a story about Marc Rousso, a stamp dealer who was trying to establish the philatelic equivalent of a stock exchange. The story questioned Rousso's ability to succeed, and Rousso was offended. He managed to wangle an audience with Malcolm—as it turned out, a brief one on the topic of stamps featuring hot-air balloons—and went from there to confront Clements in his office where Clements found him after lunch. Rousso said he'd already discussed his grievance with Malcolm and began to berate the writer for his coverage.

After Clements managed to ease Rousso out of the building, Malcolm called him in to apologize for any role he may have had in letting Rousso loose in the building. Malcolm said, "What really offended me was his nasty aftershave."

Clements was planning a small follow-up item on one aspect of his Rousso story for the magazine's Follow-Through section, but a few days later, Malcolm received an angry letter from one of the board members for Rousso's company. The name was Rothschild, not that anyone knew whether this was one of the famous wealthy Rothschilds. Still, Malcolm called Clements and said, "I wouldn't be too quick to write something about him." The implication was, Let's not risk offending someone who may turn out to be a powerful member of the upper class.

In 1987, the magazine was hit with a miniscandal that may have added impetus to anyone already thinking about leaving. Srully Blotnick, a *Forbes* columnist, became the source of an embarrassing controversy when the New York *Daily News* reported that his business psychology "doctorate" actually came from an unaccredited college and that his consumer data base didn't exist (Blotnick defended the quality of his research). *Forbes* announced the next day that the column was being discontinued, but the magazine never said why.

Not only had *Forbes* used his column, reporters at *Forbes* and elsewhere had quoted him and his data from time to time. The revelations enraged those who had accepted him as an unassailable source. Any piece based on Blotnick's now questionable numbers would itself now be questionable.

Staffers were further outraged at the magazine's decision to issue no explanation for the decision to drop Blotnick (in fact, the one-line announcement was worded to imply that it was Blotnick's decision; he "has discontinued his column," it said) and no apology for the possibility that Blotnick had deceived *Forbes* and its readers. Supposedly a much longer news release was prepared but scrapped.

Apparently, one of Blotnick's greatest supporters was Michaels. In fact, even after the column was discontinued, *Forbes* stories continued to use comments from Blotnick, apparently undeterred by the possibility that while his insights as a marketing consultant may have seemed brilliant, his credibility was questionable.

Clearly *Forbes* needed a new Michaels, revived and full of enthusiasm for the kinds of stories that corporate chiefs hate and share-holders love. Michaels created *Forbes*'s reputation for consistently producing such stories—and he'll not hesitate to tell you so. But gradually, says one staffer, "It's getting harder and harder to interest him. Now what interests him is off-the-wall reactionary extremist views. That's not good for *Forbes.*"

One example of this so-called extremism was a story by *Forbes* staffer Peter Brimelow that caused a rift between Michaels, who liked the article, and copy editors who hated it. It focused on an academic article by Linda Gottfredson, a sociologist at the University of Delaware, that discussed the implications of group differences in intelligence for employment policy. If the underlying assumptions in Gottfredson's report were accurate—for example, that blacks scored fifteen points lower than whites on intelligence tests—then the outlook for finding qualified minorities to meet affirmative-action quotas was bleak. The item caused a "copy desk revolt," as Michaels tried to get it into the magazine at the last minute. Steve Forbes handed down the order to kill the article, though it was said that Malcolm made the actual decision.

A copy of the unpublished piece found its way into the hands of the *Village Voice,* which dubbed it "racist drivel" in the May 9, 1989, issue. But the intent of the article wasn't to pass judgment on Gottfredson's controversial report on comparative intelligence levels, but simply to discuss the thorny issues it raised for minority recruitment.

The story was criticized internally as an example of *Forbes* simply using words and phrases to do what it used to do with facts gathered through incisive, investigative reporting. Queenan's AIDS story a month later was seen in the same light.

"Things like the Queenan story piss me off," says one staffer. "We have to be fresh, controversial, but a lot of the time we do it just with words. In the Queenan story, I kept waiting for the justification. Why are we listening to this guy? It was a bad story. But we do bad stories now—like a cover that asks, Are we spending too much on education? Just to be different and controversial, we take these extreme viewpoints. Certainly *Forbes* has to be different, but you have to work at it."

This staffer's decision to leave was driven by a desire for a career change, but his sense of loyalty to the organization was steadily eroded over the more than five years he worked there. Why? Forbes had "very little loyalty toward its workers. Jim Michaels probably has the biggest ego I've ever seen. He couldn't care less who comes and goes, and he doesn't treat them well. They pay well, so they think that's good enough. Either put up with it or go somewhere else."

Still, he stressed the importance of the *Forbes* experience. "If I wanted to go work somewhere else, *Forbes* means a lot nowadays," he says. "A lot more doors open to me today than would have in the past."

When he gave notice to his editor in New York, he stopped by Michaels's office to say goodbye. He knew he needed to take care in explaining why he was leaving. When one woman told Michaels she was leaving for business school, for example, Michaels was visibly perturbed and showed no interest in bidding her a fond farewell. She was puzzled until she realized Michaels thought she'd told him she was leaving for *Business Week;* she was thus able to salvage the more usual warm departure.

So when this particular staffer walked into Michaels's office, he didn't expect to be recognized on sight, having been in a bureau for several years. He was surprised when Michaels greeted him by name without hesitation: "Hi. Come on in."

With Michaels's legendary ego and fits of withering nastiness, the staffer might have thought he'd never be missed if he just quietly slipped away. "But I'd heard that even if you think he couldn't care less, he'd be hurt if you didn't say goodbye," the staffer says. "He will somehow feel hurt. There's a sensitivity in him, so it wasn't earth-shattering that when I left, he was nice to me."

Michaels was the embodiment of a common quality in many journalists: egoism welded to insecurity and mounted on a solid foundation of genuine sensitivity.

"Sometimes you think he has no social graces," the same former staffer says, "but when he's good, he's amazing. He makes stories so much better. It has to do with sensitivity and insight. When he does it, you go, Wow! That's really neat. And you forget about the times he writes nasty notes on stories."

Still, at *Forbes*, the ultimate management view was that there'd always be somebody to replace you. For the most part, at places like the *Wall Street Journal* and *Business Week*, the bias was for caring whether someone stayed or left. Not so at *Forbes*, yet the magazine was much more writer driven than editor driven, despite the view that Michaels ruled with a firm hand. Generally, stories went through no more than two relatively light edits, and as had been the tradition for years, it was the writers who generated the bulk of the story ideas.

Perhaps the most common criticism leveled at the magazine was the notion that *Forbes* didn't go after big game like General Motors and IBM. Says one former staffer, "They just don't take on these people, but it's all very well to kick the shit out of some company with a fifty-million-dollar market capitalization."

The most commonly held belief was that most big companies were sacred cows because of the ad revenue they controlled. Zalaznick disagrees. He concedes there was a dearth of hard-hitting stories about big companies, but "It's not for lack of trying," he says. In editorial meetings, Michaels regularly moaned about this. What's going on at GM? Ford? IBM?

The problem was this, Zalaznick explains. These big companies are covered better than smaller ones, so it's much harder to generate legitimate, exclusive angles on them that will remain exclusive before the competition discovers them. That's part of the price you pay for being a biweekly.

Also, the big companies tend to have much more effective defenses against even the most enterprising reporters. About the only way to penetrate those defenses is to cover the company day in and day out, reporting regularly on the company's routine business. But people don't read *Forbes* for routine company news; they read the *Wall Street Journal* or *Business Week* for that. So if a reporter from *Forbes* shows up at Exxon or Boeing, he or she will probably be arriving with a short list of trusty internal sources and access to all others controlled by a sophisticated public relations staff that knows *Forbes* specializes in the exposé.

That explains why one survey of corporate executives indicated that *Forbes* was the magazine they most feared being covered by.

Michaels would be the last person to discourage a writer from doing a legitimate negative story with a fresh angle about a top company, but *Forbes* writers are handicapped in meeting all the requirements for such pieces. In fact, Zalaznick recalls being frustrated in editing a cover story that was supposed to take a hard-hitting critical look at one of the country's top industrial concerns. Unfortunately, the writer simply hadn't uncovered the obvious roots of this particular company's mounting problems. "I spent a weekend trying to punch it up, not defang it," Zalaznick says. No one was telling writers or editors to go soft on any big companies that happened to be advertisers.

Further compounding the problem was a sort of unconscious self-censorship. "People are afraid to make fools of themselves and piss people off," says one former staffer. And it's a whole lot less threatening to one's career to write a positive story about a big company and be wrong than it is to write a negative one and be wrong.

In short, it is more the editorial mission of *Forbes* as defined by Michaels—not the owner's fear of alienating big advertisers—that hampers its writers in the effort to break big stories about corporate giants.

Ray Brady, now business correspondent for "CBS Evening News," remembers doing a tough story about Standard Oil of Indiana that was particularly hard on Robert E. Wilson, the chairman. Wilson demanded a meeting with Malcolm and Brady. "I don't know why it had to be Malcolm," Brady says. At the time, Bruce Forbes was still president.

"We met at the Twenty-one Club and he sat there blasting the hell out of me," Brady recalls.

Finally Malcolm, refusing to retract an accurate article, interrupted the harangue and said, "Why don't you just take out an ad to tell your story?"

That became one of Malcolm's stock answers to corporate behemoths who felt wronged by *Forbes*.

Michael Cieply's story of how he came to *Forbes* in 1982 and left two years later illustrates the love-hate nature of the relationship many staffers develop with the magazine. Cieply, a California-based freelance writer at the time, had reached the all-time low of his life. His marriage had failed and he'd gone broke over a book contract that soured. In the darkest moment of his despair, he received a letter from Malcolm attached to a clip of a positive "wee review" of a book Cieply had written a year earlier about the Hearst family.

For Cieply, the letter was a lifesaver. He immediately replied to Malcolm that not only did he appreciate the review, he'd appreciate even more being considered for a job. Malcolm suggested he meet with Zalaznick and set it up immediately. Soon after, Cieply was in New York, met Shelly, and got shown into Michaels's office.

"You may be able to write," Michaels told him, "but what can you do for us here?"

With that, Cieply, who had studied the magazine carefully before the meeting, whipped out a list of about fifteen story ideas and started telling Michaels what he'd like to write about.

With that, the diminutive Michaels literally grabbed Cieply by the scruff of the neck, led him into the hallway and shouted to Zalaznick, "Here's your new California guy!"

It's hard to imagine that happening at any of the competing publications. But it was the same erratic, idiosyncratic culture that ultimately contributed to Cieply's decision to leave. He could tell the magazine was moving in a political direction he wasn't comfortable with. This was the influence of Steve. In fact, years later when Cieply interviewed Malcolm for a story on the family business, he asked Malcolm about the shift to a more staunchly conservative political publication. When Malcolm responded, his voice was tinged with a severe tension: "Steve and I discuss this all the time. I'm always watching when something doctrinaire creeps in. We're alert to the danger."

It was apparent Malcolm was well aware of the shift. Indeed, it seemed *Forbes* was trying to become the *National Review* of business journalism, what with in-house Reaganite Caspar Weinberger as publisher and owner Steve a Reagan appointee as chairman of the Committee overseeing Radio Free Europe and Radio Liberty.

In addition to his discomfort with the shift to the far right, Cieply, now with the *Los Angeles Times,* had grown weary of another unpredictable element at Forbes—the ever present pressure to toughen up stories. "I was very bothered by what could happen to the odd story," he says. "You go far out on a limb and they push you farther."

And sometimes you fell off, and the editors weren't there to catch you.

At the same time, success can bring a mixed bag of appreciation. In the mid-1980s, Howard Rudnitsky and Allan Sloan won a Loeb award for a story on Financial Corporation of America and Richard Stern won one for a story on Robert Brennan and his First Jersey Securities. Malcolm gave them each $1,000, and an ad campaign was cooked up to tout these awards. The ad mentioned Malcolm and Michaels but not the writers. The only place the writers' names appeared was on the stories themselves, which were featured in photos in the ad.

Sloan went to Steve Forbes to complain about the insensitivity of blowing the magazine's horn without giving the writers any credit. Steve told him he'd take care of it, but he never did. Sloan clipped a copy of the ad from a magazine, mounted it in a cheap frame and attached a magnifying glass on the end of a string with which to discern the bylines in the photos of the stories.

Michaels walked in, saw it, and walked out muttering that Sloan shouldn't have been upset by it, because it wasn't his magazine. It was Malcolm's. One hundred percent.

13 | THE WORLD'S BIGGEST KID

"In my father's house there are many mansions . . ."
—John 14: 2

On Friday, February 23, 1990, Malcolm hosted a charity bridge tournament at Old Battersea House between the corporate America team—including Laurence Tisch, chief executive of CBS, Alan Greenberg and James Cayne, chairman and president respectively of Bear Stearns, and millionaire Milton Petrie, Chairman of Petrie Stores—and members of the British Parliament. The Americans lost but Malcolm was praised for his own fine performance.

He arrived back in Far Hills at 5:30 A.M. the next day, a Saturday, and told his houseman, Dennis Stewart, that he wanted to see his doctor, Oscar Kruesi, later in the day. It was to be a routine visit, but some acquaintances would say later that Malcolm had been looking a little wan for the previous few weeks. Stewart made an appointment, but later on he called Dr. Kruesi again. This time he seemed upset.

"He said he had looked in and was alarmed that Mr. Forbes

hadn't awakened," Dr. Kruesi told the *New York Times,* "so I raced out of my office for the Forbes home. Mr. Forbes had obviously died in his sleep. He had died very peacefully apparently."

Malcolm was pronounced dead at 4:30 P.M. For someone who liked to travel at ninety-five mph on a motorcycle, take off in a balloon in the worst weather, and sail into sometimes unsafe waters—situations in which Malcolm had numerous brushes with death—dying peacefully at home in his sleep in the comfort of his own bed was typical Malcolm: defying the odds even in death. It seemed almost too perfect to be an accident.

Denny Fleck, head of the Forbes Balloon Ascension division, was stunned when he heard the news. "I kept thinking, they'll take him away somewhere and fix him," he says. "It just wasn't possible. Somehow they'll figure a way to bring him back. Everybody needs him too much."

Liz Smith would lament, "Malcolm Forbes has been a major player in my column over the last ten years. Frankly, I don't know what I'm going to do without him."

Malcolm had spent the better part of the last twenty years of his life treating the world to adventures they might otherwise have never known. For Dennis Fleck, now forty-one years old, Malcolm had turned his entire life into an adventure—from being his chauffeur, to playing Passepartout to Malcolm's Phileas Fogg.

"It'll never be the same—never like when he was around," Fleck says. "With Malcolm, having lots of fun was very important."

A balloon-and-bike friendship tour of Brazil, scheduled for the spring, was postponed indefinitely. And a good thing, too. Had it gone off as planned, the team probably would have been in the country just as violence was breaking out in the wake of Draconian economic measures.

For the entire week after his death, the media were dominated by the event—the private memorial service the following Monday in New Jersey for family members, the enormous public memorial service at St. Bartholomew's Church in Manhattan that Thursday. "Malcolm Forbes, The Man Who Had Everything," read the front-page headline in Newsday above a photo of the happy millionaire grinning ear to ear with one arm around Elizabeth Taylor and the other around model Jerry Hall, Mick Jagger's girlfriend. Then came the talk of books and magazine articles that would settle once and for all the rumors about Malcolm's private life.

A bagpiper played "Scotland the Brave" at the private service at The Church of St. John on the Mountain in Bernardsville, New Jersey, not far from the Forbes home. Steve, immediately assuming his role as undisputed head of the family, delivered the eulogy. Also attending were the rest of his brothers, his sister, his mother, the eight grandchildren, and Wallace, Malcolm's only surviving brother in this family whose men seem destined to die far short of their eighties. The Reverend Alfred Niese, rector of the Episcopal church, presided over the hour-and-a-quarter ceremony, after which Malcolm's sons carried his flag-draped pine coffin to a hearse to be cremated. His instructions were that his ashes were to be interred on Laucala, the farthest-flung chunk of real estate in Malcolm's portfolio.

Three days later, at the memorial service in the city, St. Bartholomew's—which was selected for its fourteen-hundred-person capacity—filled quickly. Scores of photographers and camera crews crowded around the steps to the front entrance for good shots of the inevitable parade of celebrities, CEOs, socialites, and politicians who seemed to answer Malcolm's call in death even as in life.

The crowds arrived early. The ceremony was to start at 11:00 A.M., but the church was jammed by 10:30. Hundreds more than the fourteen hundred lucky enough to find seats filled the aisles, many of them forced to stand behind huge pillars and unable to see the altar. From outside came the occasional deep roar of Hell's Angels on motorcycles ("Forbes was a damn good driver," said one biker) passing by in tribute to Malcolm and the passion he shared with them. A single, unseen bagpiper was barely audible. Soon, long before the service began, would-be attendees, even some celebrities—and one somewhat disheveled woman claiming to be a distant relative—were being turned away.

Up front in the same row sat Elizabeth Taylor, former president Richard Nixon, and former New York mayor Edward Koch. David and Laurence Rockefeller were also there, along with Ann Landers, Rupert Murdoch, Joan Rivers, Lee Iacocca, John Kluge, John Sculley of Apple Computer, Washington Post Company chairman Katharine Graham, former Gannett chairman Allen Neuharth, *Fortune* managing editor Marshall Loeb, and Barbara Walters. Then there were many of the six hundred or so Forbes employees who'd been bused up from the office downtown.

Outside the church sat Malcolm's riderless red-and-gold Harley with a small American flag at half-staff and a banner of the Scottish Forbes clan.

The service started with eight Norman hunting horns echoing fully and richly throughout the church.

In his homily, the Reverend Thomas D. Bowers said that when it comes to death, "there is no way out," but as the Salvation Army says when one of its own passes on, Malcolm was being "promoted to glory." He then read these words from the Gospel According to John: "In my father's house there are many mansions; if it were not so, I would have told you. I go to prepare a place for you, and if I go to prepare a place for you, I will come again and take you to myself that where I am there you may be also."

More recent translations of this Bible passage use the phrase "dwelling places," a poetic equivalent of "mansions." Dr. Bowers apparently thought the latter would be more appropriate for this service. Certainly the house of Forbes included many mansions.

Each of the children then spoke briefly, starting with the youngest, Moira. It was clear from their remembrances that Malcolm had dominated their lives much as he had dominated every aspect of his carefully orchestrated public life.

Moira spoke of how her father told his children, "You have to do your own thing." She noted that "anyone who has received our Christmas cards over the years knows that the five of us had our differences while growing up. Some of us wore suits while others wore blue jeans. Pop was never distracted by all of this. He just loved having us around. Pop was happy to tell me I looked perfectly ridiculous in tattered jeans, but he never asked me to change."

In recent years, she said her father had talked to her about where she was headed and urged her to try to find a place in the family business, but ultimately accepted her decision not to.

He often said, she noted, that his children owed him nothing. All he asked was the freedom to give them his love and to receive it when it was returned. "In all I am, in all I have, in all I do," Moira said, "he's there, and I'm very glad and I'm very grateful."

Malcolm once said of his children, "They're our best friends and they're each other's best friends. When they went away to school, we stopped treating them like they were our responsibility. It's very hard for parents to grow up, I think. It's easier for kids to grow up than for parents to mature in terms of their kids, and not feel they have to advise and admonish, point out their faults and everything. Let your children go."

"You were hard to raise, but it was worth the trip," Timothy said, addressing his father. He talked about his father's love of freedom and concluded, "I hope your grandchildren someday will be as proud of the job they did raising us as we are of the job we did raising you."

For Kip's part, thoughts of Malcolm brought to mind three words: "Bagpipes, dumbbells, books."

Why bagpipes? He told one often repeated anecdote. It had to do with how the children were all forced to take bagpipe lessons, an excruciatingly painful requirement that led him to conclude, "If we could survive that together, we can survive anything."

Dumbbells: He recalled walking into Malcolm's office one day and finding him lifting a dumbbell, first with one foot, then the other. "Pop was not keen on exercise," Kip noted. What he was up to? "I'm lifting weights so I can keep the damn motorcycle up at stoplights."

Books: He related how one day Malcolm casually handed Kip the just-finished galleys of what would be his second-to-last book, an autobiography of sorts. Kip read the dedication: "To son Christopher, whose friendship, love, genius and wit have been instrumental in making this life 'More Than I Dreamed,' " the title of the book.

"I cried then," Kip told the congregation, "and I'm trying not to now."

Robert, who of all the children may have spent the most time by his father's side during his world travels, said, "Many years I have dreaded this moment after seeing so many others go through it and wondering how they did it without losing it."

He told of fondly remembering how on a motorcycle trip in

Norway they stopped for a meal and discovered they were being served reindeer tongue—eight of them arranged on a platter. Malcolm joked about mute reindeer attacking them on the highway. "Soon we were all hooting and snorting, dizzy with laughter," Robert recalled, and they had to leave.

He remembered clipping things he'd seen in newspapers and magazines that he thought would amuse his father. One was a classified ad that read: "Complete set of encyclopedias for sale, never used, teen-age son knows everything."

He ticked off the various roles his father filled: "Boss, bon vivant, raconteur, balloonist, columnist, happiest millionaire, leader of the pack, super this, mega that, mentor, father, grandfather, naughty boy."

He then quoted a few of Malcolm's one-liners, including this one: "As you get older, don't slow down—speed up." Then he noted that on the kitchen wall at home was this now common saying: "He who dies with the most toys wins." Robert added, "He gets the blue ribbon on that score."

Then, he thanked his father "for wanting me in the family business and giving me a chance to meet biggies as well as beefy bikers. It's been a helluva party, Pop. You've been such a friend. Thanks for the trip."

Steve Forbes was true to form—cool and under control. He began by inviting everyone to an all-afternoon reception at the Forbes building on Fifth Avenue after the service.

He mentioned his grandfather's quote from the first issue of *Forbes:* "Business was originated to produce happiness, not pile up millions." Malcolm certainly took his father's advice to heart, which explains why Malcolm liked to say, "I'll be the saddest person at my funeral."

He then went on to tell how his father's life had not been all success and pleasure. He mentioned Malcolm's bout with cancer ten years earlier and some of his near-fatal mishaps on motorcycles and in balloons, then gave a rundown of his father's failures, which seemed strange in the context of a eulogy. Steve noted, "His divorce . . . almost shattered him. As can happen, they loved each other but found it impossible to live together." By the age of forty, "his political hopes were in ruins." Other failures: the Ohio weeklies he bought after Princeton, and *Nation's Heritage,* on which he spent so much on production, there was too little left for promotion. "He never made that mistake again."

Steve then listed the best elements in Malcolm's character, as he saw them. "He never lost his almost childlike capacity to wonder, to be curious, to dream and to do. His buoyant, infectious spirit of openness, of generosity, of let's-try-it was always with him," Steve said. "When dealt a setback, he would initially look as if he had been physically hit by a punch. He would take stock—and then move ahead as if nothing had happened." Holding grudges and grievances was never part of his makeup. He was generous—many times no one knew who was doing the giving. He was especially generous with time and authority. "Only when dictating editorials did he resent an intrusion."

He praised his father's willingness as a parent to be flexible in order to "bring out the adult in us as we grew up." Among his father's most memorable pieces of advice: "Don't try to be what you're not, or you'll send yourself to an early grave."

After more hymns and prayers and Norman hunting horns, the service concluded with a single bagpiper playing "Amazing Grace"—a favorite of Malcolm's—and finally "Skye Boat Song" as the family filed out and headed downtown for the six-hour reception.

As the VIPs made their way into the bright, clear cold air outside and ran the gauntlet of flashing, whirring cameras to limos on Park Avenue, a heavyset man with a thick reddish beard and wearing a black leather jacket stood up on a wall across Fifty-first Street from the church and held up a crudely made sign. It read in part, TRUE BLUE YANKEE HIGHLANDERS, followed by some negative comments about Malcolm. He began to bellow at the top of his lungs: "He was a selfish dirty old man! He got what he deserved!" He'd shouted it twice before two plainclothes cops came out of nowhere and grabbed him, dragging him away to a cab parked half a block up Park Avenue.

Later at the Forbes building, the five children gathered in the front entrance, surrounded by samples of the family's collections, and lined up to receive the visitors. Seemingly out of habit, they arranged themselves by age. First Steve, then Robert, Kip, Tim, and

Moira. The visitors numbered in the hundreds, milling about, staring at the children, perhaps wondering how their lives would change in a world without their famous dad and his unflagging romance with the media.

Alongside their reports on Malcolm's passing, numerous publications ran sidebars listing what he left behind—a kind of bottom-line, final score crassly summing up his accomplishments. But what else would one expect? Malcolm had spent roughly the last twenty-five years of his life teaching the world the proper way to flaunt a fortune without insulting the less fortunate.

Based on a variety of sources, Malcolm's estate was far greater than the one he inherited. Estimates of the total fortune—including publications, real estate, art collections, aircraft, motorcycles, yachts, and a collection of classic cars—ranged from about $700 million to $1.23 billion. The magazine itself was valued at between $500 million (with annual profit of about $30 million) to more than $900 million (with annual profit of $65 million). But with total annual revenue of about $160 million from *Forbes, American Heritage,* and fourteen weekly newspapers, Forbes Inc. was still a tiny player in the publishing business, whose major players were raking in billions each year.

The art collection, including the Fabergé eggs, had an estimated value of as much as $100 million; real estate, $75 million; and motorcycles, cars, and aircraft, $25 million.

At his death, the estimated estate-tax bill for Malcolm's heirs was a whopping $300 million, but Malcolm had been buying huge amounts of tax-free life insurance to offset the tax bill. He also had begun to transfer assets into his children's names—about 15 percent by the time of his death.

Malcolm would be questioned, even before his death, on the advisability of spending so much of the company's cash on life insurance rather than using it to expand Forbes Inc., say, through the purchase of other media properties. But he was too conservative; he passed up the opportunity to buy *Interview* magazine from Andy Warhol's estate and instead launched *Egg,* a life-style magazine whose first issue came out a week before Malcolm died. (The critics hated it. The day before he died, *USA Today*'s Deirdre Donahue wrote that *Egg* "fries the reader's attention span with trivia. It's a dated mishmash of arch references to popular culture and obscure Gotham tidbits.")

Jim Michaels wrote of Malcolm in Side Lines in the first issue of *Forbes* after his death: "I watched with wonder as he transformed himself from a somewhat shy, bookish person into a witty, expansive celebrity. But the underpinnings never changed: the basic shrewdness and a self-deprecating appreciation for the funny and ironic aspects of life."

In fact, Malcolm probably would have appreciated the irony that at the end of his life, the very publications that had used so much space in the preceding three years to speculate on a wedding date for Malcolm and Elizabeth Taylor would begin a mad scramble days after his death to chase the rumors that he was gay.

Michaels also observed that "Malcolm loved the limelight, but it never gave him an inflated ego as it does so many." Perhaps there was an underlying insecurity that kept Malcolm's ego at bay. Perhaps his secretive homosexuality juxtaposed with his outward macho image would never allow Malcolm the luxury of feeling invulnerable as a respected celebrity.

But even in death, the supermarket tabloids were slow to give up the irresistible notion that Elizabeth Taylor and Malcolm Forbes had carried on a love affair. On the front page of the March 13 *Star,* the headline at the top read, "LIZ TAYLOR CANCELS WEDDING— Heartsick over Death of Old Flame Malcolm Forbes." (The supposed groom was someone else.) An headline inside read, "Their romance made headlines around the world." *National Enquirer* took it one ridiculous step further: "Malcolm Forbes Dies—Just Hours After Liz Decides to Marry Him."

Later that week, both publications were furiously chasing the news, as reported in the gay publication *Outweek* and repeated in *USA Today,* that if Malcolm was having a romance with Taylor, it hadn't affected his desire for young men.

In fact, one scandal sheet, the *Globe,* led its March 27 issue with this headline: "Malcolm Forbes Had AIDS & Killed Himself; His gay lover tells all." The source was George Warnock, who was paid for his story. Warnock was a twenty-two-year-old body-builder and model who claimed to have had regular weekend encounters with Malcolm at $1,500 a date from February through October 1989. (He says Malcolm first approached him at Peggy Sue's, a popular hangout for models, and that typically they would go to the town house, Malcolm would perform oral sex on Warnock, and Warnock would then sodomize Malcolm.) He concedes Malcolm never actually said he had AIDS (he says Malcolm thought he might have cancer), nor did Malcolm ever say he would kill himself (he says Malcolm "knew he was sick and had to do something").

Aside from earning some extra money—less than $1,000, the *Globe* says—why did Warnock talk to the *Globe?* He was angry at Malcolm, he says, because this rich man refused his request to help him buy a house on Long Island.

"He was paying me," Warnock says, "but I didn't think it was enough. I wanted a nice big house." Malcolm, however, told him he couldn't afford such extravagances, especially with Forbes Inc. in the midst of spending heavily to launch the new magazine, *Egg*. Warnock says he then ended the arrangement with Malcolm and went to Forbes offices to see if someone there could change Malcolm's mind. He says he told an official there he was willing to go public with his story. The official, however, responded that Malcolm denied knowing Warnock and threatened the model with legal action if his story of sex with Malcolm became public, Warnock says.

Perhaps it's inevitable that someone as publicly rich as Malcolm Forbes would be the target of such threats as a result of his desire for paid-for sex. Warnock says he heeded the threat of legal action, until Malcolm died four months later and others began to tell their tales. *Globe* editor Paul F. Levy, however, says Warnock first wrote to the newspaper about Malcolm long before Malcolm died.

On July 20, 1990, the Associated Press reported that Warnock was arrested on federal charges of trying to extort money from Malcolm via letters mailed in August and September 1989 and, after Malcolm's death, from Steve. A federal grand jury indictment handed up in New York alleged that Warnock threatened to injure "the property and reputation" of Forbes unless he received money.

Assistant U.S. Attorney Nancy Northup said Warnock was on probation for a burglary conviction. Warnock's attorney, Ian Weinstein, said he was sure Warnock would be vindicated.

Libel laws don't apply to the deceased, and Michelangelo Signorile, features editor at *Outweek,* was ready to open the floodgates. Less than two weeks after Malcolm died, photocopies and faxes of Signorile's riveting, if shrill, report were making the rounds. He had talked to half a dozen gay men who had had pretty much the same kind of sexual encounter with Malcolm—impersonal physical contact concluding with a $100 gratuity. Many of them worked for Malcolm, and most of them were sympathetic to him, saying he seemed lonely, awkward and self-conscious—that he cared whether his advances made them uncomfortable.

For *Outweek*'s Signorile, the rationale for exposing Malcolm was political. "It was a splashy memorial service indeed," he wrote. "But did the homophobes know that they were coming to pay homage to someone who embodied what they ultimately detested?"

But the most interesting piece in *Outweek* was an essay by Al Weisel, the proofreader who refused to work on Queenan's AIDS piece the previous summer. Weisel talked about confronting Malcolm—just two months before his death—at a Christmas party. Weisel was a few weeks away from quitting his job at *Forbes.*

He told Malcolm he thought it was important that famous gay people like himself publicly acknowledge their homosexuality.

"And *I* think," Malcolm replied, "it's important for people to lead their own private lives and that it's nobody's business."

Weisel countered that a huge proportion of teen suicides were gays, perhaps fearful of life in a homophobic society. It might help if there were more famous gay role models. "I think a public acknowledgment from you would do a lot of good."

Malcolm was clearly uncomfortable. Stammering, he argued that this was a free country in which no one could tell you how to live your life.

"I wasn't telling you how to live your life," Weisel said. "I was only suggesting—"

"Good!" Malcolm said, smiling. "Then we're in a hundred percent agreement."

Weisel disagreed, but Malcolm turned away. Weisel called after him suggesting that they talk about the issue again another time.

"We just did talk about it," Malcolm said angrily. "Now that's it."

In this entire exchange, Malcolm made no effort to deny that he was gay. He simply made the point that it was no one else's business. In reality, however, the intensity of Malcolm's desire for young men was sufficiently out of control to make it everyone's business. Numerous bosses, regardless of their sexual orientation, manage to satisfy their desires without imposing them on employees. Were it not for this indiscretion, coupled with his relationship to Elizabeth Taylor, Malcolm's private life might well have stayed comfortably private.

But as Thomas Stoddard, executive director of the Lambda Defense League and Education Fund, the oldest national gay rights group in the country, once told the *New York Times:* "It is generally not understood that gay people often have a prolonged social adolescence. They have to deal with questions of dating and sexual adolescence at a later stage." Most people understand when a young man comes out of the closet, but find it harder to comprehend when an older man does it. Stoddard's comments were part of a report on the case of Barney Frank, the Democratic congressman whose homosexuality became public information when it was discovered a hustler was operating out of Frank's home.

Frank, in a September 1989 interview with *Newsweek,* put into words sentiments that Malcolm might have shared: "Older [gay] people I know, because of the position they're in, tend to have companions of the opposite sex. It may or may not be necessary, but it's a very terrifying thing to live with. We grew up in a society where you're expected to laugh at jokes about the subject, and you're afraid not to."

And so, Malcolm had Elizabeth Taylor.

Malcolm once said, "Dessert had always been my favorite vegetable. To me, having just fruit for dessert reminds me of being a little kid and getting clothes for Christmas: what kind of treat is that?"

A treat for grownups.

"You could argue that Malcolm's sexual development was arrested at the age of fourteen, when his parents' marriage started to sour," says one former *Forbes* writer.

It wasn't just his sex life that seemed frozen at age fourteen. As his own children acknowledged, his most endearing quality was his childlike capacity for all kinds of pleasures. And his collecting interests certainly reflected that: toys, pictures of cowboys, pornography, motorcycles, balloons.

But Malcolm was deeper than all this suggests. He had a warmth and genuine caring for people and a complete lack of the elitism one would expect in a man of his background and privilege.

One longtime Forbes employee's fondest memory of him was that of being on the *Highlander* rounding the Statue of Liberty. Standing on the deck with Malcolm, he turned to him and said he found it overwhelming that it was on these same waters his own father had arrived in America many years earlier.

"Mine too," Malcolm replied, referring to the day in September 1904 that Bertie Charles Forbes arrived in New York and started to change the rules of financial journalism.

Malcolm once told Bob Sipchen, of the *Los Angeles Times:* "Grabbing the last piece of chicken at a family table, that's greed. . . . Donald Trump didn't buy Trump Plaza to say, 'You can't have it.' He did it to say, 'I can do it!' " His eyes bright, Malcolm clenched his fists and declared, "It's a matter of pride."

Clearly, while Malcolm played hard at the game of making money and having fun, he cared a lot what people thought of him. This wasn't just a matter of generating positive publicity. It was, as Malcolm said, a matter of pride. But he relied in many cases on money to bolster his own self-image, whether it was a $2 million extravaganza in Morocco, or $100 stuffed into a young man's pocket to ensure that the lasting impression would be that of a man who was kind and generous.

In death it would be no different. A week after he died, Forbes employees learned that in his will, Malcolm had granted all of them a week's pay and forgiven them any debts to the company of less than $10,000. The staff was awed. Malcolm, after all, apparently cared what they all thought of him; he wanted to be remembered as someone who appreciated the role his employees had played in his success. Being named in Malcolm's will touched even the most cynical employees.

"Malcolm really was a very shy man," said one longtime associate, "and I think his focus on delighting people with things—the boats, the possessions, the palaces, balloons, motorcycles—was his way of overcompensating."

Caspar Weinberger wrote that Malcolm "was a genuine hero to his sons—not, mind you, idle hero worship, but a deep and genuine affection exemplified by their lifelong association with him in his business and personal interests. . . . The Edna St. Vincent Millay poem about the candle's burning at both ends comes quickly, and correctly, to mind in thinking about Malcolm."

Perhaps Malcolm's self-effacing humor and underlying shyness stemmed from a deep-seated insecurity about his sexual preferences. "If there is a next life," he was fond of saying, "people like me had better hope the devil is not as bad off as he's painted." In the context of the public Malcolm, there was little to explain why he'd make such a comment. This wasn't an evil-hearted man talking. What did Malcolm have to be ashamed of? Did he fear that in the final accounting, it would be determined that with all his getting, he'd failed to do enough good with his wealth? That was the question a student at Princeton asked him in 1985. How could he spend so lavishly and ostentatiously in a world so filled with poverty? How does one justify the accumulation of more wealth than one could ever possibly spend?

Unlike the Forbeses, many of the Rockefeller heirs were uncomfortable in their roles as awesomely rich people.

Steven Rockefeller, son of Nelson and a great-grandson of John D. of Standard Oil infamy, responded to the above questions eloquently in *The Rockefellers: An American Dynasty,* by Peter Collier and David Horowitz. "I am firmly convinced," Steven Rockefeller said,

> that there is no rational justification for extreme privilege and the accumulation of vast sums of wealth. You cannot rationally justify it or give a good moral reason for it. You cannot defend it as socially

good that some people should accumulate huge piles of money and live in great comfort and wealth, while other people live miserably wretched lives. You cannot. All you can say in defense of your living that way is "Well, the social system makes it possible for me to enjoy this and I like it. So I support the social system that makes it possible." But I don't consider that a rational argument. It's just a selfish declaration of one's own preference.

Steven, called by some of the other family members the conscience of the Rockefeller family, went on to say that while his family had doled out about $1 billion in charity, it was not much of a sacrifice. "Giving away a million dollars when you've got a hundred million doesn't make you a better person than others."

What drove Malcolm to amass a fortune beyond his father's wildest dreams and transform himself into perhaps the world's best-known bon vivant? The pop psychologists might suggest he was unconsciously obsessed with a desire both to prove himself better than his father and to earn his respect even long after his death—to rebel and yet still to be loved. In the end, the father and son were literally worlds apart. In the summer of 1988, Malcolm purchased the deteriorating Scottish castle Pitsligo, built by Sir William Forbes in the fifteenth century, and had his father reburied at nearby Saint Kane's Kirk in New Deer. A year and a half later, Malcolm's own remains would be buried about as far away from New Deer as one could get and still be on this planet—on his island in Fiji.

It seemed that Malcolm's goal all along was to defy the odds, to end up far afield from where he began, to have his fortune and spend it too, to ignore his own internal parent, to grow increasingly youthful as he grew older. Whether he died with the most toys is debatable, but ultimately when the end came, Malcolm Stevenson Forbes had become the world's biggest kid, and, as such, by many he would be missed.

Index